The Use and Abuse of Television

of Television

A Social Psychological
Analysis of the Changing Screen

COMMUNICATION

A series of Volumes edited by
Dolf Zillmann and Jennings Bryant

The Use and Abuse of Television
A Social Psychological
Analysis of the Changing Screen

J. Mallory Wober

 LAWRENCE ERLBAUM ASSOCIATES, PUBLISHERS
1988 Hillsdale, New Jersey   Hove and London

Lawrence Erlbaum Associates, Inc., Publishers
365 Broadway
Hillsdale, New Jersey 07642

Library of Congress Cataloging-in-Publication Data
Wober, J. M. (J. Mallory)
The use and abuse of television.

Bibliography: p.
Includes index.
1. Television—Psychological aspects. 2. Television
broadcasting—Social aspects. I. Title. II. Title:
Social psychological analysis of the changing screen.
PN1992.6.W65   1988   302.2′345   88-3819
ISBN 0-89859-662-9

OR √93

Printed in the United States of America
10 9 8 7 6 5 4 3 2 1

Contents

Chapter 3
Types of Programs as Produced, Partaken, and Perceived   57

Chapter 4
Challengers: Opponents of the Screen Itself
or of Its Contents   99

Chapter 5
Champions: The Prophets of the Power of the Screen   143

The Use and Abuse of Television

A Social Psychological
Analysis of the Changing Screen

CHAPTER 1

The One Hand Clap?
Or a Sounder Way of
Understanding Television

INTRODUCTION: EXPLORING THE NATURE
OF THE SCREEN AT HOME

Capping his illustrious career, Hugh Malcolm Beville (1985)—whom we
shall encounter again—wrote a stirring and definitive defense of some of
the ways in which American television is assessed. After long service with
NBC and a full academic professorship, Beville served as Executive Director of the Broadcast Rating Council (which later evolved into the Electronic Media Research Council). Referred to as "the dean of broadcast
research," Beville has a clear and probably uniquely well-informed view of
the scene. In a telling anecdote, which he draws from a Carnegie Commission report on the Future of Public Broadcasting, (Beville, 1985, p.
234) he recounts:

> At the end of a concert at Carnegie Hall, Walter Damrosch asked Rach-
> maninoff what sublime thoughts had passed through his head as he stared
> out into the audience during the playing of his concerto. "I was counting
> the house," said Rachmaninoff. The principal test of public broadcasting's
> accountability to the community is whether anybody is listening or
> watching.

To take Rachmaninoff's remark at face value tells us only that Damrosch had had his leg pulled; to draw the conclusion that is contained in the final sentence, the passer-on of this tale Gary Steiner (1965) shows that he may have as shallow an understanding of creative musicians as he has a command of logical inference.

In this book we hope to maintain an appreciation of humor but also to be careful about conclusions and the processes by which they are attained. To illustrate this claim, let us ask some questions about the anecdote. Can Rachmaninoff have been right in implying that his assessment of events stopped short at a count of listeners? This may be partly true but is unlikely to be the whole or even the most important part of the truth, for musicians pay great attention to the applause at the end of a performance. This not only reflects their own concern about their product, but it also gives them a good idea about what the size of the house may be *next* time and whether they will have to face their peers, their managers, and their own creative selves with confidence or with contrition.

If one accepts that public broadcasting is best assessed by the "size of the house" then one might develop either of two approaches at PBS in the United States or at the BBC and IBA in Great Britain, neither of which is actually in practice. One would be to close down the PBS under the assumption that the public is better served by existing commercial and cable services. A second approach would program, as other networks do, soap operas, talk and game shows to maximize "public broadcasting's" share. Of course, these are not the aims of public broadcasting, nor is the best test of public broadcasting's accountability the achievement of some arbitrarily set quorum of audience size.

Before we leave this anecdote, it is important to pay attention to what Walter Damrosch had done. Damrosch did not find out the size of the ticket paying audience and start a conversation with Rachmaninoff on this basis; he treated the musician *as* audience, as a viewer, and to assess his (Rachmaninoff's) experience, he asked him what was in his mind. This fact should be the first lesson drawn from the anecdote. That a highly selective interpretation has been placed on the outcome—that skill and caution have to be used in dealing with subjective responses and expressions—should be the second lesson. In fact, this applies as well to objective data, which can be equally misleading if treated carelessly.

Thus far, we have encountered two ways of assessing an audience. One is simply by noting its size. Of course, this is more easily done in the concert hall or theater, though even there one has to be careful with mere numbers. Often tickets are given away to fill the house and thereby generate enthusiasm. Also, package or season sales of tickets can produce larger audiences than might have been achieved for certain shows if they had had to compete on their own account. A more accurate way of appraising a show is by asking the audience how they liked it or, as in the theater where a routine occasion has been established for this purpose, by noting the nature of the applause (or catcalls). We are not concerned in this book, however, only with assessing an audience; we wish to gain an understanding of the "Screen At Home"—a much broader problem. To do this, we will look more deeply into the phenomenon most widely called "television" (literally, meaning far-seeing, just as, in German it is called "fernsehen," although the viewer does not see anything far away— screens are all too often positioned unhealthily close—and the term does not logically exclude video-cassette viewing, or teletext). For practical purposes, television can be understood as the home screen that is used for viewing picture programs. These may have been broadcast, brought by cable, carried on cassette, or rarely, even made by oneself with a videocamera (hardly "tele", or "fern"). In English speaking countries, television services were inaugurated in 1936 (BBC in London) and in 1939 (RCA/NBC at the New York World's Fair); however, the war and the heyday of radio briefly stood in television's way.

When television began in earnest in Great Britain soon after the end of World War II, the broadcaster filled in with film of a potter's wheel because there were gaps between programs. For some time this image was more the butt of jokes than an object of interest for critics or interpreters of the new screen phenomenon. Yet with hindsight there may be more to be said about the image, and it may be better remembered than many of the programs that surrounded it. Although it may have been chosen simply as a pleasant image of creativity many interpreters saw its message as something more somber. The clay stands for consumers who were now there to be molded by the potter of the program provider; the result could be a simple but serviceable product, rarely a work of high art, but more often broken into a sharp-edged and dangerous object. The phenomenon of television (which will not be called a medium in this book, for reasons explained later) has evoked a substantial body of analysis of its production process; it has perhaps prompted an even larger literature about its viewers, and although a huge body of ephemera has been written and spoken about current programs and their participants, comparatively little of the screened product itself survives that is accessible for enjoyment or scholarship.

The phenomenon of print gave rise to the two meanings of literature, that is, the act of making written works to be shared as a widespread experience and the product itself. Less widely shared ways of creating meaningful objects have also generated bodies of work known by cognate terms; thus, portraiture and sculpture are the acts of production as well as the harvest of each particular field of work. The scripts of plays for the theater are securely part of literature, and this may be the reason why in the United States theater is known as "legitimate." Cinema and subsequently television are by implication "illegitimate." Although a few movies and television programs have scripts in print and others receive "novelization," it has so far only been print that has given screen products a widespread availability and permanence.

What does the word literature itself teach us about television? The first section, "litera," refers of course to letters; the suffix "ure" originates in the Latin past participle "us," designating the completed product rather than the act of production. This may be why furniture and caricature refer to the results of an activity rather than to a particular kind of creative activity itself. So, although the word "cinemature" has been devised and used in its own field, there is no cognate term as yet in obvious use for television. What would be needed is a word specifying the kind of signs involved, and the suffix "ture": televisture; or more fully, televisauditure; or visauditure (for the prefix "tele" is misleading, since it tells us nothing about the process which is of direct relevance to the user), or audivisiture. However, such neologisms are not only ungainly, they are also unnecessary.

The absence of the term because of the absence of the product it might refer to has been noticed by several writers, though they may in different ways have somewhat exaggerated the position. Wright (1975, pp. 6–7) argued that the products of mass communication are "not to be entered into permanent records" and are "regarded as expendable." Levy and Fink (1984, p. 57) declared that "if one criterion of artistic merit is longevity of appeal, then television's fleeting fare can not meet the test of time." Such a remark may perhaps be made more readily in the United States than in Great Britain, where there are frequent programs of great artistic merit, which certainly do have long-term appeal. However, it is also true that the absence until the 1980s of videorecorders has denied observers the means to compile a widely shared televisture. This will now change. In Great Britain by the end of 1986, several estimates agree that well over 40% of homes possess videorecorders, while in the United States the figure simultaneously passed 15%. Beville (1985, p. 275) estimated that by 1990 in the United States, 55 million homes, or 59%, would be equipped with VCR, thus surpassing cable, which he estimated would reach 52% of U.S. homes by the end of the decade. These devices, as well as videodiscs, enable screen programs to reach a mass public as retrievable products, allowing them to attain a status not won by the cinema alone—that is, to become "legitimate."

When television programs lose their present evanescent status, they will be open to more permanent and sustained criticism and evaluation. In turn, some screen products will gain a significance and value beyond that of the fleeting impressions they registered during the first television age. The public will become critics themselves and will back up their evaluations, as they do now with works of literature, music, and theatre, by buying recordings and being willing to pay to attend repeat performances where the product is experienced communally rather than privately. When programs survive in this way in public esteem and a written and oral lore is generated about them, this will exemplify one kind of evaluation and assessment of an artistic or cultural product (i.e., one which expresses ideas and feelings). Currently, the modes of systematic assessment of television are barely skeletal in public, even if they have attained some better depth in esoteric academic and even industry circles.

THE GRASS ROOT RESPONSE

What are the common modes of assessment of television in its first age, before the arrival of visual recording and the simultaneous invasion of the screen by games and other more sophisticated applications which change its character? There have been at least five such modes. First, people discuss what they see and thereby influence each other's opinions about what they have seen. This kind of assessment is like rain disappearing into the sands of the desert. It is largely unavailable to the producers, nor in aggregate to the critical community or public at large. In the live theater, direct feedback from the audience affects the players and can enhance or inhibit their performance. At one American opera performance in which the words were being displayed in supertitles the display mechanism broke down; the players did not know exactly what had happened, but they sensed a very different (and less informed) response from the audience. Even in the cinema the assembled audience can be observed as they laugh or cry, consume more snacks, or go for walks in the auditorium; their responses affect each other and eventually, albeit at second hand, reach those who made the films.

This is much less possible with television. Nevertheless, despite its currency in but small circles of shared reflections, direct behavioral reaction and comment is thus the first mode of television assessment, and there have been enlightening studies in this field. Lull (1982) observed families' viewing and worked toward a typology of their different ways of relating to the screen; Liebes (1984) used focus group discussions to shed light on the ways in which Israeli viewers of different cultural backgrounds understood *Dallas*. In Italy Capocasa, Denon, and Lucchi (1985) reported an in-home observational study of several hundred families, concentrating on their experience watching advertisements, and in England, Hobson (1982) contributed a substantial book about women's feelings about the soap opera *Crossroads*. Similarly Morley (1980, 1986) wrote about the early evening local magazine program *Nationwide* and on families' different styles of viewing. Taylor and Mullan (1986) produced a popular work on various aspects of viewers' relationships with life as represented on "the box." All of these studies have a social anthropological flavor and face a difficult problem, for if they set out to reflect the grass root response it seems consistent to do so in terms which are accessible to a wide popular readership. This may tend to obscure the discipline with which such studies may be assembled or even, in some opinions, to dilute it somewhat, but it is worthwhile to discern a particular strand of work in which a great deal of variety of popular experience can be represented.

SCALES BEFORE THE EYES OF INDUSTRY: AUDIENCE WEIGHED AS A COMMODITY

Much more prevalent and powerful is the measurement of audience size. Such a measurement, however, can actually reduce understanding of the nature of the experience the screen has engendered, or at least destructively narrow it down, if it is used as is all too common with little or no reference to other modes of assessment. Measurement of audience size produces an index unfortunately termed "the ratings." Why should we see this term as a misnomer? A simple answer begins with another question: Who does the rating, that is, rates an object to produce or contribute to a figure called the program's "rating"? Did the viewer actually "rate" the program by the mere act of looking at it? No. In no publicly known system of "ratings" assessment have viewers actually rated what they saw; they merely saw it. To interpret the act of viewing as equivalent to evaluating a program and to take the number of people who turn out to see an item as a measure of its subjective value is to make two assumptions: first, that people are capable only of a bimodal scale of response: watch or not watch—watch means good, not watch means bad; second, that the population is homogeneous with regard to taste, so that if many people watch a program, this indexes the extent to which a program has appeal or experiential merit over and above its value to a smaller audience. Both assumptions are false.

Before we assign the ratings to their proper place, we should reflect on how the term became entrenched. There may have been conscious intent to mislead at the outset. Or, the term may be a result of sloppy thinking. In one sense the term does relate to quality, albeit not as far as the viewers themselves need be concerned. It is well known in the social sciences that the word rating connotes subjective value. We rate people for kindness or diligence because we can not easily measure directly such attributes objectively, as can be done for example for height or weight. Therefore, any social scientist who participated in this use of ratings (or more correctly, misuse) has been negligent. In mitigation, the common sense notion that, given some alternatives, what people choose to do is both qualitatively and morally right, has some plausibility. Thus, the programs with the largest audiences are termed the most popular, and this term shades into the designation of intrinsic merit.

The third gloss on the term "ratings" is that it does refer to quality, but, as several writers have pointed out (Gandy, 1982), it is the seller of advertising space rather than the individual program viewer who is pleased in exact proportion to audience size. This application of the term cannot be denied, but it is not the meaning implied when the word is so often displayed in the press. Beville (1985, pp. 308–309) reports that in 1977 the largest audiences received for episodes of a regular mini-series, *Roots,* ranged from 45% to 50% of adults nationwide; these audiences were nearly twice as large as the peaks in 1984 which occurred for *Dallas, Dynasty,* and *60 Minutes.* Does this mean that "Roots" was liked twice as much as *Dallas?* Or, by the same token that *Mork and Mindy* (1979, 34%) was liked nearly one-fourth more than *Dallas* in 1984? Such notions are absurd, even though in several places Beville (1985, p. 134) argues that "quantitative ratings" do a qualitative job, or in *Time* magazine's terms (p. 240) that ratings are "an expression of democracy in action." However, perceptive observers soon realized that the audience size figures were determined not only by a program's merit but also by such things as season, time of day, lead in, and oppositional circumstances. The British television executive Howard Thomas (1962) acknowledged these facts and referred also to our third mode of assessment, appreciation indices, sometimes pleonastically called "qualitative ratings" (pleonastic, because rating means an index of quality and one should not need to double the term), as useful in complementing the estimates of audience size.

In spite of the drawbacks, audience size constitutes the "one hand clap" of the chapter title, by which the press and the public generally continue to appraise television. In the United States, Hurwitz (1984, p. 205) explained that "ratings . . . constitute the language of competition between broadcasters and between broadcasting and other media." The main city newspapers and the broadcasting press ranging from the *TV Guide* to more technical publications most commonly refer to "ratings" as indicating popularity (which is correct) and, therefore, merit (a more complex and much more dubious assumption). As an added ambiguity the HUT (Homes Using Television) definition is sometimes used as an alternative to audience size expressed in individual terms, and the two rarely agree. Thus if 50% of homes have sets switched on, it is not unlikely that at least some of the individuals in these homes are not watching, so the individual percentage or rating will be less than 50%. Although in both Great Britain and the United States, audience size estimates are not the only available measures of assessment, they are the published ones. The weekly *Listener* magazine published by the BBC carries a section labeled "Research," which consists substantially of lists of top tens (defined by audience size) for each of the four networks, backed by a short commentary. The *Times* lists the same figures, usually without comment, but the tabloid papers carry the meaning of ratings further, to indicate high audience size; "in the ratings" is accordingly the touchstone of stardom and is thus not a scientific but a quasimagical term or incantation.

Since both in the United States and Great Britain the commercial measurement contractors define individual viewing extremely generously in terms simply of being in the room with the set switched on, the individual ratings or homeviewing figures are extremely likely to be overestimates of the number of people actually watching the screen, which depends on program appeal and a variety of personal factors and social circumstances. For example, a survey (Wober, 1974) included the question "if you do sometimes watch programs you really do not want to see, why does this happen?" Among a representative sample of over 500 adults in the London region, four out of ten endorsed "I am in the room when others insist on watching" and one fourth specified not switching off when the program comes next to something they do want to see. Beville (1985, p. 148) reports a Canadian study in which 45% of respondents indicated they were casual "viewers" (in the room, aware, or noticing rather than paying attention); likewise the defunct Boston firm Television Audience Assessment (1984) found that between 40% and 50% of the audience are eating, washing up, reading, or doing something else while the TV is on.

In spite of the problems of definition just cited, firm (and therefore misleading) figures are not only commonly bandied about, but they are justified by spokespeople with high visibility and status. In the United States, Jay Eliasberg, a vice president of CBS concerned with research in the early 1980s declared "I don't give a damn what people say. I care what they do . . . If they watch it, they are satisfied" (quoted in Menneer, 1981, p. 4). Similarly, a well-known analyst in Britain (Henry, 1978, p. 280) wrote that the minute-by-minute metered diary audience size estimates available permitted "a behaviourist approach to the measurement of appreciation which I for one judge a far more valid research technique than asking people questions about what they like." Note, here, that a distinction may unwittingly have been glossed over between what people say they like in general, believe they are going to like, or, having experienced, did like. We do not need to imply negligence on the part of Eliasberg, Henry, and others, for they may be aware of these analytic distinctions. If so, however, they did nothing to make these distinctions and to cope with any consequences that would arise because of them.

In addition to the "democratic" assumptions of Eliasberg, *Time* magazine, and many others—that action is an honest token of intention and resolve—the behaviorist justification offered by Henry indicates one theoretic standpoint within psychology and one that corresponds with the sociological procedure of dealing with aggregates of behavior, which are either taken as sufficiently important in themselves, or which are used for making inferences about individual experience or intentions. In short, the ratings information on audience size (and flow) resonates with democratic ideology and with sociological and behaviorist psychological methodology.

THE CONSUMERIST VIEW: SUBJECTIVITY

In contrast, a more cognitive and social psychological approach to assessing television is to measure audience appreciation of programs. Appreciation is measured only among those who have seen programs and only after they have seen them. Appreciation is not to be confused with aspirations or intentions, which are assessed before people see (or fail to see) programs. These distinctions have been labeled by some psychologists (e.g., Palmgreen, 1984) as "gratifications sought" and "gratifications obtained"; to these terms should be added "actions sought," for it is not to be taken for granted that people always see the programs they wish to see.

There is no doubt that for industrial, scientific, and ideological reasons there has been less systematic and widespread measurement of television viewing appreciation in the United States than in other countries, notably Great Britain. The industrial background has been mentioned already; the networks sell program viewers very effectively to advertisers using behavioral data. The U.S. networks do obtain results from TVQ, which provides viewers' "overall program evaluations for programs they know along a five-point scale" (Beville, 1985, p. 143), but this information is not made known routinely, much less is it scrutinized as are figures of audience size. More interestingly, it appears, at least from Beville's account, that this qualitative information tends to reside with the networks and stations and to be used for scheduling purposes, rather than to be part of the "language of assessment" shared among broadcasters, advertising agencies, and advertisers. It is known privately among broadcasting administrators and some researchers that in some areas, data on content analysis of programs, of appreciation (sometimes from studio but also from in-home viewer samples), and of audience size are obtained and correlated; but this multidisciplinary procedure is treated as proprietary by those who support it.

It is somewhat paradoxical that in the United States, where First Amendment traditions are strong and where public opinion polling is ubiquitous, a conspiracy of silence exists about "real" ratings of programs. In contrast, in Great Britain and other countries where a license fee involves user payment for all or part of the television services available, the principal beneficiary, client, or customer of broadcasting is not the advertiser but the viewer, so it has been more appropriate to measure appreciation on his or her behalf. In some European countries, such as Holland and Sweden, these results are published, though the same is not (yet) true in Great Britain. Notably, in the United States when Home Box Office provides a paid-for service, appreciation is regularly measured, even though it is not published.

The scientific reason for concentrating on objective measures seems to be rooted in a powerful behaviorist tradition in American psychology. Stimulus-response theories seem grudgingly to have made way for a mediating role of consciousness, but one symptom of this enduring and more material perspective is the use of the term "exposure" to refer to what happens when an individual is in front of a switched on screen. Is the person exposed to the screen, or is the screen exposed to the person? Often the first meaning is implicit in what researchers write. Note that exposure is what happens to a film when a camera shutter is opened; the volition is exercised by the photographer and the film registers an effect upon it without the interfering influence of the action of any mind of its own. The television viewer may be like a film, registering perceptions more or less veridically, but much more evidence suggests that this is a deeply inadequate account of events. The viewer is active, even if when denying attention to the screen so that pictures often fall upon "blind eyes." These matters will be more fully discussed in later chapters. Here, it is sufficient to identify the scientific reasons why objective measures of television assessment, especially in the United States, have held such sway.

As to the ideological reasons sustaining audience size as the most prominent yardstick of the role and success of television programs, Hurwitz (1984, p. 207) notes "nowhere . . . do we find . . . calm reflection (on) the origins and assumptions of broadcast audience research . . . (which) is considered a thoroughly applied science, albeit one encased between the demands of democracy and technology on one side, and those of marketing and professional management on the other." Hurwitz explains skillfully how audience size measurement has responded to challenges to its utility with increases in sophistication and how it serves to ligitimate the activities of broadcasters and the viewing public (the "millions can't be wrong" argument). He provides its exponents with an ingenious argument with which to ward off attempts to include the third realm of audience assessment, the measurement of appreciation. Since all social science is the construction of frameworks of meaning and thus embodies the points of view of its exponents, appreciation measurement is but one more partisan portrayal of matters: "Despite elaborate justifications of the righteousness of their cause the qualitative research schemes proposed by various groups reflect underlying models that simply substitute one group's view for another" (p. 213). This stance, of course, implies that Hurwitz is unable or reluctant to find criteria for or ways of assessing whether the views of one group have more merit than those of another. Such criteria will be explored further, later in the chapter.

What, then, are these schemes? Probably one of the oldest is that described by Robert Silvey (1974) of the BBC who devised Reaction Indices (RIs) to express listeners' appreciation of radio programs on a scale of 0 to 100. Particularly useful during World War II in tracking public morale and its links with the ingredients of the news, the method was then extended to apply to television. After the British creation of Independent (advertising funded) Television in 1955 and its subsequent rise to a 70% share of the viewing audience, a governmental commission of inquiry (Pilkington Committee, 1960) diagnosed the pursuit of popular programming as the cause of the license funded BBC's decline in viewers. The committee recommended that the control body (the Independent Television Authority) set up a method of assessing program quality in connection with the tighter control of a more varied and demanding schedule. The ITA (later the Independent Broadcasting Authority) set up

11

a 7-day diary system by which viewers endorsed each program they saw with a position on a 6-point scale asking how "interesting and/or enjoyable" it was, providing enough had been seen on which to form an opinion. The Appreciation Indices (AIs) were transformed to positions on a 0 to 100 scale and were measured every week, either in London or in one of the other regions in turn, from the early 1970s until 1984.

While the data were largely proprietary, their existence has been widely known and results have been published in the United States (e.g., Wober, 1981d). Among other European countries France, Belgium, Holland, and Spain have all carried out diary-based appreciation measurement; Canada has also followed this practice for several years (see Aske Research Ltd., 1981). In Australia a variant of the IBA's *Audience Reaction Assessment* (AURA) approach has been developed, which makes simultaneous use of both evaluation and audience size by citing the percentages of viewers who endorse the upper options in the response scale provided. Even Columbia has embarked on systematic appreciation measurement after an emissary visited the IBA and submitted a bid based on the AURA approach to their broadcasters, winning the contract against a rival design proposed by Nielsen.

In the United States, moves began to stir toward an extended interest in this activity in the late 1970s. Carol Setlow (1978) suggested in the *New York Times* that "qualitative ratings" might usefully supplement quantitative measurements. The Aspen Institute then convened 24 scholars in the fall of 1980 to explore what needed to be known about television and to set out a research agenda (Neuman, 1981) for the time when new systems of entertainment and information dissemination would raise a host of fresh questions. Neuman reported a "renewed interest . . . in the basic psychology of the audience experience and viewer decision making . . ." (p. 7). Much of the discussion dwelt on the possible foundation of a central research body or council, which would continuously engage in evaluation and special research. Although no such institution was created, an independent company was established to tackle the first of 17 agenda points listed by Neuman, namely "how do viewers react to programs they view? . . . Do more involving programs increase the impact of the commercial messages they contain?"

The company referred to, Television Audience Assessment, Inc., was established "to develop a system of television ratings based on viewers' responses to programs" (TAA, 1984, p. 3). Note that the word ratings is used here in its proper sense of an evaluative measure. TAA departed from the portmanteau scale used by the IBA and from the particular two-scale approach developed by the Canadian Broadcasting Corporation focusing on "demandingness" and "relaxingness." They developed instead a two-scale assessment system (TAA, 1983) comprising an Appeal Index and a Program Impact Index. The Appeal Index is an almost unlabeled entity transformed to a 100-point scale from a mark given on an 11-point 0 to 10 continuum by each viewer for each program seen on a "personal program rating." The complementary measure of Program Impact is derived from answers to two scales, how much "this program touched my feelings," and how much "I learned something from this program" (both given a range of four possible answers). Although initially TAA's results clearly met with some resistance from entrenched network and industry sources, they appear to have met with more interest when it was demonstrated that high program impact probably related to less "commercials zapping" and to better recall and evaluation of advertisements. It should be borne in mind that TAA is not the only U.S. company that has measured appreciation, albeit irregularly. As well as Marketing Evaluations (the company which produces the TVQ), the R. D. Percy company in Seattle has been doing something similar for several years and, although its methods and value have not been widely publicized, they have clearly been of added commercial value over and above the orthodox behavioral data provided for their clients. More recently, Home Box Office had also assessed appreciation of its wares.

In Great Britain, following a further government inquiry into the institutions of broadcasting, a joint BBC and Independent Television consortium commissioned the production of AIs for the use of all television broadcasters. This Broadcasters' Audience Research Board (BARB) AI emerged as a carbon copy of its IBA forerunner. A decision was taken not to develop a multiscale approach, even though the TAA example and similar experiments done at the IBA had suggested its utility (e.g., Wober, 1982a). The thinking behind this latter work had been quite simple and unoriginal; it had followed the American discovery by Osgood, Suci, and Tannenbaum (1957) that "meaning" in English (and later, it was shown, in other languages) had three underlying dimensions of evaluation, potency, and speed. It seemed to follow that viewers would encounter television programs with the implicit use of such an underlying classification system. While it was difficult to conceive of a speed-based scale that would be valuable to researchers and interesting enough to subjects to motivate them to answer questions, it was clear that the existing AI scale was a composite of the evaluative and potency dimensions, which would probably repay being disengaged. The first IBA experiment, therefore, had separate samples of viewers use an interest, an enjoyment, and a composite scale; the second experiment (cited previously) had a single sample use three scales to evaluate how interesting, enjoyable, and worthwhile each program was.

It was surmised that the application of two or even three scales based on the three supposedly orthogonal dimensions of meaning would show that viewers reveal a similarly complex structure of perception of programs and, through them, of television as a whole. Although multidimensional scaling procedures have shown that for particular programs like *Dallas* and *Coronation Street* (Livingstone, 1986) there are indeed independent or orthogonal "ways of experiencing" the characters portrayed, in particular a moral or evaluative dimension and a potency or hard-soft dimension, a similar structure did not readily emerge with regard to programs taken as wholes (Wober, 1983a). Rating programs on enjoyment and impact produced generally closely correlated results. The outcome of all this may be that while people regard the *world* as "three-dimensional" (at least)—having value, potency, and activity—each regarded as separable from the others, *television* is implicitly regarded as two- or even as relatively one-dimensional. This suggests an important reason why television is felt by many to be distinct from reality, and this artificiality perhaps keeps it from having much power. The same simplicity does not emerge, however, when programs are examined more microscopically, suggesting that viewers who develop involved relationships with particular program serials may become amenable to influence from the portrayals that begin to have a multidimensional complexity similar to that of real life.

The IBA's and subsequently BARB's continuing AIs using the single evaluative scale, and the two-scale experiments of TAA and of the IBA provide a rich harvest of evidence, which complements and adds depth to that provided simply by the most complete analysis conceivable of audience size measurement. Some American examples (TAA, 1983) include two episodes of "Magnum, P.I.," which, scheduled at two different prime-time spots received audience shares of 38 and 18 respectively, but appeal scores of 75 and 77; in the opposite direction there were many pairs of shows, such as *Hill Street Blues* and *Dukes of Hazzard*, which returned very similar shares of audience size (30 ± 1) while they differed substantially in appeal, the former with a score of 86 to the latter's 68. With 10 years' weekly reports involving approximately 300 to 400 program titles per week, or well over 150,000 episode and program AIs measured, there are literally thousands of similar examples from the British evidence.

It is sometimes thought that differences between indices are the most worthwhile outcome of diversification of measurement. Yet the reverse can also be valuable. In the mid-1970s, ITV ran a single documentary entitled *Beauty, Bonny, Daisy, Violet, Grace and Geoffrey Morton*. The story of five cows and their farmer portrayed many aspects of care including artificial insemination and assistance at birth. Broadcasters and critics had been concerned that such clinically intimate scenes would displease the mass audience; the audience size figure had to be a product of trust on the part of the audience, based on limited prior knowledge of the program content, and largely influenced by lead in from the preceding program; however, the AI of 84 (10 points above average for the program type) indicated a handsome reception. The program was entered in an international competition and won.

Two American series, *Happy Days* and *Soap* were first aired in Great Britain well out of prime time but proved over several episodes to have high AIs; when moved toward more central times, they continued to deliver high shares of audience size. An opposite example occurred with the Johnny Carson show. First appearing in Great Britain in a slot well past prime time, the AIs were for some episodes in the 40s, that is, at least 30 points below average for the genre; without any indication from audience size or shares that there might be any good reason to move the item toward prime time or off screen altogether, the show disappeared from the schedules. The Japanese audience is one of the few which had failed to respond to *Dallas* (Cantor and Cantor, 1986) and a costly commercial mistake by TV Asahi might well have been forestalled by trial measurements of appreciation.

A satirical comedy, "Spitting Image," began its second series in January 1985 in Great Britain. The program is a form of animated lampoon using distorted rubber puppets of prominent political and social figures. One journalist (Richard Last, 'Rough Sketches,' The Daily Telegraph, 14 Jan., 1985) who had his ear cocked for the sound of a "one hand clap" declared "those who like 'Spitting Image' like it enormously; those who hate it simply don't switch on." Such a conclusion is simply unascertainable merely from the data on audience size. Thirty percent of an AI panel evaluated what they saw, but the bottom two response options (not very, and not at all interesting or enjoyable) were occupied by 18% of the item's viewers; the overall AI was 65, not particularly rewarding, although not necessarily unpromising for an early series episode. However, responses were so distributed that even if those occupying the bottom positions were set aside and a new AI calculated from among those who were reasonably well disposed to the program, the AI would still be only 71, two points above the week's average for the genre. The journalist was therefore wrong on two counts: Those who liked the episode overall mostly did not love it (only one in five endorsed the top option), and a significant number saw enough of it to clearly dislike it. The AI data readily showed that the episode appealed much more to younger viewers (AI 74) than to older ones (AI 48). In contrast, the American based show "TV Bloopers" gained an equal AI of 65 overall, but the distribution was less skewed toward the bottom, and only 8 points separated the top and the bottom age groups.

One area in which AI information clearly adds to that of audience size concerns what are known in Great Britain as Party Political Broadcasts (PPBs), 5- or 10-minute messages made by the parties themselves. These used to receive audience size estimates greatly subject to "smoothing out" effects linking their audience sizes to those before and after them. Not only did AIs show how little these messages were appreciated, but the numbers endorsing their opinions were a coincidental index of "subjective" audience size and suggested that sizable "zapping" rates existed. Even those who did not exit (until 1982 PPBs were broadcast on all networks simultaneously) gave these messages low AIs, in the 40s and 50s. Parties' fortunes could be tracked and even to an extent anticipated by examining the AIs of their PPBs. Although PPBs are in a sense similar to American political commercials (though unpaid for), they are also similar to programs made by the networks portraying the annual British Party Conferences. In 1984 an attempt was made by the IRA (Irish Republican Army) to assassinate the British prime minister, who escaped a bomb explosion unhurt, although five others died. The AIs for subsequent programs from that conference increased over 20 points to reach the 70s for the final broadcast in which the prime minister made an assertive speech.

Similar to AIs for such short items as PPBs are appreciation scores for advertisements. These were measured in Great Britain for some years by a company called TABS. Some of their results have been reported (Wober, 1981d) before the company changed the nature of its business, not because their results were invalid but because of the deep anxiety and conflict they evoked in several parts of the advertising sector, which found its marketplace complex enough when assessed simply by audience size. The market functioned sufficiently without increasing the information complexity of its ecosystem.

Instead of attempts to develop "tactical" kinds uses of AIs, as in marketing or scheduling particular programs, Wober has suggested (1983b), that AIs especially in the case of two-scale systems, might be primarily strategic in relating to policy concerns and that their function is scientific. Thus, it was shown in the study just cited that impact was 10 points less, on average, than enjoyment for the two program types of general information and news, but over 20 points less than enjoyment for all items in the comedy and light entertainment category. In all, the findings clearly supported those using the same methods from TAA (1983) and quite different methods of Csikszentmihalyi and Kubey (1981) that television is, as people want it to be, an ephemeral experience, mainly concerned with enjoyment. Any notable impact is (almost necessarily) limited to a few program types and, at a level matching that of enjoyment from the best programs, occurs for no more than a handful of items a week.

In a public service oriented system such as exists in Great Britain, any mechanism that links market motivations with the implementation of more demanding programs, rather than less demanding programs, will be welcomed by those who run television. This was pointed out immediately after the TAA (1983) report was received. In an unpublished article, Wober reported that high impact programs tended to deliver a greater proportion of those whom audience size measures suggested were more attentively "watching" proceedings, making "ratings" in these positions better purchases than others of equal size. The article was rejected on the basis that members of the industry would need further evidence before they were willing to make changes in their ways of buying and selling advertising space. This position neglected the fact that the industry based its existing decisions on rather infirm grounds in the first place. At issue was temporary convenience rather than completeness of available information. The market was not to be denied the opportunity to think about these matters for themselves, however, for a year later the noted television journalist Peter Fiddick (The Listener, 10 January, 1985) announced "I hereby declare 1985 to be the Year of the AI." Fiddick's observation was that some meritorious programs (in critical terms) achieved small audience sizes but very high AIs: "One run of BBC2's *The Natural World* . . . hit 90 or more every week. There is the foundation of a case for the range that a properly balanced system can provide."

Even more significant would be the effect of TAA's (1984) claim that programs of high impact engender better recall and evaluation for commercials inserted therein. Beyond this, Reeves and Thorson (1986) have reported that advertisements are better remembered and regarded not only when they follow programs of high impact but also when they precede programs of low impact. These results would extend the attraction of evaluative ratings from their relevance to program consumerist concerns to the financial motives of the advertisers. Since Beville (1985, p. 187) estimated that "each prime-time rating point represents an incremental $50 million in advertising revenue" (in 1983 figures colloquially raised to $75 million in 1986) while a study by Burke (Beville, p. 148) showed that 8% of those who chose a program recalled the last commercial seen therein compared with 4% of those who had not chosen the program but were merely coincidental viewers, it follows that knowledge of volition to see, or appreciation on having seen, programs could provide an actuarial margin of valuable knowledge. Nevertheless, this potential added value in information has not been used by both sides of the market in the United States or extensively by policy makers or even the market in Europe.

Appreciation indices have been found to be very reliable measures, as well as being sensitive to program type and content. When the new BARB measurement system was being planned, it was possible to find 858 programs for which two independent ratings were available: the AIs (appreciation indices), measured regionally by the IBA and the RIs (reaction indices), measured with the aid of a volunteer panel recruited by the BBC through broadcast notices and appeals. The correlation between AI and RI scores was 0.82, across all program types; it was higher in the film and drama (nonseries, or miniseries) category (0.85) and lower for general interest and informational material (0.66, N=222).

Probably a more remarkable demonstration of reliability focussed on the 31 programs for which scores were available, first from the appeal ratings collected by TAA (1983) in two American cities asking people to give each item a mark on a range from 0 to 10, and second, from the IBA's AI scores in Great Britain. For the latter, AIs were selected for episodes run in approximately the same time as the American fieldwork, and used three averaged episode scores per series. The U.S.-British correlation was also 0.82. The U.S. average score for these 31 items, 73.7, exceeded the British average by a small margin (71.3). The British deficit is likely to have occurred because their scale involves an explicit element of asking for interest as well as enjoyment with the former, as we have seen, tending to be linked with lower scores. The two programs with highest scores in the U.S. list, *Hill Street Blues* and *Little House on the Prairie* (86 and 83 respectively) also were at the top of the British list (82 and 80 respectively). Had data of this kind been publicly available, they could have cast a different light on the decision to discontinue making the latter series. The two items with lowest American scores in the list (*Mork and Mindy*, and *Newhart*, 62 and 61 respectively) were also close to the bottom of the British results (both 65). *Barney Miller* was the only series whose mark varied more than 8 points between the two countries, the British audience yielding a score 14 points below the American score of 77.

Apart from the heuristic function of examining AIs for specific programs or episodes (in which predictability is much more evident than any departure from sampling error variations) an example of one semistrategic use of these data can be cited. In the realm of art, an ITV series called "Aquarius" focused separate episodes on musical topics, others on visual arts (painting and sculpture), and some on drama. The items on music were preferred by a wide margin (average 76), while visual arts episodes had an average score of 68, and analysis of drama, 62. It does not follow unequivocally that the appreciation levels always depend on the type of art being explored by the program; it could have been that the reporters dealing with one realm were better than those in others. However, the differences do provide a question for further research by those who wish to make successful arts programs: Is music a more appealing muse than others; if so, what may be done to improve presentation and appreciation of the other arts?

The audience size statistic has been given credit for having a "democratic" attribution, but this credit may not be deserved. The democratic analogy stems from the realm of politics where it is closer to a matter of definition that if a person votes for a particular candidate or party, that is in itself a token of approval for the ideas associated with these exponents. With politics the structure tries to give the public a part in exercising power or rule over the society, but this is not what the public may be trying to do with television. Here, the object is to try to align the varied experiences of the public in harmony with the expressions being broadcast. If appreciation is high, one would expect that the appropriate analogy being fulfilled is not demo-cracy (people-rule) but "ortho-demo-pathy" (right-people-feel).

For the science of psychology, appreciation data offer a rich field for investigators of cognition and affect, with mood and personality as additional areas, which can be integrated with these first two by collecting suitable additional information. Just because the behaviorists made such an issue of ignoring the role of mind and experience, however, it does not mean that psychologists (who study the mind) should wish to ignore behavior. In this case, since appreciation measurement covertly discloses behavior patterns, a major opportunity is presented for integrating fields of observation that have too often remained mutually exclusive domains for different psychologists. In this sense, since patterns of viewing behavior can thereby be studied alongside attitudes to programs and, through them, attitudes toward life in society at large, appreciation measurement offers a terrain in which psychology is essentially located in a social context.

The third field of appraisal of television, then, although grievously neglected in formal scientific terms, and all too often concealed as proprietary by those organizations which do practice it, should be considered particularly promising. Together with orthodox audience size measurement, it could provide what by analogy might be called a "two hand clap." But this is to neglect two other very fertile fields of inquiry, which we must now acknowledge.

CRITICAL STUDIES:
TELEVISION AS A "NEW LITERATURE"

Our fourth estate is that which Becker (1984) in a perceptive paper has termed a "Marxist paradigm" in part of British mass communication studies. As Becker points out, this is not just a European phenomenon, but "far more of it has been going on in the United States, for example, than most people in our field realise . . ." (p. 66). The Marxist view of mass communication, Becker writes, is as a potential source of "consciousness raising." If the contents of mass communication consist mostly of expressions of a "dominant ideology" or world view of the ruling middle and upper classes, the larger working classes are either alienated from all this or, if they come to terms with or accept the dominant ideology, become victims of a "false consciousness." As an example, if women rate what they see on television with a higher overall average appreciation than is accorded by men (and this is true), then if media analysts decide that the contents being judged are not in the best interests of women, then womens' high appreciation is a symptom of false consciousness.

It is crucial to inquire about the Marxist paradigm (or its American cousin critical studies, or its French relative, semeiology) what its methods include and what they exclude. Perhaps somewhat unfairly, Becker states that practitioners "have not been greatly concerned with method, except in the opposition of many of them to what they term 'behaviorism'" (p. 75). In short, the activities of this school, exemplified in studies such as those of the Glasgow University Media Group (1976) on the presentation of news, and of Jensen and others in an anthology edited by Rowland and Watkins (1984) consist of a transplanted literary criticism. Each project is enriched by an admixture of ethnography (Jensen) or content analysis (Glasgow Media Group), public opinion polling (Jones and Dungey, 1983, on the views of ethnic minorities), industrial sociology (Alvarado and Buscombe, 1978, on the making of a detective series) or political science (Gitlin, 1981). But as Williams (1973, p. 121) claims, "the work of social and cultural science is only secondarily a matter of methodological procedures; it is primarily the establishment of a consciousness of process, which will include consciousness of intentions as well as of methods and of working concepts."

The difficulty with this seems to be that all too often if investigators are not sufficiently careful with their relegation of methodological procedures to satellite status, they run the risk of the sociologist who studies life in a hall of mirrors or of the anthropologist who records the culture of a tribe from what he hears after having called into a valley of a thousand caves. The images from sight and sound can be those of one's own projection. In fact, the Glasgow Media Group has been charged with this criticism. Hobson has been accused of neglecting mass audience feedback while being preoccupied with the sharper focus and higher magnification offered by ethnographic procedures.

To avoid the danger of wielding the "clap of the other one hand," those whose emphasis and perspective is cultural and political must draw accurately and fruitfully from the other four fields that complement their own. Such self-effacing successful eclecticism has not often been achieved, but perhaps a good example is the work of Frenchman Philippe Bourdieu (1980). In establishing a classification of cultural activities and products and aligning them with sufficiently widely sampled evidence of popular experience, many see in his inquiry a genuine effort to describe and assess part of the role of television in influencing the options for cultural and political development in society. In addition, he has drawn respect from those whose concern is more with experimental or attitudinal psychology.

The science of etymology can make a constructive contribution, as examples in this chapter have tried to illustrate (with reflections on the words literature, rating, exposure, orthodemopathy and, as we shall soon see, with communication itself), in this fourth field of critical studies. Words in current use display the courses and packages in which thoughts run and are constrained. The shape of these words and their origins give us clues as to how consciousness is currently molded; the use of verbal re-engineering may help consciousness to liberate and redirect itself from such constraints.

One may correctly suspect that an analyst of the critical studies school who uses the term "mass communication," is likely to have at least a partly false view. It may take a non-English language native speaker to be especially aware of such nuances; thus, the Polish writer Jakubowicz (1985) states that "scholars are turning away from the old concept of mass" (p. 40). Steven Chaffee and George Gerbner suggest that the adjective mass be used to refer not to the receivers of communication but "to the method of producing and disseminating its content." These observers are making the distinction between old style mass and new style minority targeted "narrowcasting." Another point is that the term communication should have meanings reflecting its relationship to the words "common" and "co-," which imply a sharing not just between those who are separately receiving messages, but between the message senders and receivers in both directions. All too often, "mass communication" really consists of messages radiated outward, or centrifugally to huge numbers who receive the content with but limited sharing between each other (though they do talk about programs seen, and assume that many others share their likes and dislikes). This observation has been made before by the British sociologist Philip Elliott and in a perspective of concern for the Inuit population of Northern Canada by Lorna Roth (1983). By the same token, there is inadequate communication between the intended receivers and the original senders—no effective centripetal traffic; these other writers have not proposed a definitional remedy. However, such a one-directed flow might better be called "admunication" (from ad: towards, and munus: service, or function). If we wrote, read about the labeled departments and courses as dealing with mass admunication it would help to highlight the problem that without good mechanisms of feedback we inhabit a nonsensical world of one or other-hand claps, a world of intention rather than of reality. Ironically, it is likely to be when people all begin to talk of admunication that a fuller degree of communication will have been achieved.

THE WORLD OF EFFECTS, SOUGHT, AVOIDED, AND ACHIEVED

The final mode of assessment of television is that concerned with effects. Here we refer to a large experimental psychological literature, as well as field studies and surveys. These are perhaps most widely known through the U.S. Surgeon General's reports (e.g., National Institute of Mental Health, 1982) and deal with the probable effects of viewing television (in the forms provided) on a wide range of perceptions, attitudes, competence, and behavior.

What can be said afresh about all this is perhaps just one point of detail and one of context. The matter of detail concerns an area of effects to which very little attention has so far been directed, other than by journalists. While most effects studies focus on those "out there" who receive messages from the screen and whose ways may thereby be changed, a smaller number focus behind the screen, as it were, on the institutions whose portrayal, because of the displays of information about them, affects their condition. Such institutions include legislatures whose proceedings are broadcast, sports whose finances and mode of organization are changed, certain performing arts, and to some extent professions like law and medicine whose performance has come to a wider and altered awareness. These institutions are reasonably well organized and sooner or later come to take stock of their fortunes under the influence of television, to make sure that the process is to their advantage, at least in the short term.

One party, however, is involved in this behind-the-screen process, whose collective position has not been widely studied (or defended), that is, the nonprofessional program participant (see Wober, 1978a). One refers here to those who volunteer to appear in games and quiz shows or who are drawn into news and documentary proceedings, but these exclude people who appear as experts whose behavior is controlled and protected by professional codes and prestige, however hard they may be pressed by an interviewer. A well-known example of a vulnerable non-professional pair, the externalization of whose privacy was accomplished in a much more radical and apparently destructive manner by television than could have occurred at the hands of the press, is that of a couple called Greta and John Rideout of Oregon (Nolan, 1981). The husband was accused of a sexual assault on his wife, and the intrusion of television news into this couple's lives after the trial may have played a part in causing them first to reunite for a time and then to break apart again. A family in England, the Waltons, who allowed a documentary "fly on the wall" camera to record for some weeks their somewhat tempestuous life also experienced subsequent disruption, which it is reasonably thought would have been less likely without the catalyzing presence of television.

The point of context concerning effects studies is that researchers in this area should operate a model in which there is a place not only for subjects (all too often conceived of and treated as objects) and processes, but also for the investigator. It is quite possible that the questions asked, or not asked, by a social scientist have some relation to his or her own personal attitudes. It is rare, for example, for researchers in the field of violence to have changed their interpretative position (Seymour Feshbach, 1971, being a notable exception). More often, what they do or publish tends to defend the position they have begun to develop. Other questions and lines of progress get sifted out consciously or subconsciously.

Here, then, is an array of effects issues, ranging from unwitting learning, imitation, or reactive outcomes for individual consumers; through effects on institutions whose fortunes may unwittingly be implicated by the attention of television; to advertisers and politicians who, in seeking to use this channel of contact, sometimes achieve their desired effects but also may find unexpected results; to a neglected but theoretically interesting group whose vulnerability makes them also important. To determine whether any of these effects can validly be claimed to exist is a challenging task, which many have accepted and a few have discharged convincingly.

SUMMARY:
FIVE DIFFERENT COMMUNITIES OF ASSESSORS

The five modes of assessing television have developed to suit the interests and needs of different sets of people, which do not overlap to any marked degree. Domestic and daily discussion helps reinforce feelings or modify ideas about experiences that have occurred; to some extent the publicity for audience size "winners" may affect such discussion, but there is no fixed ratio relating audience size to urgency or frequency of interpersonal discussions. Audience size is the criterion of particular interest to advertisers and network managers who calculate which shows they believe are economically most effective for their purposes. Audience satisfaction or program appeal, the third perspective, should be useful to the individual members of the public in their discussions, and to advertisers and network managers in their deliberations, although little headway has been made in any country to make such information more widely available. There is a minority interest in such data for social scientists, especially if it can be combined with behavioral information, and it is of value to bureaucrats involved in controlling television in those countries where such centralized controls are applied. Likewise, such information should be of interest to the strong consumerist groups in developed countries who, equipped with better evidence, could more effectively press for preferred services.

The fourth field of assessment, that of critical studies, sets out to make an impact on the political world, as well as on individuals. Effects studies do the same. Both of these, however, may achieve their goals more effectively if they were to take note of the results from within other assessment modes. To give a crude example, if violence on the screen is found to carry a detectable chance of promoting aggression (or fear) in real life, this relationship is not only important in itself, it also implies the importance of obtaining accurate information about the amount of violence that is available and viewed.

Integration of assessment methods may well be beneficial and there are some calls for such cross-fertilization, albeit surprisingly few of them. Levy and Windahl (1984) hope that with "a better understanding of activity-gratification relationships, it may then be possible to move closer toward the long-sought merger of gratifications studies and effects theory" (pp. 16–17). In the approach adopted in this chapter, "gratifications studies" are divided into gratifications sought, or needs, and gratifications obtained, or satisfaction. The latter is covered by the third rubric here, of program appreciation or viewer satisfaction. The former, apart from the possibility that gratifications sought are partly constructed as effects of early childhood viewing, is more central to assessing people than television. However, people are the underlying common element in all the five modes of assessing television, so the appeal of Levy and Windahl is seen as thoroughly multidisciplinary. More simply, the merger linking gratifications and effects theories might be encountered by others, not as a union but as a battle. The proponents on one side are those who portray viewing as selective and, therefore, as preemptive of effects; on the other side are those who have striven to demonstrate effects, for whom the idea that viewing was selective tends to undercut the force of their hard won (and often slender) demonstrations.

What, then, are the chances of having integration, or continued conflict between different methods and perspectives? As Becker (1984, p. 77) writes, referring to "those of us involved in more traditional social scientific and humanistic studies" and "Marxist scholars . . . what is needed

... is greater understanding and openness to potentially useful concepts, theories, questions and methods from the other . . . the result will be a more fruitful and rich field of communication study." There is something of a conundrum here; for, as reflective views recommended above which incorporate the observer into the field being observed would suggest, those who are well disposed to cooperation would be more likely to implement a multidisciplinary approach; the mere existence of those with other inclinations indicates that a marked degree of separation among fields will continue to exist. Hurwitz (1984) concluded his analysis by identifying a need "to elucidate the cultural processes and the social and industrial arrangements that have grown intertwined with (broadcast audience) research." But while some ask in such ways for multidisciplinary approaches, there remains a good deal of suspicion and lack of sympathy among investigators of different persuasions. Some of these are summarized by Real (1984) who looks back on an issue of the *Journal of Communication* entitled "Ferment in the Field" and quotes empiricists who disown much value in critical studies, and vice versa.

The view taken here is that it is not necessary for one only side to be correct in the debate between selectivity and effects theorists and in other such oppositions. Likewise, it is by no means necessary or convincing to suppose that either critical or, on the other hand, empiricist researchers have better procedures or perspectives. Instead, there is much more chance that all these approaches have value. Occasionally, an ideological preference of a critical investigator will neglect some evidence or incorrectly interpret something else; at other times an empiricist will come so close to the details of some process that a much broader feature of great explanatory power will be ignored. These difficulties must be overcome. In short, instead of leaving the scientist, the policy maker, the program executive, or the plain consumer with the "sound" of a one-hand-clap, the short change with which these people most often have to contend, we press for the merits of the "five fingered grasp." The five fingers are our five modes of assessing television; through a combination of all of them, the path to a proper understanding of events lies.

CONCEPTS EXPLORED IN THIS CHAPTER

Communication. With the prefix 'mass' tends to become part of an oxymoron—a term where one half has a meaning contradicting that of the other half; since information passes overwhelmingly more copiously in one direction (from centers of production, outward) mass communication may better be termed admunication.

Democratic. People "rule"—wrongly applied to the process by which audience size is used (by industry executors) to determine schedules and their contents; possibly better represented by "ortho-demo-pathy" (people feel right/good) about their screen diet.

Exposure.   Is a viewer "exposed" like a camera film, to the light of the image on the screen? Or is the screen "exposed" to the viewer? Who performs the act of making an exposure? The viewer?

Legitimate.   Theater—and by implication, what is "illegitimate"; question whether television is somehow "illegitimate" theater—for lack of live immediacy, or of substantive record of its achievements (at least, pre-VCR).

Literature.   The process of writing, and the product itself; parallels art sculpture, portraiture and hence (tele)visauditure?

Ratings.   A subjective assessment, the term misleadingly applied to fairly accurate estimates of numerical size (of audience).

Television.   Far seeing? is the distance essential?

CHAPTER 2

The Drive-In Screen and What People Will Pay to Entertain It

INTRODUCTION: TELEVISION AS A VALUED PART OF THE FAMILY

One fine October morning early in the 1980s, a television engineer from the Minnesota station WCCO called on a local family. The station wanted to persuade some families in the community to do without television for a month and to film the new style of life that ensued. The program WCCO eventually made was called *A Death in the Family*, and Dave Moore its presenter suggested (with the help of Professor George Gerbner as an expert witness) that television is a most potent presence wherever it goes. The problem of television's supposed power is a complex one, to which we will return, but before we see what it may accomplish for good or for evil, we should first note something that WCCO program makers discovered at the outset of their experiment, although they gave it little notice themselves.

At the start of the program, it was casually mentioned that among 45 people approached by the station's representatives, 27 dismissed the idea of doing without television for a month, even though this meant forfeiting the $500 fee they were each offered. Eventually, five families were recruited for the experiment, but none were willing to continue the experiment at the end of the month. In short, to have television at all was worth at least $500 a month to each of these families. What is more, WCCO made tactful use of the families' experiences in the program they made, and there can be little doubt that the publicity and the permanent record of participation constituted an additional psychological reward. For the families who declined to participate in spite of such possible financial and emotional gain, it is appropriate to set a value greater than $500 per month on the availability and use of television.

Under normal circumstances, these families were not paying anything for the use of their sets (apart from the depreciation of the capital costs, and the rate for the electricity consumed, both of which are negligible and in the vast majority of households unnoticed items). Instead, the free market, in "selling" viewers to advertisers, was giving the viewer a potentially costly present. Although this is a curious, albeit accidental, phenomenon in a society where it is generally regarded as ethically and motivationally correct for consumers to pay for what they consume, it has a close parallel in Great Britain where the ethics of consumption and payment are probably quite different.

Great Britain is known as a welfare state where the National Health Service provides an example that every citizen has a right to the best medical care available, without direct need to pay per use. Education and many museums and art galleries are financed by the state or municipal authorities from the taxes. Although these important structures that give the individual a chance of a decent life are supported indirectly by state funds, each television owner must pay a license for the right to operate such a receiver. The revenue from these licenses (after a collecting charge is subtracted) goes entirely to one of the two competing broadcasters, the BBC. The license is a cost for the household over and above the set rental or purchase depreciation and running electricity costs. Nevertheless, these amounts were not particularly large (color licenses cost £21 per year) when, in 1978 the national newspaper the *Daily Mail* persuaded four families to do without their screens "to monitor the effects on their lives." The project did not focus on the economic value of screen services and it was only from an aside that the reader might discover that one family "made no secret of the fact that they were taking part . . . only for the money . . . the £200 . . . went towards buying the lease of their house." In another of the four families "not even for £200 a month for the next five months would they agree to forego the television again." The Daily Mail did not shoot film or videotape, but they featured their families in regular stories, again providing a probable psychological bonus in addition to the monetary reward the participants had received.

Both of these journalistic experiments (as well as a French project reported by Belhassen, 1986) uncovered an important truth about the screen in the home. It has, like the hearth, taken on the role of something more than a friend. The kinds of meaning one would give to the word "value" in describing the importance of television in this perspective would tend to avoid reference to amounts of money. We would think of existential value or social value. But television is not even alive like a pet (and pets can be bought), and lawyers and insurers express even real human life, or parts of it such as limbs or faculties, in financial terms, so it is sensible to try to assess the monetary value of television screens and what appears on them.

THE SIZE OF THE MARKET
AS AN INDICATOR OF THE SCREEN'S VALUE

What, then, is television worth to those who use it? The question is rarely asked in that form in the United States, or in Great Britain. In the United States the viewing hours come free as a part of the deal in which the viewers are "exposed to" the commercials between which the programs fit. It is almost as if the networks or the advertisers might even be put in the position of paying viewers a small fee for sitting still and paying attention to the commercials, from whose effects the advertisers seek to reap their profits. It is no wonder that in this setting of transactional ambiguity the term legitimate is forfeited. Only when cable television came along did public opinion pollsters ask how much people would pay for a service that provided a marginal enhancement to what they were already getting. People were asked "if you could receive x channels of such and such contents, how much would you pay to secure each, or all of these channels?" Forecasts often turn out to be reasonably accurate, partly because the vendors then set their prices according to what the pollsters publicize, via the press.

The alternative question is rarely asked and even less often made a reality to people: How much would you pay to get back a withdrawn service; or how much would you forego so as not to have the service withdrawn? In Great Britain, such questions are never asked because the journalists and administrators act as if they know what television is worth to the individual user or family. In early 1981 the license for a color set stood at £34 per annum (the dollar then stood at $1.80=£1). When the BBC asked for a substantial increase to £50 annually, the press seemed to explode with indignation. Paul Johnson, a noted recruit to right wing thought wrote in a story entitled "Auntie BBC Whines for a £50 TV Licence" (Daily Mail, 5 November, 1981) that such an increase would be inflationary, a regressive tax "hitting the lowest paid workers hardest" and inadvisable for a government to approve for "a body which makes the task of government so difficult." The rise was affirmed for £46 and criticism evaporated. In 1984 exactly the same argument was repeated, this time in opposition to a desired hike to £65. The point is, that in 1981 the public "knew" that £34 a year (or thereabouts) was a fair price; and in 1984 they likewise knew that £46 was acceptable. Virtually no journalist in 1984 attacked the existing price; they all opposed the requested increase.

All this is a far cry from the evidence emerging from withdrawal experiments in field economics, which suggests that £200 a month (or £2,400 a year) is one way of expressing the psychological value of having the facility to receive public service broadcasting. It is usually considered that the license, which is the BBCs principal source of finance, is therefore a BBC dedicated tax. Even if this was so, it must be seen as paying for two national television networks, four national radio channels, and a score of local or regional subsidiaries. It would be more correct, however, to regard the British television license as the sum which legitimizes the payer as entitled to receive a larger system of public service broadcasting, consisting (apart from radio) of four channels of television, of a quality which users are accustomed to consider one of the best, if not the best in the world. Blumler, Nossiter, and Brynin (1986) noted that British television shows have won far more prizes over the years at international industry festivals than have competing shows from other countries. Journalists said that £65 a year for this deal was outrageous (and many readers wrote in to agree), but the experiments their colleagues have conducted at the very least raise the possibility that such amounts are perhaps one fiftieth of the true value which they should express.

Further evidence for the value that individuals place on television can be seen by noting what happens when television is introduced into a prosperous society and into a poor one. People lose little time in acquiring television sets. In the United States only 8 thousand monochrome sets were in homes in 1946; four years later in 1950 10.5 million sets were in homes; by 1955 that figure had more than tripled; in 1965, over 66 million noncolor sets were owned (De Fleur and Ball-Rokeach, 1973). Similarly, color set ownership rose from 1 million at the turn of 1962 to over 45 million ten years later. By 1960 the average ownership had reached one set per household, and ten years later the figure was approximately three sets for every two households. In the Inuit community of Frobisher Bay, nearly every household acquired television sets only six months after transmissions became available (Valaskakis, 1983). Once the set had been acquired, for the negligible added cost of the electricity (and the unseen and debatable cost in the purchase of consumer products) entertainment was available "free." Of couse, the cost of advertising (Beville reports $16 billion in 1983) is not a gift and must be recouped somehow. Although it has been argued that nothing is added by advertisers to the market prices of commodities and services, which simply become more copious and efficient, others contend, more credibly, that at least half this sum is added to individual spending, which comes to over $300 per head per year. It could be cheaper and more effective for advertisers to pay the population to attend special screenings of their advertisements and omit the programs altogether! Fortunately for the networks, no such eccentric thoughts have been advocated.

Similar figures tell the tale of the uptake of television in Great Britain. In 1947 less than 15 thousand monochrome sets were licensed; by 1950 this became one-third of a million. Five years later the number had risen fifteen-fold, and by 1960 over 10 million monochrome sets were licensed. In 1970, nearly 16 million licenses were issued, and in 1975 a ceiling of 18 million homes were obtaining licenses (BBC, 1984). This figure omits between 1.5 and 2 million additional homeowners, who are estimated to operate sets but who neglect or evade license payments. This story of rapid uptake is repeated in other countries. Sometimes authorities may be reluctant for internal reasons to develop a television service, but because so many citizens contrive to watch broadcasts transmitted from neighboring (and sometimes hostile) countries, governments realize that their populations are extremely keen to obtain screen services and generally prefer to provide them domestically. Examples include Israel, where the use of available Jordanian channels could be reduced by more domestic alternatives, and Turkey, where up to 30% of viewers in coastal regions were viewing Greek stations.

ABSENCE AS AN ORGANIZED POINTER
TO SCREEN VALUE: THE TALE OF PETER TAVY

So far, we have discussed the needs among the population for screen services as if these needs were uniform. This is by no means true, as later evidence will show. Nevertheless, two field experiments in 1984 showed how widespread was the force to acquire and keep sets, whether or not license charges were involved. The story in 1984 began in Farmington, Connecticut, where the children's librarian Nancy De Salvo was concerned by the results of recent research showing that heavy viewing was linked with lower levels of reading skill. According to one reporter (Allen-Mills, 1984) "with the agreement of local schools, Farmington embarked on a communal New Year resolution to turn off television sets for January." This may have been the resolution; but what was the response? Newspapers and television reporters in several countries took note and featured the story. Direct enquiry to Miss De Salvo and to two neighboring university research departments suggest two things: No systematic assessment of the project took place; and observance of the resolution was at best patchy, and certainly not universal. It is not easy therefore to produce abstinence from television, even in a good cause and with the eyes of the nation and part of the world upon the community.

Two British newspapers were not merely intrigued by this, but decided to emulate the Farmington project. The more intellectual *Guardian* (23 January, 1984) contented its readers with an article on how Hungary does without (its own) television on Mondays (they neglected to say how many viewed Austrian broadcasts or that Iceland did similarly until recently, when it had to fill in its own services to distract its citizens from watching U.S. Armed Forces TV). The *Express* asked readers to write in to discuss the matter, and from letters "that poured in by the hundreds" they printed ten extracts in favor of doing without television (a welcome idea for the press) and six from people who favored its continued use. The *Daily Mirror*, however, actually organized a week-long experiment. The 53-household village of Peter Tavy on the edge of Dartmoor in Devon agreed to avoid television for a week. Noting the opportunity to assess such a project systematically, psychologists at nearby Plymouth Polytechnic were retained by the Research Department of the Independent Broadcasting Authority to interview at least one person from each household, as soon as the abstinence period ended.

The reporter who set up the project knew that the village hall roof needed repair and that a committee existed for this purpose. There was in this way a coherent network whereby a proposal could be put to a whole (and necessarily small) population and connected with a source of motivation that could be relevant to all. The newspaper started by promising an unspecified amount to the hall fund; toward the end of the week a television set and a video recorder were offered to the committee, and a TV celebrity was signed up to visit the village for a story at the end of the week. Reinforcement for abstinence was provided daily in the form of human interest stories run in the *Mirror*, complete with photographs. Printed posters that identified participants were displayed in their windows; further attention was given to the village by national and even international radio and television. It became known at the end of the week that £1,000 was to be given to the village hall fund, and videotapes of interviews with villagers, and of programs they had missed were all presented as well.

The research omitted five households from the study for reasons of refusal or of professional interest on the part of the inhabitants. Immediately after the newspaper's involvement had ceased and the television celebrity had departed, 54 interviews were completed.

Partly because of the money, material gifts, and psychological rewards which had already been given, it was not possible to get people to set even a notional money value on the idea that they might have to do without television for a week. Indeed, 38 people (70%) said they would do such a thing for nothing, but 16 would not. Nearly nine in ten believed that if watching TV was temporarily made illegal, there would be widespread lawbreaking, and 35% said they would be among the lawbreakers themselves. Nevertheless, estimating the material assets to the village at £1,500 shared among 50 households, £30 per household per week had to be invested to conduct the experiment.

Rather than placing a fiscal value on their experience of abstinence, respondents endorsed two questions on Likert scales asking how much they had missed their screens and how much they might miss them if such a thing happened again. The answers were combined to yield a score on the psychological value of the availability of screen services, and this measure was related to a number of other relevant parameters (Wober, 1984a). One part of the interview consisted of a mood adjective check list to map the experience of the week; the psychologists (Irvine,

Irvine, Auburn, and Auburn, 1984) also selected items from established scales to assess personal levels of neuroticism, extroversion, and need for privacy. The strategy of inquiry, apart from the original intention of securing value estimates in fiscal terms, which could also be related to personality and mood measures, was to establish any links between these latter terms and ratings of television's psychological value.

It emerged first that more people tended to report positive (thought, activity, pleasure, warmth) mood states than those who reported negative experiences (fatigue, depression, anxiety) during the week. There was, of course, the high level of public attention to the experiment that has previously been mentioned. Extroversion levels were correlated with a higher incidence of negative mood reports and significantly, though to a lesser degree, with positive reactions. Privacy need was correlated to a still lesser degree with extroversion. Factor analysis yielded two factors characterized by positive and negative attributes, and the resultant factor scores were then correlated again with sex, age, hours of use of television and of radio, and a measure of whether reading was preferred to a number of other activities. It was found that the amount of television viewing, but not personality and mood, was linked with the rated experiential value of such viewing. This result is simple, though not necessarily obvious. People who watch television more would and do miss its absence most regardless of their other personality and communication consumption characteristics.

While it was not feasible to get direct estimates of television's personal fiscal value at Peter Tavy, the occasion did provide a plausible key to putting such questions to a representative national sample of adults. Telephone interviews were conducted with 1,488 respondents who were separated into two groups of equal size and social composition. Both groups were first told "many of the villagers of Peter Tavy in Devon recently agreed to do without all television and video for one week. Afterwards, a national newspaper gave £1,000 to reroof the village hall." Following this, one group was asked "if a newspaper gave £1,000 to a good cause that you support what is the maximum number of days you would be willing to do without television to join in such a scheme?" This type of question is an indirect valuation. The other group was asked, "If a newspaper asked you and your neighbors to do a similar experiment what is the least amount, given to you personally, in pounds for which you would do without TV for seven days?" This can be termed a direct valuation question.

These questions produced at least three remarkable results. First, both approaches produced average figures much higher than journalistic assumptions of the personal value of television, but which were nearly equal to each other, as well as similar to the indirect valuation drawn from the experience of the Peter Tavy sample itself. Both survey questions indicated that the youngest adults put a slightly lower value on the service than did middle-aged adults. The two question formats produced different results, however, among the oldest group aged 65 and over. One third of this group comfortably exceeded the suggested norm but said they might participate for up to one month (one in seven opted for less than one week, or not at all); therefore, the similar results were not the result of people merely following Peter Tavy. Supporting the notion that a substantial number of people are willing to suggest that television is worth little or nothing to them, one third of the group said they would do without television for seven days for nothing. However, one in ten would require between £500 and £1,000 personally to do without their screens for a week (Wober, 1984a).

Following accepted statistical practice, the handful of respondents who said they would need sums of several hundred thousand pounds to do without television were assimilated to a £1,000 figure for the purpose of calculating averages. Results showed that the average value suggested by the direct question is approximately £25 per person per day; the indirect question gives an average of 37 days for which people are willing to do without television for £1,000 paid to a good cause, equivalent again to £26 per person per day. These amounts come to over £9,000 per year, a figure which exceeds the national average wage per employee. Thus, it seems absurd to suggest that these calculations can in themselves point to a suitable sum at which to set the annual license.

These derived figures (supported by the WCCO and *Daily Mail* small experiments, and to an extent indirectly by the Peter Tavy case itself) are not absurd, however, in two important respects. First, the figures point powerfully to the conclusion that the current assessed economic cost of television to the British viewer is extremely inexpensive (and of course, this is even more true for the U.S. noncable viewer). Ehrenberg and Barwise (1982) estimated that British Independent Television (that is, the commercial channels excluding the BBC) indirectly cost each viewer about 1.5 pence per hour (2 cents); this calculation is based on the assumption that "if TV advertising stopped tomorrow and consumers had to pay less for their goods and services, the difference would be what they are now paying for ITV." This argument has not always been accepted; it was the view of Sir Sidney Caine (1968), once a member of the Independent Broadcasting Authority's General Advisory Council and sometime head of the London School of Economics, that people did not pay for ITV programs at all. Advertisers sold so much more, and therefore charged lower unit costs than they otherwise would have done, that not only viewers, but also nonviewers incurred no cost but experienced a saving as a result of advertising-supported television being in existence.

This view has, however, been challenged by Goodhardt, Ehrenberg, and Collins (1975) who held that advertising did not increase overall levels of consumption but principally apportioned shares of the market within itself. Even if Goodhardt et al. are correct, however, their figures of 1.5 pence per viewer per hour, at a viewing rate of somewhat over 11 hours viewing Independent Television per week, expanded to a cost of approximately £20 annually per viewer. Since there are about 2.7 viewers per household, each paid £17 a year for the license at the rates established between 1982 and 1985; adding the £20 for ITV plus £3 for inflation and the new fourth channel (established in late 1982) brings a total program cost to the British viewer, per person, of £40 per year. This cost is in addition to the cost of capital depreciation and running electricity.

In between the actual estimated cost of programs to British viewers of £40 per year and the estimated fiscal equivalent of the psychological value of having television at all, ranging from £1,500 (actual, Peter Tavy) through £2,400 (*Daily Mail*) to £9,000 (post Peter Tavy survey), an intermediate range of estimates results from orthodox public opinion surveys. Thus, the consumer magazine *Which?* (1984) asked a large sample nationally how much they would be willing to pay, per week, to support each of the four television channels, assuming that none of them carried advertising or received license revenue. The result of this was a total of approximately £120 per year; since this is per viewer, (though answers may well have differed had they been more explicit as to whether such estimates were expected to apply to each person in a household), it may mean that people thought that these services were worth £200 or more per household per year. There is no doubt, however, that, in the light of this indirect and survey evidence, the license fees in Great Britain in 1985 (£65 per household, or just over £24 per person per year) were spectacularly low. By definition, the American network commodity is even cheaper, since consumers are not asked to pay anything directly; what is less known for the U.S. case though is whether the cost of advertising is passed on to the consumer or absorbed via greater efficiency and lower unit costs. That the British claim was cheap was recognized by Ehrenberg (1985) who, in a mischievous tailpiece to an article defending the BBC and its license against the prevailing winds of press fury, proposed that the new license fee be granted not only in full, but with an added £5 per year. He justified this as a modest margin to combine goodwill with prudence, but he did not take into account the material considered in this discussion.

More recently, some research by the author, conducted while visiting a marketing course, has shown another way of assessing television's worth. Respondents were asked to estimate for each of a list of 39 well-known programs how much each was worth to them, relative to two anchor points of reference (two pounds for a cinema seat and 20 pence for a newspaper). Knowing the number of programs viewed on average, per person, within each of the main program genres (Wober, 1984c), it was possible to multiply the perceived worth of individual programs to yield an estimate of worth of the television consumed per week or per year. This estimate indicated that the worth of what was being seen was about ten times the actual cost per household. Beyond this, measures were established of amounts of viewing and of responses to a range of items that together formed a scale of "Adam Smithian" ideology. These cited whether people thought it best to have charges for museum and art gallery entry, the economic price for theater and opera, pay by consumption for school and health services, payment for screen services viewed off air and for recording on to cassette, and so on. Two relationships emerged, one being that those who viewed more tended to cite a lower worth of their viewing diet, and those who had greater support for Adam Smithian ideology also cited lower values for the items in their viewing experience. The method shows a concordance with the others cited above, in that it suggests that the worth of what is being consumed is five, or even ten times as great as the amount being paid for it in the British system. It also opens the way to relating economic concepts with psychological ones, in a variety of useful ways.

The evidence presented thus far deals with the average value of having screen services available at all. We have not as yet distinguished to any purpose any principles of differentiation that might affect the perceived values of different kinds of services. Variables at issue are the number of basic channels available, the nature of program scheduling (whether it is complementary, thus increasing choice, or parallel, thus reducing it), the presence and organization of advertising (in Germany, for example, and in the early years of commercial television in Great Britain, there were advertising magazines of commercials linked together; this is in clear distinction from an approach which permits advertisements placed in program breaks), and the social controls applied (for example, no violence is allowed in Swedish television). These and other variables could well have substantial and interacting effects on what people think screen services are worth. In addition are questions of cable, video recorders, and satellite additions. Such additional facilities may increase the perceived values of total screen services in a variety of ways, including (though it is unlikely) multiplicative, monotonic (additional features raising perceived values as though by the increase of units equal to those defined by the first ones), or more likely a diminishing additive appeal.

The foregoing discussion has dealt with two distinct, but obviously connected, aspects of personal value. One is the *psychological* value in terms of a need for stimulus that screen services seem to provide most persuasively. This psychological value will be shown in the next chapter to take a variety of forms, so that certain kinds of material are more extensively used than others, though the different forms (or program types) tend to provide similar levels of satisfaction. The other aspect of personal value is expressed in *economic* or monetary terms and refers to how much people are prepared to pay. In the next section, this aspect will be examined in relation to the ways in which screen services are provided. To some extent, what people are willing to pay must also be related to the habit people have acquired over three decades of being conscious of paying very little for a commodity which, if absent, would have to be replaced with other goods and services, like books, magazines, cinemas, theaters, and bars, which would cost the individual considerably more.

METHODS OF PAYING
FOR SCREEN SERVICES

The four principal methods of paying for television include advertising, licenses, central grants, and what has been called "pay per view" (Young, 1975) but which may more usefully be labeled PACT, Payment According to Consumption of Television (Wober, 1981). The technical details of the first three arrangements are known well enough to require no further elaboration here; PACT, however, needs a brief explanation. It was thought for some time (Young, 1975) that it would not be possible to collect revenue unless there was cable connection to sets (in which case there could be central metering and billing of consumption, as there is currently with telephone systems); however, it was soon realized that even off-air broadcasts could be metered by devices within sets, which would be needed to decode broadcast signals that would be aired "scrambled." Such a system was in fact operated in California by a company called Selectv (Pottle and Bortz, 1984) even though it was later discontinued. Many journalists have suggested that this system is too expensive or fallible, so that users would be tempted to fit illegal decoders; others have been less negative. Widespread evasion and tax avoidance already occurs with license systems, but meters are successfully operated for electricity and gas supply and are also being fitted to assess the cost of water consumption.

Without referring to PACT metering systems, the engineer Townsend (1978) declared "the question is no longer 'what is possible' . . . almost anything materialistic is now technically plausible." Soon afterward a trade periodical carried an article (Nemo, 1980) suggesting that every set be provided with a descrambler linked to a meter. Another periodical (TV World, 1980) carried a news item saying that three British companies had announced that they had devices of this kind that could be used with off-air (that is, broadcast, not cabled) transmissions.

There is thus no doubt that PACT is technically feasible, even for broadcast TV. So far, American and British companies wishing to use PACT think in terms of selling new services via cable or, in some cases, relayed by cable after capture from satellite broadcast; however there is no reason why the device could not also be used to pay for public service channels. This was almost realized by Scott (1980) who argued that "the BBC should broadcast via satellite a scrambled signal which would be decoded by a machine rented from the corporation . . ." Clearly, what could be done for satellite in the future could have been done at the time for existing terrestrially broadcast signals. Indeed, this has been firmly advocated by Peacock (1986) who chaired a committee set up to consider ways of financing the BBC. The committee proposed that all new sets sold should be required to have sockets that enable cheap devices to be fitted whereby "encrypted" signals (Peacock makes a distinction between encryption, which is more sophisticated and scrambling, which is evidently more readily evaded) can be decoded for viewing, at a price registered on a counter. Peacock favored a system by which an era of "electronic publishing" would eventually be ushered in and backed a plan of pricing per program as the groundwork for its accomplishment (some method would have to be adopted to allow brief 'test' viewing of a program without incurring payment).

The interesting matters at issue concern the methods and levels at which services should be priced. The options proposed by Nemo are precise and elegant and follow a practice that suits the operation of cable systems providing major units of viewing such as films or major sporting events. Nemo suggested that each program should be individually priced, and the meter would sum up a cost over a time period such as 3 months. This way "beneficial" (such as informative or educational) items could be given a low "incentive" price, with higher costs put upon self-indulgent fiction, especially where it is expensive to produce.

Two drawbacks to this pricing scheme include the technical complexity of meters needed to cope with a wide range of price codes at the receivers' end and the difficulty, economically as well as politically, to allot a price code at the point of distribution to each program. There would likely be a great deal of argument among departments as to whether news merited the same (low) pricing as current affairs, whether every newscast deserved an equal price, and so on. This complexity could conceivably become a challenge rather than an inhibiting drawback, and the resulting marketing tumult could provide an arena like that in the cinema industry, which in some respects television would increasingly come to resemble.

An alternative pricing scheme for implementing PACT could be to make a flat charge *per day* for use of the set. The screen would in this way resemble a large newspaper, like the Sunday *New York Times*. For a flat fee, a great deal is purchased, only some of which is used. This system both provides for satisfying majority tastes and allows room for providing for minorities. This would be simpler for the technology and cost of meter construction, as well as for the micropolitics of production. Both these methods of pricing PACT per program per day involve a variety of economic, administrative, and social psychological implications, which will be useful to examine and interrelate. In considering these options, a primary purpose will be to point to the psychological features of PACT arrangements, since these have been neglected hitherto. The cultural, administrative, and economic aspects of payment methods have been examined, though usually in a piecemeal fashion by numerous journalists, but at least one text (Owen, Beebe and Manning, 1974) has made an integrated examination of all of these fields.

There are three good reasons, at least, for which to conclude that Owen et al. (1974) had not said the last word on their topic. One is that a decade has passed since their work was published, and much change has occurred in these years with the development of new methods of providing screen services. Second, the central focus of their book is economic, paying little attention to psychological notions; thus they have a section on "measuring viewer satisfaction" in which they develop three measures of satisfaction, none of which are psychologically realistic. Thus, these measures neither make nor even evidently realize the distinction between expressed choice (or what the viewer says he or she wants to see, and which some psychologists term "gratification sought"), and evaluation or satisfaction, which really must be measured subjectively after viewing has occurred. To the economists, the users' exercise of first instead of second choice is an index of greater satisfaction. The next chapter, however, will show that it is difficult to proceed usefully with such assumptions. Finally, the authors discuss some administrative and structural matters with an insufficient grasp of their complexities. Thus, they look at "public television" as a possible answer to complaints about American commercial TV and hold up as an example "most European countries" which "place great emphasis on the use of government-run or government-supported systems of broadcasting," giving the BBC as an example. The latter example is incorrect and neglects two points: that the BBC is not government supported or run, and that Independent Television in the UK, while paid for commercially by advertisement, is nevertheless a public service system. Similar hybrids of commercial support linking a public service ethos under indirect nongovernmentally run systems of social control have been achieved in several European countries.

At this point it would be useful to think of a chart, which would lay out diagramatically the four payment systems (by advertisement, license, central grant, and PACT) and the four perspectives in which these systems should be analyzed (economic, administrative, cultural, and psychological). One view of the payment systems could be that they are qualitatively different and impossible to arrange in any linear order; another position could be that an underlying continuum may exist, on which these systems might be found to take an orderly position. Such a continuum may be implied in the philosophy of Adam Smith, who held that a dignified relation exists when the user of a commodity or a service pays for that use, while at the other end of the continuum is the more Marxist view that to each should be given according to his need, with a central pool of state or communal institutions collecting resources and then redistributing them. In this view, PACT stands at one end of the continuum, embodying a condition of direct reciprocity between user and the payment to the provider of the commodity used; next comes the license system, in which it is the users only who pay, though not at the exact point of use, nor in direct ratio to the amount of use. Such a system is seen also in the purchase of season tickets for transportation systems or for series of orchestral concerts, or even in the case of health insurance. Third, the government grant mediated through treasury disbursement of tax revenues has both nonusers and users paying indirectly for goods consumed; the point of payment is so far removed from that of use, and so thoroughly enjoined with other directions of expenditure, that it

		Concomitants		
Payment Method	Economic	Administrative	Cultural	Psychological
Advertising	Flexible income Rich if economy prospers No cost evasion (directly) Vulnerable to foreign intrusion	Tendency to skeletal permanent structures; bought in material, from independents Organisation faces *two ways* (to public and advertisers)	Adverts symbolise choice in a free society Need for social control Entertainment > information > education	Tends to devalue service Maximises usage/waste Encourages *conformism* or ritualism
Licences	Stable income, inflexible High collection costs, evasion occurs Allows tax indexing (though as yet unused) Vulnerable to foreign intrusion	Prompts large, bureaucratised production machine (good for some genres) Broadcasters demand control	Payment symbolises duty to pool resources in a sharing society Ent. ≥ info. = educ.	Does not devalue service, but condones waste Encourages *conformism*
Central Grant	Stable income, inflexible No direct collection costs or evasion Tends to occur in poor, or totalitarian countries Hides cost to public Vulnerable to foreign intrusion	Size of institution reflects size of country's economy Control in hands of regime	Programmes symbolise subservience of viewers to authority Info > ent < educ	Devalues service, permits waste Could see conformism, or other modes, but encourages *rebellion*
According to Consumption	Flexible, dynamic High collection costs No evasion Displays cost to user *Protected* from foreign intrusion	Suitable for large and autonomous production institution	Programmes symbolise choice of expression in a free society Ent > info = educ	Encourages economic, planned viewing; discourages waste Enhances value of service Risks retreatism or rebellion, but encourages innovation

is difficult for people to perceive links between the initial payments and the benefits eventually experienced. Finally, advertising is such an amorphous way of spreading the collected revenue to pay for consumption via the distribution of public goods that paradoxically, in the capitalist societies where it is primarily found, it may be considered as exemplifying the Marxist pole of the system continuum. Research will be described in a later chapter (Wober, 1985a) that provides support for the empirical validity of the existence of a continuum of this kind.

PAYMENT METHODS
AND AN ECONOMIC PERSPECTIVE

Any success in understanding or measuring the intensity with which gratifications are sought from the screen, or the psychological and corresponding fiscal values of such facilities, is incomplete and in a way pointless unless it is linked with a further understanding of the economic, administrative, and cultural systems within which such gratification pressures are exercised.

In the economic perspective the different payment methods have major consequences for flexibility or stability of income for program providers. Advertising provides a payment system that is flexible rather than stable; if the vendors want stability it has to be introduced by vigorous selling activity. During the mid 1970s after the quadrupling of the oil prices rocked world economies, there were fears that television budgets might be tightened, but broadcasters' sales teams pressed the argument, with some success, that when selling is tough, advertising becomes more important. The conventional view that the television market sells only a narrow range of products is quite wrong. A layperson might associate television advertising with washing powder and convenience foods, but one authoritative review (AGB, 1979) reported that the sum of the percentages of gross revenue then generated in Great Britain by the top ten "product groups" was 37%. Over 60% of television advertising revenue in 1978 was generated by a range of at least 30 product groups, not one of which had a share greater than 2.3% of the whole. Later data show that the same diversity persists through the mid-1980s and may even have increased. This diversity, whose symbolic value illustrates that choice is a feature of Western societies (though the balance between the freedom that the choice confers and the responsibilities incurred is less visibly brought into focus), may be a feature of the mass appeal channels, which exist in Britain and the United States, dominating screen use through the 1980s. As channels become increasingly numerous and segmented, with Hispanic and other ethnically targeted services in the United States, or with music, news, and sports channels via satellite and or cable, the diversity of advertising that each channel might be able to develop would be likely to reduce. This would reinforce channel images and could have some similar effect in intensifying segmented patterns of channel use.

In Great Britain, the revenue generated by one national network from advertising was £363 million in 1978, a year in which the BBC's license-based system generated not more than £345 million; by 1984, the Independent Television System, expanded to two channels, took in over £900 million, while the BBC licenses generated £750 million. The United States has approximately four times the population of Great Britain (220 compared to 55 million) and approximately four times the number of television households (88 million compared to 20 million). Reflecting these ratios, the gross television network advertising revenue in the United States in 1982 according to one source (Television Digest, 1984) was $5.8 billion; at an exchange rate of $1.80 = £1, this is equivalent to £3.2 billion which is somewhat over four times the estimated U.K. gross television advertising revenue in 1982 of under £0.8 billion. Since in the U.S. the gross advertising revenue rose from $3.2 billion in 1977 to $5.8 billion five years later, this growth represents an increase of over 10% each year, effectively over the ordinary rate of inflation. Beville (1985, p. 202) points out that to network sales should be added national spot and local advertising sales which were estimated for 1983 to be $7.0, $4.8 and $4.3 billion each, respectively. To this, Beville added $0.4 billion, which advertisers spent for cable commercials, giving a total of 16.5 billion dollars on screen commercials, in 1983. Note, that these figures represent payments for screen time but appear to exclude the cost of actually making the commercials—another large sum. All these figures suggest that flexibility in generating income has been, and continues to be, quite adequately, even handsomely, realized both in the United States and in Great Britain.

In Great Britain, healthy revenue has enabled the advertising-supported system to establish a new channel, with the public service goal of providing for minority interest groups not hitherto served by television and complementary, rather than competitive scheduling. The new channel has achieved many of its goals for minorities and has advanced to an 8% share of overall viewing hours, while revenue across both channels remains buoyant, and award winning programs such as "Brideshead Revisited" and "Jewel in the Crown" have been created. One of the daring feats of Channel Four is to have mounted hyperlong programs, including a reconstructed trial of King Richard III, Nicholas Nickleby, a Wagner biography, the U.S. Superbowl football game in the middle of the night, and other items that run from at least 3, to 5 hours at a stretch. Increasingly into the late 1980s, this channel has provided programs of magazine, documentary, and drama genres reflecting the lives and needs of the gay population.

All this flexibility in programming is sustained by a buoyant income, generated by diverse product groups, in contrast to the constrained finances of the BBC, which has undergone major trauma every few years when its license levels are reset. If economies are stable with negligible inflation and a license is set at a confortable level, then conditions may allow reliable major future product planning at the BBC or similar public service broadcasters in other nations. License systems share the potential advantages and disadvantages of the rigidity or stability of income levels with those institutions supported by direct treasury grants. The treasury grant was at one time advocated by Young (1975) who noted that it could minimize the losses suffered as a result of evasion of license payment. Unfortunately, tax evasion also exists to quite an extensive level, and it is not convincing that treasury finance would necessarily be a more efficient means of supporting broadcasting than would any other method, licenses included.

The great drawback in free societies to a government-granted broadcasting system is that the piper would want to call the tune; for all the defects said to characterize broadcasting in free market systems, in which freedom is held by critics to be something of an illusion (e.g., Gerbner, Gross, Morgan, and Signorielli, 1982; Schiller, 1981), it is nevertheless thought to fulfill the role of an independent information source. Where government grants are the means of financing television, they tend not to be generous. Third World and Eastern bloc broadcasting systems have not developed reputations as sources of such good programming that their audiences resist a strong desire to see imports from the West. Nor do they provide a source of program exports, which could generate demand abroad.

PAYMENT SYSTEMS
AND TRANSBORDER PROGRAM FLOWS

A macro feature of economic relevance that distinguishes the four payment systems is whether they are vulnerable to foreign intrusion. What does this mean? Foreign intrusion can make itself felt in two ways. One consists of imports that are willingly and openly brought in. The other consists of satellite transmissions that a country may not purchase or transmit for itself but which nevertheless may become available. A society with advertising-supported television, depending on its own buoyancy and size, will not necessarily be secure against such foreign intrusion. The advertising system depends on and exemplifies a free market ethos; as such, it would be opposed to bureaucratic controls excluding foreign material. While the U.S. networks have never bought British program series (though they may purchase news material or coproduce items), independent stations and the PBS have tried to use such European material, partly to express cultural and to maintain financial independence from the networks and their associated nexus of producers (Cantor, 1980).

Networks that collect advertising revenue are not in any position, other than by direct program competition, to resist encroachment by foreign satellite. It is not inconceivable that offshore companies might secure satellite broadcasting rights grounded in Central America or Caribbean countries and use channels thus obtained to offer either Hispanic programming of an anti-U.S. nature or conventional entertainment programming in English. Such channels would either seek their own advertising customers, or they could be sustained by governments hostile to the United States. Either way, the U.S. advertising based system would be open to a degree of cultural intrusion. This would not apply, of course, to a wired cable system, provided this was only to sets without the ability to receive off air.

While these concerns about cross-border intrusion may seem arcane to the U.S. view, they have, of course, been a fundamental problem for Euro-Canadians, vis a vis the United States, and less often and widely realized for Inuit Canadians vis a vis the mass to the south (Valaskakis, 1985). Even European countries, hitherto relatively culturally secure and self-assured, have become concerned. The U.K. *Press Gazette* (for 11 July 1986) reported a statement of the Council of Europe which said "while viewers may be happy about the impressive growth of the number of television channels available, governments are not. They are worried this could jeopardize the future of the European audiovisual industry and the cultural identity of individual countries and Europe as a whole." The EEC Commission had submitted in April 1986 a proposal for a directive, to lay down by law in member states various provisions which would include that internal broadcasters would have to ensure that a minimum of 30% of their programming time, apart from news, sports, game shows, advertising or teletext, would be reserved for EEC product and at least 10% should be first broadcasts (i.e., not reruns). The 30% would rise to 60% in 3 years after implementation of the directive.

The individual viewer may tolerate foreign intrusion, thinking it to be insignificant, but unaware of the extent to which a mass of seemingly insignificant decisions may combine to form a substantial and unwelcome challenge. Growth of foreign car purchases proceeds in units, but eventually it may threaten domestic production and yield widespread economic repercussions that individuals did not anticipate, but which would have caused them to act differently in the first place had they known what might ensue. It has been noted that British car purchasing is extremely eclectic, quite different from the behavior of the French market. All over the western world people buy Japanese cameras and their and Taiwanese communications hardware, where price and quality are the main determinants of purchase. Thus, foreign presence in a nation's television environment depends on cultural readiness to use the product and on technical circumstances, such as satellite overreach, which are difficult or impossible to exclude, even should a government wish to do so, provided that domestic televisions are open and designed for financial systems involving advertising, license support, or even direct treasury grant.

Only one payment technique is relatively invulnerable to foreign intru sion because it is a lockable system. This is the PACT approach to financing. Since it involves the use of descramblers in order to use signals involving codes applied by licensed broadcasters, only those imports which the system controllers decide to buy can enter the system. External satellite broadcasters may learn to use domestic codes, at which point the latter may be changed, or at any rate they may be designed to be different from those in operation in neighboring countries. Use of appropriate codes could be defined as keeping within copyright laws; in effect, domestic broadcasters and their viewers operating metered receivers equipped with credit card type recording devices would be acting within a legitimized system, and foreign satellite intrusion would exist both in transmission and in receipt as infringement of copyright and attract legal action. This is by no means to say that such a system would be desired in the United States or in other western democratic societies. It is merely to discuss an attribute of a system that enables it to function in a particular way. Such an attribute could well be desired by, for example, some countries in the Middle East and the Far East, who wish to conserve their national cultures and to minimize distrusted intrusions; it might even be welcome in countries such as Belgium and Holland where the national systems are heavily encroached on by outside activity, which becomes internalized to the possible dilution of a nation's original identity.

PAYMENT SYSTEMS
AND FURTHER ECONOMIC ASPECTS

The most psychological of the economic aspects of the four different payment systems concerns the visibility of the cost of use to the consumer. Like the treasury grant, advertising's cost of production and consumption is hidden, or at least not obvious, to the consumer. This means that the consumer cannot relate the use of a commodity to the cost involved in producing or in obtaining it. These are conditions best suited to waste. Thus, just as where water or electricity supplies are inexpensive and paid for by some other person, lights and running water are left switched on without concern, so too, television, where financed by a means distanced from the consumer, will tend to be left switched on and, by a reciprocal process, will receive little attention. In contrast, PACT systems display the cost of the product to the consumer. Two forms of PACT do this in different ways, and it is important to distinguish their different consequences.

Where payment according to consumption is organized in a relatively gross manner, by a monthly fee for a channel or set of channels, once the fee has been paid, items on those channels may be left on without being viewed as waste; however, there is likely to be a residual tendency to scan the schedules to see what is available and assess its value, and to some extent to plan viewing to make the most of the money spent. If the system exists in tandem with an amorphously financed (advertising, or treasury or charity granted system, as with PBS) source, then while prudence is exercised with regard to the sources and material for which money has directly been paid, waste may still be the fate of the nondirectly bought product.

Waste should be seen here as a concept that has both economic and psychological aspects. The economic features have been dealt with by economists (Owen et al., 1974) but the psychological aspects have not often been examined. Studies of satisfaction (see Chapter 3) have documented how much is viewed but not appreciated and, hence, could be considered as waste of time and experience; some research has shown that people view quite a lot of what they did not want to see in the first place or miss what they would have liked to have seen. All these cases can be seen as defining waste, though perhaps because the term has something of a judgmental or moralist tone, it has not been used as a central way of examining what is used to good purpose.

One of the conceptual differences that has to be clarified between the economic and psychological perspectives involves what is to be understood by the term "demand." As used, for example by Pottle and Bortz (1982), and economists generally, the term refers to behavior, to what people have bought, or used. Thus they say "results suggest that demand for premium channels of nonbroadcast programming is strong and increasing." What this means, in economists' terms is that purchasing and use of such commodities is increasing. In contrast, a psychological view of the term would take demand to mean what people want, or gratifications sought. It is quite different to say of this notion of demand that it is increasing, for this implies that an underlying need is changing, rather than that an existing need is merely finding new outlets.

Once we have made the distinction between the two different views of demand, we can say more clearly that a PACT financing system, by displaying cost to the consumer in a precise manner related to the consumer's actions, is likely to minimize waste of the commodity and to provide a direct way in which demand (understood in the psychological sense) is related to demand (seen economically).

The pricing of direct payment systems is almost certain to rest in the hands of the suppliers rather than to be regulated by some central authority. This autonomy makes it flexible, and prices can be raised where psychological demand is strong enough, so that substantial incomes can be achieved. It is this flexibility that makes these systems feared by those more indirectly financed, such as by licenses and treasury grants, which generally tie themselves to less wholly populist schedules and which are culturally, administratively, and economically less flexible. Nevertheless, as has been pointed out, there are various forms of the PACT financing system which can afford different degrees of protection for minority elements in a schedule. Payment per program offers such protection, while payment per month provides such a broad bridge that the system resem bles that created by the license. Payment per channel is more like that per program and very strong populist channels would be generated in contrast to weak minority channels; the former would have little or no incentive to carry up-market fare, such as concerts, among the game shows and soap operas. The system which might work best for all factions is pay per day, the users' flexibility lying in the option of cutting out some days' viewing, a phenomenon not uncommon where television is viewer rather than advertiser driven.

The flexible payment systems, where income is determined by the broadcasters, develop conditions where the broadcasters become distinct from the program makers. Though broadcasting companies are likely to become rich in prosperous economies, they still may not want to develop greatly in established size, lest in leaner times they might not merely slim down, but collapse; thus, they commission much work from independent and semi-independent contractors. The latter may sometimes seek to strike up political attitudes, but the broadcasting companies can isolate these to some extent by encapsulating them in presentation as outsiders. If need be, they can commission material that opposes any case being made by a particular program. The broadcasting institutions which do, or might, get their income from advertising or from PACT are therefore likely to develop a chameleon-like posture in which their political color is taken from the surrounding society and does not stand out from it.

PAYMENT SYSTEMS AND CULTURAL PERCEPTIONS

One of the administrative or structural consequences that may flow from flexible systems of finance is that the types of program making which thrive on an established team ethos may be harder to achieve or to carry out well. Thus, comedy or drama may prosper when large groups of creative people are employed over a long time by the same body and can work together and trust the resources in depth of the institution. However, a broadcasting company that does not keep creative teams of substantial size together (and which thus avoids the doldrums when they are not producing anything worthwhile) may fail to kindle that creative harmony in its contractors which translates to the audiences as excellence in programming. While the same balance between depth of team resources and the stimulus of newcomers is sought by successful football teams and orchestras, few manage to get it right. The point here is that skeletal structures in broadcasting companies must harbor an ethos more like that of a hotel than of a successful residential college. The former may lack in solid creativity, while the latter may become stodgy.

Culturally, two flexible payment systems (but not the treasury grant) imply a symbolism of the choice that consumers (and voters) have in a free society. The advertising system brings advertisements to the fore as symbols of purchasing choice. This accent on the marketplace beyond the broadcasting field clearly invites some mechanism of social control so that the programs do not become mere vestigial adjuncts of the advertising. One such control lies in the discrimination of viewers themselves, who might not watch if the proportion or nature of straight programming was overwhelmed by the advertising function. Of course, if audience sizes fell as a consequence of excessive advertising time, the market itself would seek to restrain this time in favor of editorial material. If the society does not trust the discrimination of viewers or wants to move the performance of the system to some distance from that at which people view "too much" or not enough of "the right" kind of (usually informative) material, institutions will be set up to control the behavior of an advertisement financed system. While this is an administrative feature on the one hand, its cultural aspect on the other is that it symbolizes a judgment about how viewers might behave and another about how they should.

The two less flexible payment systems entail a symbolism that can be seen as a cultural feature in its external appearance or as a social psychological process of informing users where they stand in their social system and how they relate to their broadcasting services. The license system, if properly explained (though it hardly ever is, at least in Britain) symbolizes the importance of a legitimate relationship between consumer and supplier. It symbolizes an equal status among users so that anyone who pays a license can consider themselves entitled to receive broadcast services of a reception quality and range of contents equal to that enjoyed by any other license payer. Therefore, while in the United States there may be a smaller motive to supply strong terrestrial signals (at considerable cost) to small outlying communities, this is not so in license funded countries where there is a strong obligation on the broadcasting authorities to bring equal services to all license payers.

This obligation holds for the advertising supported ITV system in Great Britain, and although neither the commercial broadcasters nor their controlling body receive any revenue from the licenses, the latter have to be paid by any consumer who might wish to view (or even whose set may be equipped only to receive) ITV programs. The ITV system, though receiving no reciprocal return from the license revenue, has to fulfill complex social obligations commonly defined under the term Public Service Broadcasting, in return from which it receives the right from Parliament to sell audiences to advertisers. It is essential to grasp that the license is in name, and potentiality, a legitimizing device rather than a tax and that it does, or can, symbolize a relationship between consumer and provider that is a socially regulated one. The analogy can be drawn between a license payment system and a game or sport regulated by rules and referees; in contrast, the purely advertising supported system (where it is not associated with a licensed one) more closely resembles a war. The casualties are said by many researchers to be the public who experience a range of ill effects as a result of their mildly pleasurable indulgence.

The other less flexible payment system, the treasury grant, symbolizes the subservience of the viewer to authority. In such a system, the commodity one uses is bought by some distant initiative, without much consideration for the consumer's expressed wishes. Of the triad of purposes of information, education, and entertainment, the treasury grant is likely to give priority to the first, with education also likely taking precedence over entertainment. A license system, if it exists on its own, may be regulated to allow some priority to educational and informational goals, but as soon as it must coexist with a flexible payment system, even if the latter is socially regulated as in European countries, some accommodation is most likely to occur so that entertainment gains in prominence.

In advertising financed systems, entertainment takes precedence over information, and informing (because it is easier to do in an entertaining way) takes precedence over educating the viewer (which implies the application of some minimum of intellectual effort on the part of the viewer). A PACT system on the other hand, which can be free of advertisements, allows programs rather than commercials to be symbols of choice in a society of people free to spend their time and money as they see fit. Approximations to such systems are already available in video cassette recorders and cable systems, and the evidence in the next chapter suggests that the fuller exercise of free choice in a situation where people will have to pay for each such transaction will lead to a heavier patronage of entertainment to the neglect of education and all but the most entertainingly presented information. (This has been dubbed in Great Britain the "wall-to-wall Dallas" syndrome.) With VCR the top ten (or twenty or fifty) sales lists provide good indication of what that sector of the public, which purchases these items, really values. In Great Britain, thriller and horror movies top the lists. With cable, however, a package is being bought so once the cover charge is paid, there is some incentive to make the most of the purchase by using it all. In these circumstances, people will want to buy a cable channel which suits their particular interests, and moreover, one which is not cluttered with unwanted material. Surveys have proliferated which ask people what they would pay for different kinds of new services (music, movies, sport, round-the-clock news) as well as what value they set present broadcasting services.

In the United States, Arthur D. Little (1980) estimated demand for a multichannel DBS service in a variety of conditions. Survey results were used to assess the attractiveness of available pay TV services (as experienced in late 1979); the results were then extrapolated to simulate or predict demand for new channels. Pottle and Bortz (1982) referred to what they considered shortcomings in the Little study even though they considered it the "only major study using empirical data which has attempted to estimate consumer demand for a multichannel service in competition with cable." Using Nielsen data they concluded that "consumer demand for non-broadcast program options is strong and increasing," but that "the value attached to subsequent program services is less than that accorded the first." This apparent paradox can be resolved by noting that the first (economists') use of the word demand has a different meaning from the idea expressed in the second conclusion, namely that the psychological demand (or willingness to pay) for each one, diminishes with additional services.

While this American research appears not to have distinguished among the contents offered by the new channels, in Great Britain AGB Cable & Viewdata (1983) questioned over 2,000 people who had each been sent an illustrated booklet explaining the nature and attractions of different proposed new cable channels. Over half the sample were willing to pay £5 per month (that is, £60 per year, well over the existing license rate, and in addition to it) for a basic service which would consist of the four existing public broadcasting channels but with added films, music and sport; over one fourth would pay another £5 a month for an extra premium service consisting of newer films and special sports events. British survey results between 1980 and 1985 dealing with the declared intentions to buy videocassette recorders have corresponded remarkably well with the numbers of people who report ownership subsequently. Thus, in 1981 8% said they had VCRs and 6% said they were likely to buy one in the next year. In 1982, 18% reported ownership and 9% willingness to buy, so that in 1983 it was no surprise that 27% declared ownership. In 1984, the figure rose to over 35%, and it was estimated that 43% would have the use of such machines in 1985. If these results show that survey estimates have some predictive power in the case of VCRs, this reinforces the value of such data in the task of forecasting the actualization of demand for cable television.

THE PHILOSOPHIES EMBODIED IN DIFFERENT PAYMENT SYSTEMS

Entertainment (as the next chapter shows) is the goal favored by consumer demand. Thus, advertising and PACT systems not only symbolize but also constitute arrangements where the consumer, rather than some indirectly appointed authority, is the arbiter of what should be provided. In this sense, these two payment systems are more democratic. This is not to say that consumers know, demand, receive, and use what is best for them in the sense of not yielding ill side effects; indeed, they may well command and consume much that in indirect ways is dysfunctional—the screen equivalent of junk food.

This review of some of the cultural implications of four payment systems illustrates a fundamental ideological difference in how viewers and their powers of discretion and choice are regarded and handled in different societies. The two alternatives were recognized as far back as the philosopher Plato. Here, the two models can be called the clinical and the forensic. The term forensic is based on the Latin word forum, the place where citizens of competence and awareness gathered to discuss and help determine the course of policy and of public affairs. The forensic model is what prevails outwardly in the United States, being carried over from the political world to the broadcasting one. It implies that the viewing public is to be considered as having exceeded a necessary minimum level of competence and understanding so that "people know what they are doing" both in respect to immediate gratifications sought and obtained, and as regards any subsequent consequences that ensue. This view means that any possible harmful consequences of viewing habits or experiences are considered by society to be adequately anticipated, avoided, or accepted by the viewers. The possibilities that television viewing might diminish reading and writing skills, might shorten patience, or might prompt aggressive behavior or callousness are by implication part of the responsibility of the individual viewer to avoid or to accept.

In contrast to forensic model, the clinical model takes its parallels from medical and public health practice. Just as the Food and Drug Administration may decide on expert technical evidence that a particular substance is dangerous to health and withdraw it, or a doctor decides to withhold information from or prescribes action or treatment for a patient which the patient might not choose, a clinical model of mass communication administration makes specialist decisions on behalf of its viewers' welfare. Some of these decisions are not what the viewers would themselves prescribe. Thus, in most countries other than the United States, Australia, and a few others it is common for informational or more demanding programs to be given scheduling positions which they would never have won in a system determined by market forces; programs overly violent, containing excessive obscene language, or sexually too explicit are not aired; and stringent rules apply to maintaining political balance and avoiding ethnic disharmony. All these decisions are made not by, but for viewers because there is an underlying assumption that not all viewers could or would make the same decisions if left to themselves.

It is not altogether true that in the United States there are no interventions made by a central authority on a clinical model. In the early 1950s blacks were portrayed in programs such as "Amos 'n Andy," in "step 'n fetch it" roles, which were demeaning. Such portrayals received no First Amendment protection when civil rights pressures caused them to be abolished. It must be acknowledged that this was not intervention on behalf of blacks accomplished by a bureaucratic central authority, but it should also be noted that the reform applied more particularly to the men. Black women as well as white women are still portrayed in roles demeaning to their sex, which are not subject to a clinical approach to control, so that a male oriented culture is still supplied, to answer its demand, with images of male power enjoying and enjoining female submissiveness.

Atkin (1986), in describing elements of social control on the options available for cable programming, cites a number of cases in which legal action has been taken, at a state or city level, with varying degrees of success. For example, in Austin, Texas action was taken against a group which aired a Ku Klux Klan program on an access channel. What is noteworthy is that no powerful and concerted action restrains programming at a federal level. Indeed, in attempting to explain why CBS dropped "The Smothers Brothers Comedy Hour," Metz (1975) indicated that Tom Smothers had complained about partial expurgations to senators and FCC officials and commented that "name calling, even if it reaches the press, is forgivable. But going to the Feds—whether the FCC or Congress—is not playing the game."

By distinguishing between the forensic and clinical concepts of control, one can see that at a cultural and administrative level, they correspond with particular methods of financing screen services. The treasury grant very obviously and the license more subtly symbolize or give the means to exercise clinical models of control. Advertising, in its public market orientation, and PACT systems, still more clearly through their private financial covenants with individual consumers, exemplify the forensic control model.

PAYMENT SYSTEMS
AND A PSYCHOLOGICAL PERSPECTIVE

This leads to the psychological properties of payment systems, the final plane in which they should be studied. We have seen that advertising finance tacitly encourages waste; screens may be left switched on with little attention being paid to them. Thus, no money is paid directly for such encounters, and the situation is also likely to cause consumers to feel that payment for such services is not even worthy of consideration. A program on such a service starts off being like a plastic package for a mass produced food; it is rapidly discarded as waste and forgotten. A program brought to the viewer in this way has to make an unusual impact to surmount the handicapped ambiguity of its conception. The viewer is placed in a relationship of "other-directedness" (using Riesman's term). If he or she does not like what is on there is no justification for complaining; it was put there by tastes and perhaps for tastes other than one's own. Not surprisingly, Beville (1985, p. 139) reports a "Values And Lifestyles" research model in which two thirds of viewers are characterized as other-directed; over half of these, called "belongers" are the heaviest TV viewers. In the scheme of another American sociologist who modeled relationships linking the individual with the surrounding society (Merton, 1957), this kind of viewer relationship can be seen as "ritualistic" in which the product of the broadcaster is used, though the goals being pursued by the broadcaster (of showing the viewer certain commercial messages) may not necessarily be accepted.

The treasury grant, producing broadcasts at no immediate cost to the viewer again prompts waste and careless use of the commodity. The viewer's relationship could become conformist (if one accepts both the goals and the product of the broadcasters), ritualist, or retreatist, where the viewer rejects both the goals and the product offered from the broadcaster. The treasury grant system is likely to engender devaluation of the service, especially where the grant has been sparse and has led to meager fare. In regimes where the goals of the broadcasters, that is, the political schemes their work is designed to reflect or to serve, are rejected by viewers, conditions develop described by Merton's term of rebellion. In this adaptation, the viewer substitutes personal goals, rejects the proferred product, and either does something else such as not watching television, or seeks a foreign transmission whose ethos is preferred to that of the viewer's home service. Such conditions are found in parts of East Germany where many viewers can and do watch West German television.

The psychological concomitants of the license relationship are that the product is likely to be valued since it has been paid for, but as a homogeneously extruded product rather than as discrete units of varying nature. Toothpaste is certainly a strange analogy for as good and varied a service as that provided by British television. Yet the service is paid for in bulk, and at an extremely cheap rate; so for spans of time it could indeed be left on without attentive viewing of the purchase because what goes by unnoticed incurs no added expense for the viewer. The Merton adaptations found here could be those of conformism, ritualism, or retreat by having no sets (in practice, in Great Britain only about 2% of households).

With a PACT system the purchaser is not usually buying in bulk, getting the chalk with the cheese across the whole week. This is the only payment system which actually discourages waste and by so doing encourages active, planned viewing. While other systems can be said to promote "other-directedness" in viewing behavior, the PACT systems develop an "inner-directed" approach. In Merton's model, adaptations encouraged here would include conformism and innovation. The latter is where the goals of the apparatus are accepted to provide visual experience, but the user provides new means or ways of using the set. Uses of the set for video recording, Teletext, or computer extensions are innovations for instrumental purposes; TV games are innovations with expressive purposes. The point is that when the license is paid, the viewer is tempted to feel that the product should be used even though this may mean just receiving it on the set and wasting the experience. With specific payment, the user is motivated to scrutinize what has been paid for. The next chapter shows that there are modest or low take-up percentage rates for several types of programs, implying considerable waste since many programs are available which are not viewed. The hypothesis would follow that in a true PACT system (such as pay per view, or cable where channels are specifically defined by their contents and only those are bought which the purchaser favors), take-up percentage rates based on those who have particular interests would be higher, regardless of program type, since only those viewers who wanted to use particular types would pay for them.

One effect of PACT should be a greater control over children's viewing. To promote this result, a rate would be set on programs, or on the day charge that would contribute noticeably toward a monthly or quarterly bill. This would bring about vigilance over cost, and discussion among users possibly to limit the number of days for which the service is purchased. Although not generally appreciated, the statistics which report that American viewers watch television (or more correctly are present in the room with the set switched on) for 6 hours a day every day have succeeded in producing an illusion that everybody views every day. This is dispelled by statistics of daily reach of all television services currently available in Great Britain which show that on a typical day well over 10% of the public have not viewed at all. The same is almost certainly true in other countries.

Because user-free television days exist, a constructive step is to devise or apply a payment system which recognizes and harnesses this fact; people should not have to pay for those days on which they do not watch. Once this becomes explicitly known, then discussion will occur within families to determine which days should be nonviewing, and the broadcasting schedules will be more actively scrutinized to come to the decisions on which days to purchase. The proposal is, of course, no more puritan than that which holds that people should not eat steak on every day, so that eating on some days costs less than on others.

The symbolic message carried by PACT appropriately priced is one of conservation and thus of responsibility in the use of resources. It is likely to be fiercely opposed. One of the arguments notes that old and poor people are the heaviest viewers, for whom television provides an important substitute for an active social life. To deny these people a cheap prop, especially after they have become so accustomed to it would be heartless (and politically unwise). The simple and humane resolution of this difficulty, apart from noting that habituation to vegetative viewing is not positive, particularly for old people, would be to grant a sum added to pensions, welfare, or tax transactions that would be equivalent to the cost of, say, 3 hours' viewing a day, or 4 days a week or to index the meter cards from these peoples' sets so that their bills would be reduced by the appropriate factor.

The revenues generated by a payment by program viewed option are difficult to determine but would create strong pressures to maximize populist programming to the detriment of attempts to vary the available wares. However, with a day rate version of PACT, it is feasible to assume that an average of at least 5 days' use per week for 50 weeks would be viewed; if this was priced at 25 cents per household per day, it would cost the household $62.50 per year and would raise $5.5 billion across the 88 million households in the United States, approximately equal to the gross revenue generated by network advertising in 1982. In Great Britain a price of 25 pence per day per set, assuming the same frequency of use at 250 days per year would cost each household £62.50; since there are 20 million television households this would yield £1.25 billion a year, well beyond that the BBC requested in 1985 (it collects much less from monochrome sets). Such an income would leave a comfortable margin to pay for the controlling authorities which maintain scheduling, political balance, and other consumerist standards not only on the BBC channels but also on the commercial ones. A part of this revenue could also be used to subsidize senior citizen preferential rates and other schemes of assistance where needed.

Though PACT systems have been described here as flexible, for industrial planning it is necessary to have some predictability, which can be achieved by setting the rate so that the revenue generated noticeably, but not greatly, exceeds that which would be yielded by licenses. This would be visibly fair and would build in the necessary incentive for discretionary use. It is this feature above all others that is the strongest asset of a PACT system, for it promotes a consumer relationship in which many of the harms alleged by some researchers to accrue from passively manipulated viewing would be inhibited. This perspective has not been developed by most writers, who associate license or treasury grant funding with systems of social control of television, and link PACT systems (as in cable or subscription TV) with open markets in which products of dubious aesthetic standards can flourish. Here, on the contrary, PACT is seen as well suited to supporting a mass communication system subject to social controls.

To examine the British model further, if PACT was harnessed only to BBC program consumption, it would lose that quality the license has of underpinning a legitimate viewing environment in which controls are applied also to the commercial channels. However, if PACT was based on a day rate, then it would be quite appropriate for the money to be used for such joint control purposes. In Great Britain, this would have the effect of increasing the IBA's independence from the commercial system it is set to control, in contrast to the interdependent relationship that exists at present in which the IBA receives rentals for transmitters it supplies to the television and local radio broadcasters whom it franchises. Carrying these analyses some steps further, it would seem that for countries of the size and prosperity found in most of Western Europe, many parts of Latin America, some parts of Asia and Africa, and in Australasia, some combination of PACT and advertising systems (PACT and licenses do not complement each other; rather, they are alternatives) would ensure public service television channels of high quality and variety, whose use is economically determined to symbolize and express both individual responsibility over the use of resources (one's own, as well as those created industrially) and the exercise and enjoyment of free choice in free societies.

SUMMARY

Countries with established television services nearly always provide them extremely cheaply, and most users have internalized this benefit to the extent that considerable reward or compensation would be required to forfeit such an asset, even for a short time. However, partly because people have become accustomed to enjoying a major service extremely cheaply, they are willing to pay more, though not dramatically more, to the extent of the full economic representation or money cost of the psychological value of the asset for what they already have.

The prospect for providers of cable and other add on subscription services (the word subscription should refer only to voluntary payments for an exclusive service rather than to mandated payments for an inclusive service) has up to now been assessed by asking people what they would pay and also by studies of the experiences of cable companies which provide specialized channels as in the United States. Video cassette recorders offer an additional parameter by which willingness to pay can be measured. British surveys in 1983 and 1984 regularly showed that at least 30% of those sampled and often much more said they had the use of a VCR (the official industry measurement contractor equally regularly turned in estimates 10% less than the average of others). British and Swedish surveys reported that VCR use was split in favor of taking items off air (descheduling), perhaps three times as many hours being given to material acquired than to material that was hired. Rent of a VCR and the prices of tapes for recording programs off air, plus hiring movies cost in Great Britain in 1985 between £15 and £25 per month, which (at £180 to £300 a year) far exceeded the cost of a color license and ordinary TV set rental (£150 to £180 a year) which must be paid by VCR owners in any case if they retain aerials for off-air reception. This evidence reflects our demonstrations that there is much more "money in the pot" for a large segment of the population than has hitherto been extracted by orthodox payment of license fees. This money has also been neglected by advertising-supported systems that hide the cost of programs in prices for other goods and services. The cable companies have, on the other hand, begun to tap this revenue.

The addition of video cassette recorders to television presents a formidable combination, since there is much surplus programming on air or cable which viewers can not use because of clashes or of personal unavailability. This programming exists as a cheaply bought or free though untapped asset which can be harnessed on tape. Furthermore, the video cassette recorder gives the user the feeling of control over technology, more so than does the TV set fed off-air or even by cable, which allows one to choose between, but not also to stop, delay or re-view programs.

These considerations, together with studies (as described in the next chapter) of the patterns of use of different channels, program types, and of programs themselves provide the necessary information to judge which kinds of people are likely to be driven by what kinds of requirements in being ready to pay, to what extents, for new screen services. There is, of course, much scope and even need to know more about the "what kinds of people" question; so far, the small study at Peter Tavy briefly tested three personality measures, but other scales such as measures of locus of control, needs for achievement, affiliation, sensation-seeking and privacy, and authoritarianism will all help to understand the different motivations for, and thus potential values of, having devices which concentrate on information (such as Teletext) or on entertainment at users control (such as VCR) or on entertainment more in the providers control (as with TV or cable) or on psychomotor skills and intellectual challenge (as with certain video games or computer facilities) or on affiliation (as might occur with video telephone). At the moment "progress" is being made by entrepreneurs who often believe in a market without having adequate guidance for doing so (and who often, as with certain U.S. cable operations, fail) in a climate stimulated by ideologues (some of whom, for instance, want to make broadcasting "free" like the press) with civil servants and politicians inserting industrial, cultural, and administrative interests into the mixture. It would benefit all these factions if more attention was also given to the social psychology of the situation for the users of viewing devices and services. This we shall do in the next chapters.

CONCEPTS EXPLORED IN THIS CHAPTER

Absence. Of a service or a facility provides one pointer to its value.

Clinical. A model of the viewer implying a low degree of awareness and competence for control, hence leaving room for an elite who may take control, to a greater or lesser extent, justifying this as in the viewer's own interest.

Cost. Viewing of "nonpay" TV has hidden costs, passed on through the price of goods and services, to viewers and nonviewers.

Democratic. Ideology underlying preference for certain payment systems implying that viewers have, and express collective choice of and control upon the contents of the market.

Forensic. From forum. A model of the viewer implying a high awareness and participation in control of events that affect the self.

License. Not a fee or a tax but a *legitimating* payment regularizing a relationship between user and provider in a system of social order.

Merton's Paradigm. American sociologist holding that the modes of ajustment of the individual to the social context are identifiable as distinct patterns and include conformism, ritualism, retreatism, rebellion, and innovation.

Payment Systems. At least four can be identified: Pay according to consumption (PACT), license, treasury grant, and advertising.

Subscription. A payment usually voluntary for an exclusive service rather than mandatory and applicable to (almost) universal users of a service.

Value. Worth has a psychological as well as an economic dimension.

CHAPTER 3

Types of Programs as Produced, Partaken, and Perceived

INTRODUCTION: THE NEEDS FOR
AND USES OF CATEGORIZATION OF FARE

Divide and Rule: the Roman adage has been presented as a hard pre-scription for empire builders, reflected in St. Matthew's observation that a house divided against itself will fall. But perhaps the precept had an-other meaning of which the Romans themselves were well aware, and which can serve as a useful lesson for political and communications scientists today. This meaning is based on understanding division not as a destructive but as an intellectually creative act. Thus, Caesar divided Gaul into parts so that each was meaningfully and administratively sepa-rate and amenable to order. The same is the object of scientists, to classi-fy phenomena into sets and types so that their behavior may be more effectively understood, predicted, and ultimately controlled.

To see the relevance of this observation to the study of screen use it may help to imagine an opposite to the Roman precept: "unite and re-lease" or "corral and create." The image thus created is of a different kind of empire building, that of the edifice of wealth. It is noteworthy that the former strategy has been more characteristic of a number of phenomena in Europe, including the way in which television has been handled, while the latter has been more characteristic of the United States. To divide, classify, order, and administer has been more of a European way with television, leading to lists of program types each subject to quotas and positioning rules, and of which particular effects may be suspected. In America by contrast prominent theorists (eg., Gerbner and Gross, 1976, pp. 175–177) have emphasized the homogeneity of television's essential nature and have held back from the notion that it could be regulated. It is not necessary of course to follow scientific division and analysis with onerous political constraint; and the former can be productive in other ways, for example in educating the public toward the realization of a forensic model of consumption and away from the clinical perspective more characteristic of European television regimes.

To ask whether television's contents are homogeneous invites a look at their origins, and by their varied sources one recognizes strands that are still effectively separate. From theater and cinema television took plays and films, while from vaudeville came variety formats to the screen. Both cinema, radio, and the press were sources of television newscasts and current affairs (see Altheide, 1976; Schlesinger, 1978). Since from the beginning, television was screened in homes rather than in public places, at least in the United States and northern Europe, the "parlor games" and quizzes of yesteryear were rapidly worked into a wide range of lastingly popular game shows. Soap opera was taken over from radio (see Cantor and Pingree, 1983) which had in turn developed it from print. Since television so swiftly reached millions of consumers the serial and developing format, rather than the single and repetitively conservable form of the live theater, was favored.

Television has also invented its own new forms of content. Thus, docudramas have crossed current affairs with soap opera, while the miniseries such as *Roots* and *Winds of War*, which attracted the largest audiences of 1977 and 1983, and later the *Thorn Birds* has explored the development of a story across from four to a dozen episodes while amplifying the effect of the content by concentrating the scheduling to reach vast numbers of viewers simultaneously. Electronic devices of image manipulation including color changes, spatial rotation, reversal, split images, magnification, and superimposition have made new art forms of presenting titles, credits, station logos, and other linking material, as well as burgeoning with music into a family of entertainments much wider than the best known "pop videos." Electronic flexibility has also helped the development of humanoid puppets and rubber creatures, which have been given roles both in children's entertainment and information, as well as in adult political satire. Another achievement of television has been the exploitation of personal privacy (see Wober, 1978d) which takes place in several ways. Apart from the relatively trivial solecism of embarrassing the participants in game shows are clinical explorations of medical, psychiatric, or legal matters where television presents operations, explicit childbirth, encounters with the mentally ill, people in court proceedings, prisoners, and people at home with their families.

In examining the varied array of television's contents it is also useful to observe what has not thrived on the screen. Thus, in probing the term "soap opera" (Wober (1984g) asked what the significance of its "opera" component might be. The musical content of this genre is far from central, and the interpretation offered was that the label was developed "partly as a joke, not so much intended to explain or contain as to conceal with contempt." In fact, serious musical concerts and opera have not become common on mainstream network television; nor have they been a viable part of cable packages. The different positions of such programming in the United States and Great Britain becomes evident by comparing the annual reports of Nielsen (1984) and of the IBA (1984). In the former, prime-time material is categorized into main drama and information, with no mention of an arts or culture category. The latter report points out a "current affairs and general factual, arts" category, as well as an adult education sector and in detail describes a wide range of operas, concerts, and programs of arts explanation and analysis.

Quietly substantiating the differentiation of programming into separate types is the fact that hybrid forms have been weak or rare. Soap opera and comedy have occasionally been crossed, but the former needs a gravity which the latter obviously rejects, so hybrids soon regress to one of the parent types. In the mid 1980s, *Remington Steele* and *Moonlighting* explored a realm combining those of adventure and comedy, as did *Minder* in Great Britain. *Hill Street Blues* had elements of soap opera, adventure action, and situation comedy. However, these hybrids are distinguished by their rarity as well as their quality. Although ABC sports used the phrase "the drama of athletic competition" in its approach to televising the Los Angeles Olympic Games, fictional drama about sport remains drama, while live or recorded sport for all its dramatic nature remains actuality, separate from fictional drama. More convincing an example, docudrama is a succesful new hybrid of news and drama, but the enterprises in this field have tended to be of a "one-off" nature and have not established on off-air channels their own regularly filled slots or times. Nor have they established their own channels on cable in quite the same way as has occurred with soap opera or action adventure.

Thus, television offers a wide range of content, which has been extended by cable with its "adult" (some may take this as a curious euphemism for material that is, in its unbridled nature in another sense, juvenile) erotic programs and its specialist music. One question posed by all these contents is how they can be categorized; another question is what audiences may do with these goods. We have seen in the previous chapter that the vehicle that delivers such goods, the screen, is undoubtedly of great value in two senses; people want it a great deal, and although they do not usually have to pay much for it, when tested by deprivation, they suggest that they would be willing to pay much more than they have hitherto been made to do. By making appropriate distinctions, we will now be able to develop a better idea as to which parts of the output of television are more desired (as ideals, before they have actually been used) and which parts are more extensively consumed.

In the first chapter, we discussed five ways to assess television and screen material; here we will use five ways of categorizing programs, which sets to a considerable extent correspond to each other. The first perspective of assessment was that of grass roots opinion, reflecting what people thought about programs; here we will formalize a cognitive approach to program categorization. Next we examined the interest taken in audience sizes, and this affords another way, through recorded patterns of actual behavior, of exploring the existence and definition of program types. A third perspective involved audience appreciation as a mode of assessment, and this affective or evaluative type of measure provides a corresponding opportunity for the emergence of groups or programs. Fourth was mentioned the critical school of program studies, which was concerned with the making of screen material and the industrial and organizational circumstances that determine the kinds of significance placed before the viewers (or at least, in the view of media sociologists); this categorization uses the same ways of deciding that screen contents can be grouped together. Finally, there is the effects field of assessment; but here, this does not translate into an obviously similar approach to program typing. We can deal more easily with the idea of motivation; what people say they want to see reveals patterns. However, since viewers' motivations to an important extent limit or determine the conditions in which effects may occur, the constructs of motivation or selection and of effect are unified in the perspective usually termed "uses and gratifications" theory but which here is replaced with the label "needs and gratifications" theory. The difference is important because "uses" is an idea being treated separately here under the heading of behavior; needs and gratifications are emotional conditions and structures which are preconditions to action and behavior but which do not always produce or correspond to behavior which could be described with labels similar to those of the emotional states. Therefore, the motivational method of typing programs is worth considering independently of the behavioral evidence. To summarize, here are the assessment perspectives of Chapter 1 set alongside the different ways of constructing the menu of the screen and its fare, which occupy the present chapter. The categories can luckily and appropriately be labeled with each of the first five letters of the alphabet to facilitate easy recognition and remembering.

Chapter 1	*Chapter 3*
A. Appreciation	Affective: patterns of feeling, having viewed programs
B. Behavior, Audience size	Behavioral: patterns of viewing experience, duplication
C. Critical, content-counts	Sociological: organization of production, encoding
D. Discussion, First hand experience.	Cognitive: ideas on similarities of programs
E. Effects	Motivational: what people set out (want) to see

Not all these approaches will be given the same amount of attention here. More attention will be given to those cases where there is something new to report which is not available in the literature. This is one reason why the items will not be dealt with exactly in the order shown in the chart.

A SOCIOLOGICAL APPROACH
TO DISCERNING PROGRAM TYPES

In distinction to the views that television's content is homogeneous based on analyses of essential messages or structural features said to be contained therein, the industry makes more specialized distinctions in its operations. A network would not inquire with Mary Tyler Moore's or Norman Lear's companies for sports programs; comedy, drama, and other kinds of products contain a great deal of specialist experience and skills in their construction; therefore, it should be possible to discern some groupings of production and administrative institutions which would correspond to a taxonomy of program types. In the United States, however, the industry seems to resist regimentation; in Great Britain it is much easier to see an industrial structure which relates to program type or genre. The differences in the two systems may well reflect the greater economic and political ideal of flexibility in the United States with a tradition of desire for order and social control in the latter.

In the *Broadcasting Yearbook* (1984) the three major U.S. networks ABC, CBS, and NBC list their executive personnel and display their organization; all three list only three broad program areas of internal concern—news, sports, and entertainment. What they do not make they buy; and as explained in the previous chapter we see here large but relatively skeletal organizations in an advertising financed system in contrast to which the British Broadcasting Corporation (BBC, 1976) lists thirteen separate groups or departments involved in program production (much more than in foreign purchasing, which is limited in Britain by customary quotas of around 15%). These thirteen segments are drama, light entertainment, current affairs, outside broadcasts, general features, science and features, music and arts, documentary, children, religion, schools, further education and community programs. While these segments do not have the same weight, the list points to a much more specific industrial segmentation than is discernible in U.S. network organization; this segmentation yields greater possibilities of control and stronger momentum for stability.

In viewing the American industry, Gitlin (1982, p. 437) refers in a section on "genre" to a "sensitivity to shifting moods and group identities in the audience"; in similar vein Mosco (1979, p. 37) had remarked "it is more useful to view the entire process of structuring a complex problem as subject to much uncertainty, rather than to specific guidelines"; he continues "organisational pressures lead people to think in narrow terms" (which he dislikes, and wants to overthrow, so he concludes) "is it too bold to suggest that Western bureaucracies might benefit from periodic Cultural Revolutions?" However, in spite of this discomfort with order, American analysts do find themselves using generic terms to describe production realities. Cantor (1980) refers in title to Prime Time Television but rapidly (p. 23) specifies this more narrowly in saying "this book is about prime time drama . . ."; while she refers to four major categories of drama—the western, the detective or mystery, situation comedies, and general drama—these are systematized more broadly (p. 30) "to distinguish the situation and domestic comedies from the action adventure shows." These differ in the production process in several ways, being made by different companies, the former often using studios and live audiences, the latter doing without audiences in outdoor location work. Dominick and Pearce (1976) add that organizers of Emmy Awards look for some industrial segmentation to enable some kind of fair comparisons to be made of product and producer excellence.

A paradox in this portrait of apparent flexibility and variety is that economic pressures may have diminished the opportunity to translate industrial structural variety into corresponding diversity on the screen. Thus, Head (1976, p. 214) documents the costs (in $th) per "rating point" as being for Comedy 4.0, Variety 4.2, Westerns 4.0, Feature Films 4.6 and Public Affairs 12.3. To achieve the clarity and understanding afforded by this analysis, program type categories had to be used; and further, Head recorded the changes brought about by enforcement of the Prime Time Access rule, when drama dropped during the relevant day part from 46% to 5% in four years, comedy fell from 22% to zero, while game shows rose from 11% to 66%. Foster (1982) looked back on the 1970s with the bleak impression "as the competition grew greater, there was less and less innovative programming and more emphasis on tried and tested sitcoms and programs about crime. The single most important development was the miniseries, of which ABC's *Roots* was the most successful example".

In summary, program types undoubtedly exist at an industrial level, enabling administrative decisions to be made (even if they backfire) and an order and segmentation of phenomena to be perceived. With new screen services carried on cable and separate satellite channels, the diversity with sports, news, children's, music and movie organizations can be observed. However, within the handful of program types there may be an apparent choice but at the same time a considerable homogeneity across alternatives. In the world of cars there are several types such as sedans, sports cars, compacts and the like, and several makes within each type; but each make is unsurprisingly similar to its competitors. In the screen world there are similar bionic thrillers, super-vehicles (a talking car, a superfast helicopter), and other look-alikes in each genre. Moreover, ambiguities occur across types. Is wrestling a sport or (as is suggested by Wober and Dobie, 1978) a form of vaudeville? Are chess, world series baseball, international cricket between the West Indies and the old colonial power England simply sport or news, drama, or politics in admixture? Some of these questions can be resolved merely by following administrative precedents; but in refining and making use of an undoubted industrial or economic level of reality, it may be useful to have recourse as well to other methods of categorizing programs, to which we now turn.

THE COGNITIVE PERSPECTIVE ON PROGRAM TYPES

To add the view of the viewer to that of the program maker one approach is to ask people whether, to what extent, and in which cases they regard programs as similar or different. This level of analysis can be called cognitive, as one has not yet assumed that viewers may prefer one group of items over another or that they may do anything particular about such possible preferences. Unfortunately, over three decades of television research, there is still not always analytic clarity about this matter; thus Webster and Wakshlag (1983) outline a theory of television program choice but, in lamenting a "troubling lack of theoretical clarity" (p. 436) have themselves left out this cognitive level of analysis when they link their concept of "viewer needs" with "program-type preference." Yet, in order to have preferences for one or another program type, one first has to perceive their separate identities, and not all people may perceive types in the same ways. Thus, any preference patterns that come to be described and measured may be partly defined by perceptual categories. To make this more concrete with an example, a person might say they want this evening to relax and see a good "drama;" one family member could take this to mean a classical novel brought to the screen, such as *Pride and Prejudice;* another might take drama to mean modern mini-series, and others might assume it means something with crime and action in it.

We have said, earlier on, that a forensic model of the viewer prevails outwardly in much of the discussion about the role of the viewer in the United States; this outward model will now be examined more closely. The task of establishing viewers' ideas of how programs are aggregated into types was tackled in detail relatively early in the history of television, in Great Britain. In the United States, broadcasting has been developed principally as a commercial enterprise with viewers considered as the commodity by advertisers and even by many academic researchers, implying the use of a clinical model, as objects being "exposed to" messages in order to study effects that may thereby be imprinted or set in motion. For industrial and ideological reasons previously addressed, there may not have been a strong reason to establish cognitively defined program types. In Great Britain however, in the mid 1960s the infant Independent Television Authority was given explicit requirements by Act of Parliament to enhance the respectability of the commercial television sector for which it was responsible. One way to do this, as was pointed out by Ian Haldane (1970, p. 59) its first Head of Research, was to "research into the state of public opinion concerning the programmes."

To do this, Haldane set a first goal of establishing "viewers' vocabulary about programmes, to define general dimensions of evaluation applicable to all programmes, and to identify clusters of programmes which are similar from the viewers' standpoint" (p. 60). Using over 200 rating scales and a list of 130 then running programs, factor analyses yielded a 9-factor solution for one set of data and an 11-factor solution for a parallel set. In a second stage, all the programs then being shown on three channels were rated using 12 scales combined from these two factor analyses. The resulting profiles of attributes were cluster analysed, and solutions varying in simplicity from a 2-cluster to a 20-cluster version were produced. Bearing in mind the institutional realities of program production, a 6-cluster solution was chosen as offering an effective definition of program types for use in Great Britain.

It is interesting to note that in the United States a very similar approach to that reported by Haldane was carried out nearly 10 years later (see Beville, 1985, p. 150). Jack Landis of Marketing Evaluations carried out a large study for the CPB and "documented the viewer's ability to discriminate among programs based on particular appeal elements." Over 250 descriptions (delightful, witty, boring, etc.) were used to profile 96 commercial and public television programs, using a national sample of 3,000 respondents. Seven basic dimensions were revealed by factor analysis, each with a positive and negative aspect. These aspects comprised providing knowledge or providing distraction, giving fun or building tension, provoking desire to watch or not to watch, being suitable for family or adult viewing, containing realistic and familiar or unfamiliar people, generating emotional or cognitive involvement, and having visual emphasis on beauty or auditory emphasis on wit. Even if this was the real way in which people encountered programs which would set the perspectives in which they reacted to the commercials associated with the programs, Beville reported (p. 151) that "industry interest in TV Factor Ratings . . . . was not forthcoming." It has to be said that program makers in Great Britain were not first in line either, to obtain such ratings, which were compiled for "public service" rather than primarily for industrial reasons.

It is useful to distinguish between what Haldane's researchers called factors of program perception and clusters of programs. Each factor consisted of a set of scales on which people assessed numbers of separate programs; it is easy to name factors where the constituent scales have a recognizable similarity. Thus, one factor was labeled information and was characterized by scales such as thought provoking/relaxing; other factors which resembled program types included one called romance (scales for women/for men; soft/hard,etc) and another labeled humor. One factor that presented instructive difficulties included scales such as involves crime/has little to do with crime; American type/British type;

violent/gentle as well as unbelievable/believable and fictional/factual. The researchers had first thought of labeling this as a realism factor, but they noted that other scales—unrealistic/realistic and fantasy world/real world—did not load here but did do so with the information group. The distinction, therefore, emerged from viewers' perceptions between believable fiction and informative reality, a classification which will contribute to assessment of theories of television's effects in later chapters.

The six clusters of programs first identified included entertainment (which included a soap opera still running nearly 20 years later, *Coronation Street*, but which centered on quizzes, game shows and variety), pop (*Batman, The Monkees, Dr. Who,* etc), crime/violence (*The Virginian, Danger Man, Z Cars, Till Death Us Do Part*, later screened as *All In The Family* in the United States, and the *Frost Programme*, seen as disturbing and adult), women's romance (*Peyton Place, The Forsyte Saga* and other soap operas), intellectual (including political documentaries of the time, and, perhaps surprisingly, cricket), and sports (excluding cricket, and wrestling, which lodged with crime/violence). These viewer-implied categories conflicted in some cases with judgments which paid more attention to a sociology of production and program procurement. Frost (1969) realized that the utility of a system of classification strictly based on viewers' cognitions would be limited, since it was subject to change as these perceptions altered, providing difficulties both for research and administration. For example, it is useful to have comparative assessments of economic and hedonist effectiveness of program types, both across types and over the years; it is also useful to examine whether there is segmentation of viewing behavior across types and whether experience with particular program types may relate to a variety of effects television is alleged to have on perceptions of the real world and on behavior.

The program taxonomy eventually established within the ITA (later the IBA) and which was used until early 1985, when program appreciation measurement was taken over by a consortium including the BBC, comprised the following types: adventure/action (series), soap opera, sport (including wrestling and cricket), comedy and light entertainment, news, general interest and information, films and drama (single items and mini-series) children's programs, and a residual miscellaneous group. Later work (eg., Colbert, 1976; Douglas and Wollaeger, 1982) suggested that the comedy and light entertainment group could be split into several distinct parts based on different patterns of evaluation as well as of perception. These subgroups would include zany comedy (symbolic of social disruption such as *Soap, Monty Python,* etc.), situation comedies more symbolic of harmony, quiz and guest chat shows, and music and band shows. The general interest and information category could also be meaningfully split into political documentary and discussion, the natural world including anthropology (*Cosmos, Life on Earth, Survival, The Disappearing World*), and domestic magazine shows (consumerism, gardening, local history, etc.). The fact that there are always marginal cases of programs that resist easy categorization is welcomed as a sign of a healthy broadcasting system because it suggests that program makers are innovating with new forms. But, just as the categorization of a new dish to a position on the menu influences consumers to consider it as an entree, dessert, etc., so with new television formats the scheduling and presentation help teach the public how to regard the new item. What is much more significant than the problem of what to do with category misfits should they occur, is that such misfits do not often occur. Thus, in 1984 it could have been possible for a program maker to have devised something neither just sport nor soap opera or news, based on the Olympic Games in Los Angeles. In fact, nothing so innovative occurred.

Noting that while in the United States *I Love Lucy* is universally perceived as a situation comedy but that in Saudi Arabia the same program might be seen as "the spear point of the Women's Liberation Front" Gould, Johnson and Chapman (1984, pp. T7-T8) press forward two strong arguments for their alternative approach to program analysis. First, they expect a rapid internationalization of television via satellite and video cassette, leading to a need for some kind of economic and research Esperanto of program description. Second, they claim that the "few Annual Reports of broadcasting organisations . . . are worthless because the data upon which their categories and percentages are based, have never been properly defined." They offer an elaborate hierarchial system of classification of attributes by which each program could be placed not just in one pigeon hole, but tied to a number of branches and even twigs of a great tree of meanings which they display. This system has a blackcloth dimension, including labels such as "welfare," "day to day things," and "economic things," which others might see just as a Dewey type system of allotting contents into departments. The system also has a traffic concept, including labels such as "cultural exchange," "education," "values," "entertainment," and "information," which others may recognize as a kind of purpose classification.

The work of Gould et al. invites several critical rejoinders. Their analytic scheme would be very expensive to carry out in any one country, let alone in several, and there is not enough reason why any organization in one country would wish to embark on such a project. Next, it would be meaningful to perform the task in one country mainly if it was also being done in exactly the same way in most other countries. There is little chance of achieving this degree of coordination. The scheme really calls for an international organization to carry it out. UNESCO is the only appropriate body, but events before 1987, including studies performed indirectly for UNESCO under the aegis of the International Association for Mass Communication Research on cross-national flow of news in television, tended to dismiss earlier concerns about "media imperialism." These arguments had been based on assertions that news tended to flow into weaker (Third World) nations from stronger ones. Investigation did not support such assertions of whether this news was about the former or the latter. While the case for concern about media imperialism was flattering in this way, events during 1987 affecting UNESCO's leadership suggest that those who hitherto supported the "free flow of information" ideology (the anti-media imperialists argued under the slogan of a "right to know" ideology) would gain the upper hand. In effect, Gould et al. have proposed what appears to be an elegant but impractical system, whose thoroughness ensures its interest for those who are concerned with understanding in any depth how the screen and its contents are managed.

The entertainment and information type distinctions previously mentioned were reflected in Great Britain in the Broadcasters' Audience Research Board (BARB) appreciation service that replaced the IBA's independent system in 1985. But while BARB made new distinctions reflecting cognitive realities and economic ones in separating home made from imported fiction, it collapsed the IBA's two previously separate entities of soap opera and adventure action within the domestic and foreign fiction types. The BARB taxonomy may be more suitable for revealing appreciation scores and type norms to the networks; it is less suitable when seeking to use the data to assess effects theories, as will be shown in several examples. Ultimately, industrial organization will have to adapt itself to reflect and serve the realities of how user demand is organized (the travails of all-news cable channels, culture stations, and video discs illustrate the losses that can be suffered by those who neglect such realities). Achieved demand (durables bought, or programs viewed in general, consumer behavior) will have its roots in expressed demand (what the consumer says he or she wants to buy, or view) which in turn is likely to be linked with consumers' perceptions of the market (cognitions of the commodities available, and of the groupings). From this cognitive level, we can now turn to look at preference measures of what viewers say they want to watch.

MOTIVATION-BASED METHODS OF TYPING TELEVISION CONTENTS

The third basis on which to detect groupings of programs is probably that on which the most work has been done. Here there are two approaches to the problem. One asks people *why* they want to watch particular programs, or what their *needs* are that television programs might meet. The second approach is to ask *which* programs people want to watch and from this evidence to assemble sets or types of programs based on common preferences.

Preference questions can be asked in a number of ways, and unfortunately the meanings are sometimes ambiguous. For example Roe (1985) asked Swedish viewers to say whether they "dislike very much", down to "like very much" each of 15 program categories. Roe describes the results as indexing preferences, but analytically it should be seen that the answers may well have reflected evaluations reached after viewing. Since for program types, as distinct from single items, preference formation is likely to be based on the experience of evaluations, this ambiguity may not matter very much. Even so, it may be true that a person has a desire to see comedies, a need or preference for comedy; but the habitual fare in the category may be disappointing so that it reduces the mark given in a liking scale. This kind of ambiguity may partly explain why Roe reports "entertainment programs, quizzes and serials, three categories apparently loved by program producers (judging by TV output) do not arouse the audience to strong feelings" (1985, p. 28). Nevertheless, Roe lists 6 of the 15 categories for which there were significantly positive correlations between his measure of liking/preference, and amount of TV use, the top three being serials, quizzes, and entertainment. Since heavy viewing may be an index of program seeking, this is one sense in which these entertainment types are preferred. What is clear is that conceptual distinctions are needed at the outset so that measures can tap each stage in the orientation of users to screen material.

Individuals vary regarding their basic level of need for arousal or relaxation. Arousal may be produced or kept at the person's optimum level by enduring personality structures; by the management of stimuli that are sought out; or by fear, anger or other emotional changes whether sought or unsought. For these reasons, people have been asked how often they watch television for excitement, information, or relaxation; which of several message systems they prefer to use for satisfying such needs; or which needs are more important at what times of day. All such questions concerning screen material are general whereas questions about peoples' needs are individualized. Such approaches are limited by the fact that people may not be totally aware of their needs or be willing and able to report them accurately. This, of course, is of particular concern to critical theorists, many of whom do not trust the public to know what is best for them.

Unfortunately, the approach that has been most concerned with the psychological component of how and why people use television is termed "uses and gratifications" theory (Blumler, 1979). Even though a psychologist (McGuire, 1974) contributed to early work on this theory, focusing his work on motivation, followers continued to be preoccupied with the term "uses" and the behavioral measures that such a word suggests (Katz, Blumler and Gurevitch, 1973). The theory would be more usefully termed "needs and gratifications," both terms dealing at the same level with motivations and their satisfaction or discharge, with the behavioral measures of use mediating between start and end states of motivation, emotion, or affect. Meanwhile, results from studies of patterns of motivation or need, implying their requitement by viewing certain types of program, can be reviewed.

Early analyses (Kirsch and Banks, 1962; Swanson, 1967; Wells, 1969) used self-reports of viewing or claimed preferences for specific programs to produce clusters of program types. After objections by Ehrenberg (1968) that some of these clusters may have been artefactual, reflecting channel loyalty and scheduling regularities (though these, argue the networks, merely skillfully reflect audience needs), what Webster and Wakshlag (1983) term a second generation of studies on patterns in program preference was achieved (Gensch and Ranganathan, 1974; Rao, 1975; Frank, Becknell and Clokey, 1971). Such studies statistically controlled for variation attributable to scheduling characteristics, and unsurprising clusters or types such as drama, situation comedies and news emerged. Webster and Wakshlag feel bound to say that many such studies "fail to make a distinction between data on program preference and (those on) program choice" (1983, p. 442). In short, what people say they want to do is not necessarily what they actually do or what they say they do. Nor are any of these accounts necessarily congruent with how pleased they are with what they have done.

Apart from Roe's work, which exhibits some of this conceptual blurring and omits controls for scheduling, a second generation example from Great Britain by Segnit and Broadbent (1973) is worth examination because of its size, reputation, and the attention paid to it by Ehrenberg and his colleagues. Segnit and Broadbent have been associated with the Leo Burnett advertising agency, which, in turn, has had connections with the research approaches linked in the United States with Yankelovich and other agencies interested in life styles and psychographics as ways of attending to differences among consumers. In this approach, 7,000 adults were asked for each of 53 programs whether they "really like to watch" (as well as a number of other questions). Comparing the percentages who like to watch one item with the percentages for each of the others affords a way of assembling pairs and families of programs with high support in common. Six main clusters appeared labeled adventure, sports, light entertainment, current affairs, children's programs, and a group called cult items (resembling the zany comedy, and with which one might associate later titles such as *Fawlty Towers, M.A.S.H.,* and *Hill Street Blues*).

Segnit and Broadbent repeated their study in 1975. Examination of the results (Aske, 1977) revealed clustering similar to that previously found. Women and men proved to disclose very different preference patterns, much of the separation of sports and soap opera clusters being attributable to this demographic difference. One ambiguity with this study is that the question "really like to watch" may refer in part to a satisfaction incurred after viewing, rather than purely reflecting what people "want to watch." In the 1975 data, for example, about 35% of adults said that they "really liked" to watch the 45 items listed, whereas about 55% said that they did not watch them at all. This leaves only 10% who could be said to be viewing casually rather than purposively. If this is correct, it implies there is little waste in time spent and patterns of viewing support a rational model of program choice. Yet other evidence, for example that provided by Goodhardt et al. (1975) who cite the Segnit and Broadbent material, suggests that much viewing is casual. It is more likely that both the "really like to watch" and the "do not watch at all" figures are both overestimates in which respondents confuse (because the researchers have allowed them to do so) what they want to do with what they actually do.

Other available evidence, however, reflects less ambiguously what people say they would and would not like to see. The IBA (1974a) polled a national sample about whether they would like to see more or less of each of 11 sorts of programs. The assumption was made that people agree on what these categories mean. Thus, some might think documentaries meant nature and travel programs and say they want to see more, whereas others might take the meaning as political and say they want to see fewer. If people regard television as a homogeneous entity (the so-called moving wallpaper of some critics), there would have been similar numbers of people wanting more or less of each sort of program. This was far from what was found. At the top of the list came documentaries, of which a plurality of one fourth of those questioned wanted to see more over those who wanted less, while for sport 5% more wanted to see less. Major differences in expressed demand for different sorts of programs were found between women and men and between people of different ages and social classes.

In an opposite approach, Wober (1974) asked people to cite any kinds of programs they would not want to watch. The most salient result was that whatever people understood by the term "daily life/hospital serials" prompted 11% of them to say they would definitely not want to watch such material. Seven other type labels each drew no more than 1% or 2% of people who would definitely not want to watch. This study suggests that people are broadly tolerant of program material across a wide range and are not deeply committed to avoiding programming (except to a small extent soap operas among men and sport among women).

A very large study probably focusing on viewer motivations, but also touching upon behavior, has been reported by Espe and Seiwert (1986) who used data from a Eurobarometer survey conducted in 1981 in six European nations. Respondents were taken through a list of eight program types and asked to give a mark on a scale from 1 to 10 "how much interest you have" in each type. It seems likely that in German and French the meaning of *interest* is identical with that in English, though the referent for terms like "series and serials" (soap operas? action adventures?) or "documentaries" (*Cosmos*? political documentaries?) could have varied between countries. As well as the interest measurements, respondents indicated their overall weight of television viewing in hours per day, and these data were then analyzed in great detail. In four countries (though not Great Britain and Luxembourg) a type of viewer emerged who declared strong interest in entertainment and films and who watched television heavily. In all countries, high sports and informational program interests corresponded with relatively light reported viewing levels. The study suggests that, depending on national cultures, heavy viewers are not undiscriminating but form into types characterized by certain configurations of declared interests. Espe and Seiwert

(1986) suggest that with increased program supply (cable and satellite channels programmed to reflect particular interest configurations) the "differences between user groups could be strengthened and reinforced" (p. 323). This points to heavier viewing of action adventure by adventure lovers, of sports by sports lovers, and so on. The corollary is for less diverse experience for many individual viewers and a corresponding increased chance for viewing to accomplish "effects" by reinforcement, whereas previously these had been mitigated by dilution.

As with the total television deprivation studies examined in the previous chapter, a useful opportunity for examining viewing preferences indirectly occurs when, for some unusual reason, the pattern of supply has been interrupted. During 1979 the ITV network experienced an 11-week strike. Toward the end, one survey (TV Times, 1979) asked people to name any programs that they had particularly missed. The two items mentioned most were the major soap operas *Coronation Street* and *Crossroads*. Fewer than 10% missed the national newscasts (which they could receive in any case on BBC), but fewer than 5% missed the local newscasts which are a much more prominent feature of ITV than BBC. A similar survey (Wober, 1979b) asked half a national sample what they missed and the other half what they looked forward to. Again, about 20% missed or looked forward to a soap opera; smaller percentages missed and looked forward to films, drama series, and comedy entertainment. Exposed to this kind of question grounded in actuality, the often found apparent preference for documentaries disappears, suggesting that the response may be affected by social desirability.

Children and teenagers may be one segment of the population more candid about its preferences. In the United States, Rubin (1977) asked groups aged 9, 13, and 17 to list their three favorite programs. Coding revealed that adventure-drama and comedy series won the most preferences. Children's entertainment was favored by 9-year-olds, but not thereafter. Virtually no children cited educational material as their favorite viewing and the same was true (except among a few 17-year olds) for news. Very similar preference patterns had been shown among children aged from 5 to 12 in three regional surveys in England (IBA, 1974b).

One important feature of program clustering, which most simple preference studies overlook, and which helps to emphasize the difference between cognitive and motivational levels of analysis, is that within any single perceived type there will be motivational variation linked with perceived quality. People recognize that certain programs are comedies (or are supposed to make them laugh); people may wish to see comedies (or to be made to laugh); and they therefore wish to see good comedies and not bad ones. Once they have evaluated a comedy series as poor, viewers are not likely to be thinking of this or similar series when giving preference judgments in favor of comedy. A study that demonstrated this distinction (Wober, 1979a) took 20 programs deliberately selected to represent well-liked and not well-liked material from each of seven program types. These items were combined in 190 pairs, which were divided into eight sets judged by independent samples of viewers who said, for each pair, which of the two they would prefer to see. Alternatively, respondents could say the two were equally attractive, or equally uninteresting. By this method news programs were more often said to be preferred than were other types, and comedies were the least often chosen type. This study pointed to one reason why simple preference studies may not easily provide popularity hierarchies in which most commonly viewed or liked programs correspond to what people say they want to see. The reason in many British schedules is that quite often strong comedy shows may find themselves in competition with weak adventure or soap opera, thus providing a different prospect to that of a weak comedy against a well-liked adventure or soap opera.

A second kind of discriminator of appeal within a program type was explored in a study of news (Wober, 1978c) in which respondents were asked how much they felt they knew about as well as wanted to see material about each of nine topics. On some topics, for example the Royal Family and the Middle East, there was a more marked correlation across individuals between interest to view and claimed knowledge; on other matters, such as Northern Ireland and immigrants' affairs, fewer people wanted to see coverage and there was a less marked correlation with claimed knowledge. Results and their patterning were closely similar in samples in two separate regions, providing some validity for the notion that in news and documentary programs all is not equal in terms of what people want to see, partly related to what they feel they already know about.

For over a decade, a number of studies have used program type preferences as a pointer to predicting actual viewing behavior. Thus, Wells (1969), Frank et al. (1971) Lehmann (1971), Bowman and Farley (1972), and Owen et al. (1974) in the United States; Darmon (1976) in Canada and Rosengren and Windahl (1972) in Sweden have reflected some of the British experience discussed here, in showing that there are some generally distinguishable predispositions to see material, which can be identified by distinct types. Nevertheless, a number of explanations have been offered as to why preferences do not simply translate into patterns of choice or behavior. These include limitations of viewer availability (Webster and Wakshlag, 1983), group influence on viewing options (Barwise and Ehrenberg, 1982a, Lull, 1982, Webster and Wakshlag, 1982), and differences within program types in terms of interest or knowledge and appeal.

However, since people take their preferences, organized partly in terms of types, to the range of programs offered, this fact is increasingly realized and embodied in ways in which the material is newly marketed. Thus, cable channels often segregate their material into channels, reflecting notions of program type; and video cassette sales and libraries categorize their material by type as well. Some of this segmented marketing has turned out to be an expensive failure; one way of avoiding failures, not just for marketing but also in consumerist and other perspectives in which more cultural protection or control is desired, is to examine carefully the ways in which users have behaved with existing network television. To this body of evidence, we will now turn.

BEHAVIORAL EVIDENCE ON PATTERNING
IN THE USE OF TELEVISION

The lay person's view appears to be that people simply pursue the programs they want to see. Such a view, if it exists widely, is what is addressed by the regular publication of 'top tens' and hierarchies of programs determined by audience size. It is dramatically clear that some programs achieve higher audiences and even shares of audience against most available competition, while others do not. In recent years more than half the nation has seen mini-series programs such as *Roots, The Thorn Birds, Shogun,* and even single items such as *The Day After.* Most other programs do not reach such wide audiences.

To illustrate the fact of individual program appeal it can be useful to examine instances where that appeal is seriously reduced. In Great Britain March 1985 marked the anniversary and imminent end of a major strike in the coal mines. The ITV channel chose a Friday prime time to replace a soap opera and an adventure thriller (*Dempsey and Makepeace,* featuring a U.S. police officer on assignment in London) with a more than 2½ hour documentary on the strike. For the hour before the strike program average ITV audience size was down 15% from the week before; averaged across the first 2 hours of the documentary, the audience was 65% down on the levels the week before. The strike program was then interrupted for the regular newscast and this experienced a 35% drop from its audience the previous Friday, illustrating a "disinheritance" effect. It is not necessary from this particular case to generalize to conclusions about program type affecting audience size, even though many among the audience did not wait to find out what the program was like but departed from it immediately. It does illustrate that while there are some programs that more people watch, there are others that not only fewer people watch but probably actually avoid.

At the next possible level it may be claimed that viewing is patterned, at least to some extent, by program type. Type is evident cognitively and motivationally; such predisposition is unlikely to have no effect whatever on behavior. However, many researchers have either minimized the role of program type in patterning activity, or have denied it explicitly. Thus McQuail, Blumler and Brown (1972) emphasized that viewing was largely determined by patterns of seasonal and daily activity, with expressed needs not well matched with viewing behavior. More substantively Goodhardt et al. (1975, p. 48) studied thousands of duplications (the percentage of those who, having watched one program also watch another) and concluded "there is no special tendency across the population for people who watch one program of a given type to also watch others of the same type," a position which they maintained five years later "with the partial exception of sports programmes, the attitudinal clustering by program types . . . does not reflect what people actually do by way of the programs they choose to watch" (Aske, 1980). This denial of the role of program type was largely accepted by Hirsch (1980a), though he provided no independent evidence for taking this view.

The question of whether program type is of any force in predicting behavior can have importance both for marketing and for social policy. In selling advertising, if part of the variance in audience size is attributable to program type this can be a valuable aid in planning campaigns. For those systems where television is required explicitly to maintain political balance it would not be effective if opposing statements were each developed in separate episodes of a documentary series, for only just over half of those who saw one side of the case would be likely to see the opposing case in the second program, which itself would have an audience of whom about half would not have seen the first program. Political balance, if it was really to be maintained in the minds of viewers, would have to be achieved by presenting both sides of a controversy in a single episode. This constraint is strongly opposed by critics and program makers, while the statutory requirements upon broadcasters both in the United States and Great Britain do not accept its validity. The paradox is that while the existence of the regulations accepts a clinical model of the viewer, for whom some expert care has to be taken, the substance of the regulations implies that viewers are forensically competent.

A more parochial concern for broadcasters is that if dedicated audience flows across series, let alone program types, can not be taken for granted, then narrative style should accept that some updating of the story should always be supplied.

The Aske group (ie., Goodhardt et al., 1975), while agreeing on the pull of particular programs but denying a similar power for program type, do acknowledge the phenomenon of channel loyalty. This applies to a modest extent for the major networks, but practically not at all for a minor channel such as BBC 2 in the United Kingdom or the independents in the United States. If it is true then that individual programs and the program environment, such as channel, each partly determine audience size, some convincing explanation seems necessary to explain why no such role exists for program type. While the problem has not been tackled explicitly by Aske, other writers have tried to resolve the difficulty. One possibility pointed to by Wober (1981d) is that Aske's duplications have been calculated on a basis of the proportions of the whole population who are found in common across two program audiences, but that typically only three fourths of the population are available (at home) to see programs in common across the two episode times. Webster and Wakshlag (1983, p. 438), noting the Aske case, suggested that "if there is no special tendency for viewers of one program to watch another of the same type, it is probably because there is no special tendency for the same people to be watching television when both programs are on." Actual relationships should be investigated by calculating duplications on a basis of common available, rather than total viewer, populations to provide a correct comparison between duplications involving pairs of like-type and unlike-type programs.

An alternative, which reflects something else that Webster and Wakshlag say, in "positing viewer availability as a cause of program choice" (1983, p. 437) is that there may indeed be patterning of viewing behavior by program type, but that Aske have not sought it appropriately, and have therefore not found it. Indeed, quite opposite to Webster and Wakshlag's idea is the case that program availability, and hence the possibility of program choice, may help determine viewer availability and through this, viewing behavior. While Aske have always used the program as their basic unit of analysis, a complementary method is to take the viewer as the basic unit. A difficulty here has been that American academic researchers have often used telephone interviews for assessing behavior, affording but limited depth of recall (eg., Tan and Tan, 1985), while industrial measurers of audience behavior (Nielsen and Arbitron in the United States and Japan, Audits of Great Britain in the United Kingdom, Teleskopie in Germany) have concentrated on the program as unit of analysis, with sophisticated individual level data relatively difficult and expensive to obtain. A major exception to this situation, however, has been the IBA's system of *Audience Reaction Assessment* (AURA), which began regular weekly operation in 1973 and ran uninterrupted until the start of 1985. The AURA system sent diaries each week to enough people in one of the ITV regions to receive back at least 500 completed returns. Each diarist gave each program they had seen a mark on a six-point evaluative scale (how much you found this interesting and/or enjoyable); responses were weighted on a scale from 0 to 100 to calculate an Appreciation Index (AI) for each program.

The AIs have been tabulated in weekly reports organized into seven (adult) program types (largely determined by the work described in the previous section). For each program type a weighted type average AI has been calculated, so that, for example, an individual program AI for a sports item can be compared with the sports norm rather than with that for news programs, or films and drama. The system worked well and provided the model for a joint BBC-ITV system initiated in 1982, as well as for other systems in Australia and, on an occasional basis in the United States and elsewhere. McCain (1985) has described how many European countries have research on viewer appreciation of programs; the data in some of these countries are even published. Beville (1985) reminds Americans that the networks have used TVQ for many years and continue to do so, although the data are proprietary and not published. Almost as important as the AI scores has been the fact that the data provided coincidental estimates of audience sizes for individual programs, as well as patterns of viewing for individuals.

Because the ecosystem of British television has been of sufficient complexity to provide theoretically interesting situations, but has not been too complex to elude precise measurement, the week long AURA databases have provided good test beds on which to examine issues in the realm of viewing behavior theory.

For each individual, it is known how many programs he or she endorsed in the week, within which types, on which channels, and in what sequence; further, appreciation is known for each program. Demonstrating the feasibility of this data source for studies of viewing behavior as well as of appreciation (Wober, 1976 May) an immediate result was to demonstrate that, contrary to the views of many critics (which could still be found among some a decade later) individuals were not loyal to one channel every day or every week but typically watched two or more channels each day; that BBC2, then widely considered a minority channel was actually used by a majority of the population each week (as is also the case for the PBS in the United States); and that the shares of viewing attributed to each channel by this method were very similar to those published by the official industry contractor using its diary-validated set-meter system.

With the AURA diary as a basic instrument of exploring patterns of viewing behavior alongside appreciation the scene was now set for a series of studies, which have flowed from the IBA's research department, developing in scope as they continued. These data not only afford an account of viewing behavior and its accompanying experience, but by the addition of short extra questionnaires a wide range of other attitudes and even personality attributes have been measured, all of which may be analyzed together with the information on viewing.

The first range of questions tackled was that of any evidence of segregation of viewing behavior into patterning by program types. It was soon shown (Wober, 1978b) that younger people are heavier viewers of programs containing violence than older viewers; younger people are not heavier viewers overall and tend to be less heavy consumers of news, corresponding to a similar result in the United States (Poindexter, 1980). Not surprisingly, women on most weeks see more soap operas than men, whereas men view more sports. Apart from these demographic differences, when the 1979 strike hit ITV, the diary was available to track any responses in behavior patterns to the now altered amount and proportion of programs broadcast within each of the program types customarily analyzed. Studies in other countries had tackled a similar question concerning adaptation to increases in availability. Thus, Hulten (1979, p. 15) from Sweden reported that over the decade 1965–1975 "the overall composition of programming offered remained relatively unaltered . . . as did total viewing time. Viewers' choices, however, shifted significantly towards a higher proportion of broad-appeal programmes such as weekly series, films and other fiction." From Belgium, Geerts (1980) described what happened when added channel availability altered both amounts and proportions of material of different types that were on offer. Viewing of material labeled "religion" and "culture," although now open to greater opportunity and choice, actually decreased; viewing of sports and of quizzes increased by a greater percentage than the increased availability of these categories.

A major study was also organized by UNESCO (1981) in which three weeks' television provision and use were examined in each of seven countries: Belgium, Bulgaria, Canada, France, Hungary, Italy, and Japan. The amounts provided in each of several program categories and the extent to which each of these types was used were all measured. A feature of this study was to control for program clashes where two items of the same type were on at the same time on different channels, thus reducing gross availability to a measure of usable availability. Using these methods, substantial differences between countries in what were called corrected audience indices per program type were found; for example, in Bulgaria news was more fully used than it was in Belgium. However, in all countries "fiction-based entertainment programs" were used more than other types. Educational and religious material fared poorly, as did "other information programs." News took an intermediate position.

The AURA study in Great Britain showed that during the 1979 strike adventure action availability fell by 70%, while actual viewing of material of this type fell by only 39%. Comedy and light entertainment availability fell by nearly half, but viewing of this category increased by nearly one fourth. After the 11 week strike, adventure action and soap opera viewing both increased, though not to the full extent of the restored greater availability. Restored greater availability of comedy and light entertainment was evidently unable to increase the amount of this type already being consumed. After the strike the availability of sport, news, general interest and drama material all increased, but the amounts of viewing of these types actually fell in comparison to their rates of consumption during the strike. These results, unlike those of UNESCO were based on gross rather than net measures of program availability, since it was argued (Wober, 1980c) that a comedy on two channels at the same time was two chances to see a comedy with a real option otherwise of not viewing at all. The overriding point was that the viewers did not adapt to changes in availability in a way that ignored program type; type was very much a part of the patterns of adaptation to the new situation.

Differences in appeal in terms of the amount of use made of different program types were then noted over a whole year's data (Wober, 1980a). Seasonal variations plotted on a chart showed that these were but minor variations in an index termed the "take up rate." This was a measure of the number of programs seen per individual, within a program type, divided by the number of programs available in that category. The take up rates were greatest for action adventure and soap opera, followed by comedy, drama, news, sport, and last of all general interest and the miscellaneous section. This study, though huge in volume needed some refinement, as it embraced material at all times of the day. Ehrenberg (1968) had objected that differences attributed to program type may be artifacts of scheduling practices in different day parts. A second study

(Wober, 1982c), therefore, examined 13 weeks' data, making a distinction between prime time and all time calculations. The first result was that program types attracting larger audiences when no restriction was placed on time of day also attracted larger audiences for prime time only. Conversely, material watched by smaller audiences over all timings was also seen by fewer in prime time. The major staples of entertainment attracted by far the largest audiences especially when the "dilution" of afternoon and late night post peak hours was removed.

More recent work in this vein was done with data surrounding the establishment in Great Britain during November 1982 of a new national network Channel Four, which, taking advertising gave the Independent system two channels to complement the two operated without advertising by the BBC (Wober, 1984c). The procedure was to examine eight weeks' diary data preceding the arrival of Channel Four, with eight weeks' data immediately following its start. To parallel these periods eight chronologically similar weeks were taken before and eight after after the launch anniversary in 1983 and running into the start of 1984. Several measures were devised including one of week's reach, one of take up and one of percentage take up. Reach refers to the percentage of the panels who saw at least one program within a type during the time measured, which was a week for each respondent. Take up refers to the number of programs viewed per person, again calculated within each program type separately; finally, take up percentage refers to the number of programs viewed per person on average across the sample, divided by the number of programs available that week, again calculated separately within each program type. Reach can be seen as expressing a sociological interest about the spread within the society, or within particular demographic parts of it, of each program type. Take up is more of a psychological measure, and percentage take up is a measure that should interest both social psychologists and economists, for it relates individual behavior to the environmental context, and it expresses for different goods (that is, here, program types) the extent to which they are used. The calculations were made across all data for all times, but the results shown here are based on prime time data only.

It is clear that most people make use of at least some material from most program types at some time during each week. Nevertheless there are marked and recurring differences between the program types. This perspective shows that comedy and light entertainment is the most popular, in the sense of the most widely used program type; at the opposite end of the scale are soap opera and sport, which, it has been noted before, are of more particular interest to women and men respectively. Thus, while 64% of men made at least one use of soap opera in an average week (34 weeks were involved, in all, in the above figures), 78% of women did so; while 71% of men viewed at least some sport per week, only 53% of women did so. It may be said, though without much force, that reach was down in the year after the introduction of the new channel; however, the differences are small and with variations in programming and other ex-

TABLE 1
Measures of Reach for Seven Program Types

Program Types	Periods			
	A: pre C4	B: Post C4	Year Post A	Year Post B
Comedy, light entertainment	95	96	91	94
Films, drama (non serial)	94	96	90	91
General interest, information	89	84	80	84
News	87	85	80	81
Adventure action	75	78	73	72
Soap opera	70	75	65	70
Sport	63	53	56	49

ternal factors, not much should be made of the kind of chronological variation seen here.

It should be borne in mind that, though these results might be taken as offering a pointer to underlying truths about human needs and interests and how they are expressed, they are at the same time likely to reflect two further aspects of individuality. One concerns British culture and traditions of behavior—one aspect of which is perhaps a lower level of interest in politics than may be found in some other countries. Thus, Italian interest in politics may be greater than that found in Great Britain, with a commensurately greater consumption of news (Phillips, 1986); particular stages in a nation's life are also expressed in following news—as is found in Israel, where attention to news is very widespread. Other cultural traditions will also affect the balance of interests in and access to different forms of fiction; thus, it has been pointed out (Hawkins and Pingree, 1980) that American light viewers of television probably see more violence-containing programs than do British heavy viewers.

This points to the second source of variation among cultures: availability (and location or scheduling) of program material. However, the multiplication of channels and the spread of VCRs increasingly negate this source of cross national differences; where Sweden had maintained a broadcast environment containing relatively little violence, more recent access to cabled satellite-supplied material from foreign sources has increased viewing of music videos (Roe, 1985) while VCR has brought an increased reach of access to movies containing violence (Roe, 1983). Reach, however, is not the only useful measure of program use, and an index of *volume* of use per viewer is also important and has been devised.

Take up percentage is an index of effective realization of demand, which looks at the use made of what is available. The figures reflect prime time only, so scheduling differences across the major time periods and

TABLE 2
Measures of Take up Per Cent For Seven Program Types

Program Types	Periods			
	A: pre C4	B: Post C4	Year Post A	Year Post B
Soap opera	32	24	21	23
Adventure action	25	27	19	20
Comedy, light entertainment	21	16	13	15
Films, drama (nonserial)	17	14	13	11
News	14	11	10	11
Sport	13	10	10	9
General interest, information	8	4	4	5

differences of viewer availability do not affect the picture greatly. A minor but remarkable result is that for adventure action, on the arrival of the new channel there was no decrease but an increase in effective use made of the program type. Figures for average numbers of items viewed per person per week make it clear that in period B it was an increase in personal viewing, matched with more programs available, that gave the increased take up per centage.

Apart from this isolated result for adventure action, when more programs came on air with the new channel, because the amount of viewing per person did not increase correspondingly, the percentage take up figures fell. The detailed figures of numbers of programs viewed per person in prime time show that while for adventure action and comedy and light entertainment people viewed more after the advent of the new channel, for news and general interest material they viewed less. The idea of providing the new channel, propelled into being by a lobby of critics and program providers, was that viewers would have more specialist interests met, and viewing would become more selective. One index for such an eventuality should have been that appreciation of items seen in the new dispensation would increase. This can be examined later, but with the evidence on behavioral trends it seems that if selectivity has been applied, it has done so more effectively in the realm of entertainment than of information. This provides a pointer for what would happen with the advent of new screen material with video cassette and with cable channels. Catalogs of stock of video rental shops show the contents are primarily drama and entertainment, with very little if any component of hard information. The first British cable use survey (AGB Cable and Viewdata) based on diary measurement shows that mainstream entertainment was the content of most new viewing time, with the channels providing more demanding material losing out more than the channel providing the strongest entertainment competition—the advertising funded ITV.

In the light of comments made just before Table 2, these results may not foreclose the possibility that program types may be used or taken up in different proportions in other broadcasting environments. The United States has had a viable market for a 24-hour satellite news channel. Yet this viability should be examined to see whether it rests on a high reach with a relatively low take up (as is more likely, given the scheduling patterns of news on US terrestrial networks) or on a lower reach but heavier take up among its users. One of the keys to answering this question lies in an understanding of individual differences in needs and in consequent patterns of use.

The audience does not view programs as a homogeneous unit. Partly generating the program types whose existence has now emphatically been demonstrated in terms of behavior as well as of cognition and motivation, different kinds of people make heavier use of different program types. This can be demonstrated with reach, as has been mentioned in some details above concerning sport and soap opera; it can be demonstrated in terms of take up rates; and it can be demonstrated with the take up percentage which relates what is viewed (taken up) to *what is available* (the number of programs viewed, per person per week, divided by the number of programs broadcast that week, of that type). The next table is based on eight weeks' data a year after the period following implementation of Channel Four. (Whereas Table 2 dealt with prime time only, these results reflect use of total broadcast time).

As we have noted before, women make more effective use of soap opera, while men do so more for sport. Older people make more effective use of news, in terms of the proportion of items available that they watch. As in the United States (Poindexter, 1980), adventure action is more fully used by younger than by older adults, which, given that the latter tend overall to be heavier viewers, is a noteworthy though small difference. Films and drama, with a somewhat higher percentage of material taken up than general interest and information, tend to have less noticeable

TABLE 3
Demographic Differences in Uses* of Programs, By Type

	Soap Opera	Adventure Action	Comedy Lt. Entertnmt	Films Drama	News	Sport	General Interest
All adults	19	18	13	6	9	8	4
Men	16	18	12	5	9	10	4
Women	22	18	13	7	8	6	4
16–34	18	19	13	7	6	6	3
35–54	16	17	12	6	7	6	3
55 +	24	18	14	6	13	11	5
ABC1	15	16	11	6	8	6	3
C2	21	19	13	6	8	7	4
DE	24	20	15	7	11	10	5

* take up percentage, defined above

and linear relations between demographic and percentage take up measures than is found with other program types (for example, as with sport, across socioeconomic status). While the evidence thus far has depended on measures taken within individual weeks, or arranged across weeks, one study has shown panel-type stability of behavior disclosing the reality of program types, across weeks. In an election campaign project (Wober, 1984e) a London panel recorded its viewing on 2 weeks separated by 1 month. The average correlation between the number of programs seen in any one type and the number seen in any other type in the separate week was 0.3; this documents the general underlying difference between light and heavy viewers. However, the average correlation between the number of programs seen in each type with the number seen in the same type during the separate week was 0.73. This indicates that, apart from a general propensity to view much or little regardless of type, those who watch more of a certain type are more likely to segment their viewing similarly on another occasion. It should be clear now that two kinds of determinants of audience size or segmentation of behavior are established: those in relation to individual programs and those in relation to program types.

A third level of screen content differentiation is that of channel. It has been shown by Goodhardt et al. (1975), both with American and British data, that channel loyalty exists as a phenomenon more markedly in Great Britain and much less clearly so in the United States, unless one includes minority language stations. Here, what can be added is a demonstration of how patterns of viewing by program type and channel are related together, as well as tendencies to watch any one channel together with each of the others.

The points of interest here involve the possibilities of either system loyalty or of cultural loyalty. The first implies that people who watch more

TABLE 4
Common Use of Channels Across the Introduction Of a New Channel

	Period Examined			
	A: pre C4	B: Early C4	Year Post A	Year Post B
No. of weeks	3	7	7	7
ITV × C4	—	.14	.17	.13
ITV × BBC1	.02	−.01	.04	.12
ITV × BBC2	.01	.03	−.00	−.01
C4 × BBC1	—	.14	.15	.20
C4 × BBC2	—	.31	.32	.28
BBC1 × BBC2	.41	.31	.38	.41
Average sample sizes	487	534	563	565

commercial television in its established mainstream channel ITV would tend also to watch more Channel 4. This might be due to habit, to some similarities of climate created by the presence of advertising, as well as for more practical reasons that two channels under some element of common control share common program start and end times, some joint onscreen promotion, a common program journal, and some repeats of episodes of a series carried first on one channel then later in the week on the other.

These system considerations are very evident in the case of common uses of the BBC channels, and both system and cultural climate or ethos differences may be evident in the near-zero correlations between ITV and the two BBC channels. When Channel 4 began, a relationship was immediately observed with ITV, but this was paralleled by a relationship with BBC 1, and well exceeded by the links between weight of viewing of Channel 4 and BBC 2. This last result points to some cultural loyalty, with people who partook more of the relatively more up-market or demanding schedule contents of BBC2 finding common ground with Channel 4. What seems to have happened subsequently is a confirmation of the links between ITV and Channel 4 viewing, with no change in the absence of links between ITV and BBC 2. Channel 4's cultural ethos type relation with BBC 1 has increased slightly and is still in evidence with BBC 2. Thus there are clear signs of both system loyalty and cultural loyalty. The latter may not be wholly a matter of ethos or of sensibility but rather may have something to do with the materials scheduled on each channel. Light can be shed on this point by examining correlations between weights of viewing to each program type and channel.

People who watch more ITV have tended to be heavier viewers of all types of programs particularly of soap opera, and comedy and light enter-

TABLE 5
Links Between Amounts of Types and of Channels Viewed

No. of Programs Viewed, in:	Numbers of Items Seen on:			
	ITV	C4	BBC1	BBC2
Comedy	.61	.35	.32	.28
General interest	.39	.34	.47	.50
Films, drama	.42	.37	.27	.23
News	.54	.06	.47	.13
Sport	.38	.15	.30	.35
Adventure, action	.50	.17	.17	.07
Soap opera	.71	.15	.01	.00

(Partial correlations, holding age, sex, class constant; averaged over 17 weeks' data in 1983)

tainment. Heaviest BBC1 viewers have also tended to be heavy users of general interest and information material including news, but these viewers have not been more or less frequent soap opera viewers. This is not only unsurprising but also an encouraging sign of the validity of these data as measures of viewing behavior, since the overwhelming bulk of soap opera items were at that time shown on ITV. In 1985 BBC 1 began to compete in soap opera with a major new show, *East Enders*, while late in 1986 the daytime hours, hitherto empty or used for schools' broadcasts, teletext pages or various other more specialist elements were assigned more general programing, including imported soap operas. These new schedules are likely to have altered the relationships shown in Table 5, though figures are not available at the time of writing to document any such changes.

In its first year the viewing time accorded to the new channel did not exceed 5% of the total per week, so it is not likely that the relationships between program type and channel viewing across the period examined in Table 5 (which spans 1983) would have altered markedly. However, by the end of 1984 Channel Four typically received 8% of total viewing time and a chance to alter the relationships between itself and other channels and reciprocally between other channels themselves may have begun to be detectable. Two changes for the weeks examined in 1984, over those considered in 1983 (which had seasonally similar positions) can be seen (see Table 4). First, a significant link has emerged between ITV and BBC 1 viewing; second, Channel Four may have come to share its viewing slightly less markedly with BBC 2 in exchange for a stronger affinity with BBC 1. These patterns of development point to a mainstreaming phenomenon in which those who watch more of one popular channel (BBC 1 or ITV, which have over 30% over 40% of weekly viewing time respectively) also tend to watch the other. The new channel has become used more like the mainstream channels than like the original minority one, BBC 2, which took less than 10% of weekly viewing, even though it reached 60% of the population at some time during a week.

This British evidence (and it is not easy to know where comparable evidence exists elsewhere, relating program type, channel and individual viewing data) shows that it is possible to have a program ecology in which people pursue certain programs and avoid others, pursue certain program types and others to a lesser extent, and favor certain channels or sets of channels. The reasons for channel loyalty must include some identification with an atmosphere thought to characterize a channel; some realization of personal suitability of a channel's scheduling practices; and some response to shared program start times, information, and promotion that exists for each of two pairs of channels. The behavioral patterns discussed here are a most important part of considerations, which will be examined later concerning the possible effects of television and options for influencing such processes away from causing harm and toward creating benefits.

SUBJECTIVE EVALUATION OF VIEWING
AS AN ASSESSMENT PERSPECTIVE

When appreciation indices became available in the early 1970s in the independent television sector in the United Kingdom (the BBC already had its proprietary reaction indices), people in television companies and the advertising industry found them a tantalizing prospect. Their hope was to be able to predict audience size for new programs, for to do so, even to a small extent better than by existing (mostly wait and see) methods, could be of real commercial value. The first step was simply to correlate appreciation with audience size; however, because extraneous influences on audience size, such as channel loyalty, promotion, competing programs, and, it can now be affirmed, program type were not controlled for, relationships were negligible (see Goodhardt et al., 1975). This suited the ideology and the methods of those who preferred the objectivity of the Neilsen and AGB type metered measures of audience size. In addition, early attempts to explore the utility of program evaluation started with the multiscale apparatus that Haldane and his colleagues had devised. Using bipolar scales such as sad–happy, if a comedy was accorded a mark in the sad range of the scale, program makers felt such an outcome was absurd and, as a result, retreated from descriptive appreciation indices. The process of withdrawal was reinforced by the fact that the audience size estimates were, and still are, referred to as ratings, creating a somewhat ambiguous impression that audience size itself was an index of subjective, as well as economic, merit.

From time to time, however, applied researchers returned to these data to see what could be done with them. Thus, Prue (1979), the Media Research Manager of J. Walter Thompson in the United Kingdom, obtained IBA (AURA) appreciation indices for over 70 programs, taken only from the light entertainment type and shown only on the two major channels; he had also excluded single special programs, quiz programs, and guest shows whose appeal after seeing them (as distinct from previous desire to see them) might depend on idiosyncrasies of the particular episode. Within these constraints Prue was able to show a positive relationship between audience size and appreciation scores. Prue was aware that appreciation not only might give some indication of future audience size, but it might also give some indication of effects of program climate on the effectiveness of advertisements seen alongside the programs. At that stage Prue believed that a halo effect linked program with advertisement appreciation; on the other hand he also thought that recall for the content of an advertisement on the day after the program was negatively related to appreciation for the adjacent programs.

Similar results have been reported by Barwise and Ehrenberg (1982b) from the United States. Using a five-point liking scale and a mixed list of 20 programs (eg.,*Dallas, 60 Minutes, Hello Larry*) they reported a 0.8 correlation between liking and audience size. They added to this demonstration with different measures of evaluation (good of its kind, really like to watch) and different measures of claimed viewing, such as how recently an item was last seen. Overall, they claimed that "the marked relationship between liking and viewing can hardly be in doubt" (p. 10). However, what can be in doubt is whether their measures of liking referred to appreciation specifically after having seen a program, or to something much more general and prospective such as "really like to watch." Barwise and Ehrenberg refer to "attitudinal responses" as though these are consequences of each viewing experience and agree that there "are systematic differences in the liking of different types of programs" (p. 22); thus, although they reject the idea that audience sizes have anything to do with program type, they claim that there is a positive relation between appreciation and audience size (for particular programs).

These, then, are some indications of the existence of interest in appreciation measurement, to which it must be added that the broadcasters in a system of public service provision of programs use the data as one of their indices of quality control. On occasion, public statements are made by people in the industry who infer judgments about program quality from what they observe about audience size. Thus, Colin Clark of the British Masius advertising agency declared [in Marketing Week (13 September 1983)] "the audience is becoming more selective and . . . we at Masius have always maintained that the *quality of programming* has been the major factor in falling audiences." This allegation is based on the validity of the claim of falling audiences, which appeared at the time to be the case. However, the published audience size data from the industry's contractor are not fully corroborated by other evidence (for example, it was said in the industry that Channel Four audiences were at that time often greater than the official figures estimated); in late 1983 and afterwards audience sizes even by official measurement proceeded to increase. More likely, the clamor at the time had its origin in the further threats posed to the daily newspapers' advertising sales by the arrivals in 1982 of the new Channel Four, and in early 1983 of breakfast TV; such a motivation was aknowledged by an article in *The Times* (4 April 1984) headed "Newspapers United to Declare War on TV Giants."

The IBA's appreciation indices were recorded, with few changes in technique, for 12 years before they were discontinued in 1985. A portmanteau-type question was posed namely, "how interesting and/or enjoyable was . . ." the program you have just seen (enough of to have formed a judgment of it); and a six-point scale was used. For some years news was treated as a week long entity, but then the results were broken out separately between weekday and weekend news. The average AIs for all viewing have been calculated for each of seven distinct program types; these results afford a longitudinal record relevant to the history of television in Great Britain.

These results substantiate Barwise and Ehrenberg's observation that appreciation relates to program type; previously, Goodhardt et al. (1975)

TABLE 6
Appreciation Norms for 12 Years of British Television

Year	Sport	General Interest	News	Soap Opera	Adventure Action	Light Entertainment	Films Drama
1973	77	80	77	76	73	72	71
1974	78	75	77	76	74	72	70
1975	76	75	77	74	74	72	69
1976	76	76	76	72	73	72	70
1977	77	77	76	72	71	72	71
1978	77	77	75	71	71	72	72
1979	79	77	77	73	71	71	72
1980	77	77	76	71	70	70	72
1981	78	77	77	73	71	72	71
1982	76	76	76	72	72	71	71
1983	76	75	75	72	71	72	71
1984	76	73	75	72	71	72	71

had established that a difference of over five points between two AI scores each for a single program, if they were based on at least 50 observations each, was likely to be significant. The figures in Table 6 were derived from between 15,000 and 20,000 thousand programs per year, which have been assessed by panels accumulating some 25,000 raters per year, each of whom views on average about 35 times per week. Although the differences between average scores for various types are small, and differences across the years are small, it would not be wrong to consider three point differences as reflecting real variation in aggregate experience.

The overall differences of five to seven points between sport and general interest material on the one hand, and films and drama on the other, differences moreover which occur regularly across all the years, must be considered real.

If some of the difference between program types can be linked with different standards of rating or generosity between people of different age, sex, or class, who actually view these materials to a different extent, this kind of discounting does not so readily apply to differences across the years. If the agency spokesperson was right about deteriorating program quality, then it should be most manifest in the general interest type, and to a lesser extent in soap opera and adventure action. It could still be argued though that program quality was falling if it was true that viewers become habituated in their judgment and give material a score now that they would have rated more poorly in years gone by. Such an argument would suggest that television has debased viewers' powers of discrimination in the realm of quality. It might also be true that, if program quality was falling and viewers were thus to some extent turning off their sets, it is the substantial segment who do not mind or notice diminution in quality who deliver these ratings, which have remained relatively stable in several types (sport, news, light entertainment, films, drama) across the years.

Such explanations, however, are not parsimonious. It is simpler to conclude that there is little reason to consider that, in four program types, there has been any effective diminution in quality; and that in three types there has been a small, though significant diminution in satisfaction across 12 years. There are good reasons why films and drama (the latter including single plays and short series), which are often seen in the hope of getting satisfaction, which is in some instances not attained (but in others, exceeded), receive lower appreciation scores than do the other types. A symbiotic adjustment is to be expected in the case of soap operas, where a substantial familiarity exists, and there might be reason, therefore, to expect high appreciation in this type. Soap operas, however, attract a large audience (Table 2), which means that they are seen by both heavy and light viewers. Light viewers tend to award somewhat lower appreciation marks for what they see, thus diluting the appreciation aggregate for soap operas. A similar situation exists for the type of sport.

FROM ONE DIMENSION
OF APPRECIATION TO TWO

Psychologists in America in the 1950s showed that the meaning for most words and ideas could economically be mapped by an underlying structure of three dimensions: evaluation, potency and speed (Osgood et al., 1957). Any idea would have just so much or so little of each of these three basic properties, which together would describe a substantial part of the meaning in that idea. Bearing this in mind, it is easy to note that the IBA's AI assessment scale is a neat package of two of these dimensions: how interesting relates to potency or impact and how enjoyable relates to goodness of appeal or value. What becomes of speed? How fast or slow paced are given programs? Much less is known about this dimension of program assessment, and what it may reveal about the art and experience of screen communication. The third dimension may offer a rich field for future researchers to explore; meanwhile we can see that researchers in the first two fields have been quite productive.

In the United States, a germination point for systematic studies of evaluation was a conference run by the Aspen Institute in 1980. The journalist Carolyn Setlow (1978) explained clearly why the commercial networks were not and would not be interested in qualitative ratings; she also explained how simplistic and deficient was the measure only of behavior. She detailed the work done in several overseas countries and prophesied that it would require some federal agency or private foundations to develop and implement a system of quality ratings in the United States. This is precisely what happened. A company called Television Audience Assessment (TAA), founded that year in Cambridge, Massachusetts, embarked on production of quality ratings concentrating on two dimensions of assessment (see Beville, 1985, p. 155).

From TAA, Roberts and Lemieux (1981) reported a preliminary study involving 1,600 people telephoned in Springfield, Illinois. The survey explored responses to programs that had just been seen, measuring evaluation, attention, planning for viewing, and a number of other points. Two scales began immediately to emerge, indicating appreciation (not in the two-dimensional IBA sense) and impact. The next study (TAA,1983) expanded to 3,000 subjects in two markets who mailed back diary sheets with which they had been supplied daily over a two-week period in 1982. Each program seen received a personal program rating (called appreciation) score on a scale from 0 to 10, and two other four-point scales "this program touched my feelings" and "I learned something from this program") yielded results, which were combined to give an impact score.

At this stage TAA (1983) asserted that appeal was useful in predicting audience loyalty across episodes, whereas impact scores could be of commercial value because they indicated intraprogram loyalty. This meant that viewers were less likely to leave the set (or channel) during commercials for a high than for a low impact program. TAA proposed an index to be called *Proportion of Viewers In the Room for all Commercials* (PIRC), which they said was linked in a linear relationship to a composite of impact and appeal. Knowing the PIRC, an advertiser would get nearer to knowing the number of viewers actually found by the commercial (rather than the number estimated by orthodox measures of audience size). To underline what advertisers should be concerned about, TAA reported that 46% of viewers of low impact programs left the set during commercials compared with 26% of those viewing high impact programs.

It may be ironic that in a communications environment where great importance is placed on freedom of information, pressures and anxieties evidently existing within the television industry restricted information about the PIRC index. Beville makes no mention of it. TAA had to reinforce the validity of their case and next (TAA, 1984) published results of a laboratory study on this topic. Two conditions were set up, one of an informal viewing room more like a home, with distractions of magazines and snacks available, and a more formal theater style viewing environment. People saw hour long programs into which commercials had been inserted. It was shown that the environment mattered much more than did the programs in affecting attention to programs, as well as recall and credibility of commercials. Higher impact scores, more so than appeal ratings, linked with better recall for commercials while impact was more effective than either environment or appeal in relating to intention to buy the brand advertised. The work of Thorson and Reeves (1986), mentioned in the previous chapter, closely supports TAA's findings.

These American results pose both a challenge to the industry and an opportunity for public service broadcasters. The challenge is whether the buyers and sellers of television advertising will take up these more sophisticated methods of assessing the flow of audiences to add to (not replace) existing measurement practices. If high impact does produce a better advertising climate, then an environment will be created in which there is less casual viewing of material that makes very little impact on viewers, and that some may consider to be a waste of time.

In Great Britain a number of studies have paralleled the explorations of TAA. In March 1981, three surveys were placed with viewers by Aske (1981). One sample assessed its week's viewing experiences on the Appreciation Scale used routinely by the IBA. A second sample assessed its viewing of the same schedule only on a scale of enjoyment, and the third sample focussed only on interest. The result was that where enjoyment was greater than interest, the former tended to match the appreciation score; when interest was greater, it matched the score. Aske concluded that the Appreciation scale was effective for measuring either or both enjoyment and interest and that the similarities in these three modes of assessment probably outweighed the differences between them.

This was not the only possible view of these results. It is likely that if people deal with a single scale, whether it is in terms of enjoyment or of interest, they use that scale as a more broadly evaluative device than its particular label implies. What has to be done is to get people to use at least two scales simultaneously so that a contrast in evaluation, if it exists, is made explicit. To explore subjects' stamina in the use of several scales, a supplementary diary sheet covering one day was added to the usual appreciation diaries during one week in November 1981 (Wober, 1982a). Viewers were asked, in addition to showing how "interesting and/or enjoyable" each item they saw had been, to say also how interesting, how enjoyable, and how worthwhile the programs were. This procedure certainly opened up differences between two scales; for example, programs which were more interesting than enjoyable were all informational, whereas the opposite occurred only for entertainment material. Worthwhileness correlated more strongly with enjoyability than with interest.

There was a noticeable drop in the number of programs assessed on the experimental scales, suggesting that multiple tasks probably overloaded some respondents. The next two projects (Wober and Reardon, 1983), therefore, used two scales with one sample of people during the same week as the twin appreciation scale was fielded among a separate sample. This was done twice, at the beginning and end of a month in which a new channel had been started. Many differences between the results from the separate scales now appeared. The four channels had different levels of impact and enjoyment overall, with the new channel initially particularly low on the latter. Differences between E and I scores revealed variations in response to programs and to program types accored by different demographic sub-groups. This British work had no need to seek possible commercial applications; the initial purpose was to have improved instruments with which to help judge the success of the new channel, which had been set social goals of appealing in new ways to existing audiences and of satisfying interests that had not hitherto been well satisfied by existing channels.

One of the potentially important results of a subsequent two scale survey (Wober, 1984a) was to show that adventure action programs clearly received the lowest average impact score of any program type. Since programs of this kind set out to make their appeal through pace and impact, their failure to register well on this dimension suggests that, at least among adult viewers, this category of programs for all its overt violence is emotionally discarded. This study also measured viewers' experience of visual and auditory imagery, and these practices revealed one way in which the two evaluative scales operated differently. People with stronger visual imagery tended to record greater impact from actuality program types, but this was not so evident with entertainment types. Auditory imagery practices did not relate significantly to either enjoyment or impact ratings.

As a footnote to the outcome of two scale evaluations, a file of American appeal scores was available from TAA with which it was possible to compare contemporary British ratings. For 31 American programs also screened in the United Kingdom, appreciation scores were averaged across three weeks; the U.S. average for the 31 shows was 74 to the UK's 71 for the same items. At the top of the list in both the United States and Great Britain were *Hill Street Blues* (86) and (82) respectively and *Little House on the Prairie* (83) and (80) respectively. The high U.S. appeal score (and potential export value) of *Little House on the Prairie* was not widely enough known in the United States to save that series from extinction on grounds of flagging audience sizes (although the high appeal, with what TAA claim is a better chance of repeat viewing may have enabled the program's audience to have been better sold as a segmented target group). Overall, the U.S. appeal results correlated 0.74 with the U.K. appreciation ones, suggesting that evaluation of merit, even across program types and countries, albeit ones that share a considerable awareness of each other's screen fare, is a reliable process.

SUMMARY: DRAWING THE MAPS
OF TELEVISION TOGETHER

We have looked at five different ways of mapping the territory of television. Do these perspectives all show congruent pictures of a single underlying phenomenon? Or do the perspectives reveal separate, though overlapping, phenomena? By no means have all the combinations of perspective been tackled by researchers. In a project similar to some American research by Neuman (1981), Himmelweit, Swift and Jaeger (1980) explored the possibility that the sociological and cognitive frameworks were linked. Seeing "the audience as critic," samples of viewers rated programs on a great variety of scales and the underlying patterns were identified. The cognitive structures, or ways in which "the audience" thought about programs were shown to be complex, as are the views of professional critics. But the project was limited in that the respondents did not assess real episodes of real programs, but merely their titles on paper. Likewise, the exercise was not repeated among a sample of critics to show whether the lay and the professional frameworks were similar.

Viewing these efforts 4 years later, Newcomb and Hirsch (1984) judged that this kind of work was "just beginning," though it did point to ways in which viewers and critics might or might not overlap in their perceptions. Following this, Alexander (1985) showed that teenagers did not interpret soap opera episodes altogether in ways which critics had supposed were dominant in the content; it was not surprising, therefore, that such young viewers did not reveal any effects of the supposed thematic contents of soap operas. In turn, Livingstone (1986) reported a study of viewers' conceptions of *Dallas;* elements of this revealed a marked morality component of the series, with different characters occupying different positions along the continuum. Independent of the morality realm was a potency issue, revealing how hard various characters were. Incidentally, no speed continuum emerged clearly from Livingstone's work as discriminating between characters or as applying to the series as a whole. The structure of meaning of *Dallas* for viewers was thus displayed and corresponds quite well to how it has been described by critics. In an independent enterprise Liebes (1984) presented focus group discussion analysis of the experience of *Dallas* for Israeli viewers. Instead of adopting a declaratory approach, as many critics have—often quite perceptively and usefully done—Liebes allows the structures of meaning of *Dallas* (again with a strong morality theme) to emerge as being constructed somewhat differently by viewers according to their own existing cultural backgrounds. The television screen thus becomes partly a mirror in which the picture is composed of what is broadcast but which is colored and shaped to a considerable extent by the culture of the environment in which it is viewed.

The kind of authority assumed by those who have been called critics here, is exemplified by Hartley (1984, p. 121) who announces "it seems to me that the dirtiness both of television texts and of individual readers is a matter worth looking into further." This uses the word dirt in a British rather than an American sense, despite its appearance in an American book, and explores the very interesting notion that dirt means lack of cleanliness or clarity, hence ambiguity; and by its management of the ambiguities it presents that television has power. Hartley christens his new discipline "videology" and offers an analysis of the news scenes as examples of what it offers; it is more likely a feature of the ambiguity to which he refers earlier, that another viewer (or reader of Hartley's essay) might construe these episodes differently. Unless the television image then is to become a mirror of several reflections, of critics and of nonprofessional viewers, all superimposing the colors and shapes of their opinions and standpoints upon the broadcast content, it may be advisable to negotiate some agreement among the critics and viewers. This process is called audience research and is more or less adequately done by discussions and formalized questions.

Uses and gratifications theorists (eg., Palmgreen, 1984) have looked for links between the patterns of demands or needs, those of uses, and finally those of appreciation; however, one must be careful in examining these studies to distinguish whether the measures of uses (that is, behavior) have got close enough to records of actual actions, or whether, as happens not infrequently, the measures of use are really of reported use, which are possibly confounded with influences from what people like to think they have seen. Thus, Barwise and Ehrenberg (1982b, p. 10) who were looking at links between appreciation and behavior, wrote (p. x) "claimed frequency of viewing . . . was subject to very much overclaiming" partly at least because people "merely think or even just say they like what they watch." Nevertheless, Barwise and Ehrenberg reported on American evidence that when one controlled for time of day and type of program there was a positive relation between audience size or share, and audience appreciation.

British work on this particular linkage provides similar evidence (Wober, 1984c). Using the AURA database in which appreciation and viewing records are two features of the same diary endorsements, average correlations per viewer per week across 17 weeks' data in 1983 appear in Table 7 below. The average minimum number in each of the measurement pairs was 327 viewers. Thus, for example, in one week 300 people may have seen at least one sport program and rated it (others saw more, and among these sport viewers a correlation was computed between the number of items seen by each person and the average appreciation given by each person for the items they saw). In another week 350 people may have seen at least one sport item, and so on. From Table 1 it will be

TABLE 7
Appreciation and Amount of Viewing by Program Type

Within Program Type	Average Correlation*
Adventure/action	.10
Soap opera	.21
Sport	.10
Comedy, light entertainment	.03
News	.15
General interest, information	−.04
Films, drama	−.01
across all types	.01

* simultaneously partialling out age, sex, class

recalled that sport is the type reaching fewest viewers, so in a week in which 350 may have seen at least one sports item, 450 viewers may have seen at least one light entertainment item. The effect of this fluctuation in sample size is to some extent mitigated by having 17 weeks' data pooled; it may be safe to treat indices of .10 and over as departing from zero or randomness. It should be noted that in this procedure, those who have not seen any of a given program type during a diary week are not eligible for an appreciation estimate (though this is admitted in other research procedures) so the correlations here will tend to be flattened. It may be taken then that positive and quite significant correlations exist for soap opera and news, between actual amount of use and appreciation (per episode, after seeing each one). Modestly significant links, albeit of very small size, are indicated in the cases of sport and adventure action; for comedy, general interest, and films and drama there are no significant links between amounts of viewing and liking.

These results are not dissimilar from earlier those presented by Barwise, Ehrenberg and Goodhart (1979), which were based on 8 weeks' AURA data. In their study the program was the unit of analysis, whereas in the results above the individual viewer was the basic unit. The viewer yields two kinds of scores: number of programs endorsed and average appreciation accorded to them. The program has two similar attributes: the number of viewers who endorsed it and the appreciation they accorded. Calculated by programs, at a time when there were only three channels in Great Britain, the Barwise study reported a substantial difference between prime and nonprime time results; for the former, correlations within two broad program types (information and entertainment) averaged 0.6 for the two popular channels, and 0.3 for the minority (BBC 2) channel. Away from prime time the correlations between audience size and appreciation fell to 0.2.

Another way of demonstrating a link between appreciation and behavior is to compare penetration figures with appreciation measures. Unpublished studies show good correlations within programs, or across them, between these two indices. This means that if a show in its early episodes has greater appreciation among a particular segment of the audience it is likely that a greater percentage of that segment will view it. Typical examples would involve off-beat comedies such as *Hitchhikers' Guide to the Galaxy, Soap, Fawlty Towers,* or *Spitting Image.* These have markedly higher appreciation among younger than older viewers and correspondingly larger penetration figures. An attempt has been made (Menneer, 1984) to extend this approach to the audience as a whole, so that shows whose early episodes have good appreciation scores are observed to build audiences. The evidence presented appears to be selective, however; Menneer shows how appreciation remains constant for shows where occasional episodes have markedly smaller audiences because of special events shown on the main opposing channel. Thus, he argues, good appreciation reinforces a program's claim to its place in the schedule or at least defends it by showing that exceptional lapses in audience size are not due to the program itself but to external circumstances.

Reviewing such results and introducing new data, Wakshlag and Wober wrote (1985, p. 188) that "evaluative scales whether global or preferably separated into their main components of meaning, show continued promise as behavioural indicators." The new direction of analysis was to define "dropout," which was currently available in terms of quarter hour audience size measures; thus, the difference in the second over the first quarter hour gave the dropout figure. (Negative dropout meant that the audience size had grown). Gandy (1981) had used this method in the United States to show that for over 500 half hours studied, the dropout was greater for shows featuring violent content than for nonviolent material. Wakshlag and Wober (1985) were able to find, for 83 shows, independent measures of audience size, appreciation, and separately of enjoyment and impact (these last two indices from the same fieldwork instrument). None of the three qualitative measures correlated with dropout, although appreciation and enjoyment did separately relate positively with audience size for entertainment shows.

Further, work by Wakshlag and Wober went on to use much finer behavioral data, in this case dropout measures calculated across the first two three-minute segments of programs. This material, as yet unpublished, produced a similar picture—that dropout is related to structural features such as channel and start time; but audience size, in controlled dayparts (and within program type) does relate to appreciation. This suggests that known appreciation level, within these program type, daypart and channel constraints can actively contribute to determining audience size. The relevance of this for "philosophies of control" was discussed by Wober (1984f) in relation to the uses sometimes made of public opinion survey testimony.

The point made here rested upon the lack of resemblance between five hierarchies of program types, three of them evaluative, one affective, and one behavioral. Two philosophies of control were discussed. One termed "forensic" or explicitly consumerist holds that what people say they want to have provided for them is likely to indicate what they will consume. One simple example refutes this theory; viewers say they do not want to see reruns of old shows or films, but they still provide large audiences for much of this kind of material. The second philosophy holds that people may know their minds, but their actions frequently belie the patterns of their beliefs with the consequence that program schedules may or should be planned other than by concentrating on satisfying explicit consumerist requirements. The data discussed are in Table 8.

In this case the measure of the effectiveness of use made of program types has no significant correlation with a profile of demand across types. Taken this broadly, the effectiveness of use criterion relates significantly and negatively with measures of appreciation and of impact (broadly supporting the contentions of Barwise and Ehrenberg, 1982b).

TABLE 8
Alignment of Five Measures of Program Assessment

Rank Orders for Types:	Measures				
	Want	Use	Appreciate	Enjoy	Impression
Soap opera	6	1	4	2	4
Adventure/action	4	2	7	4.5	7
Comedy, light entertnmnt	1	3	5	6	6
Films/drama	3	4	6	3	5
News	7	5	3	7	1.5
Sport	5	6	1	1	1.5
General Interest	2	7	2	4.5	3
Source:	1975: % wanting to see more of said types, shown	Table 2 above	1983 appreciation index average		1983: Wober & Reardon

Better appreciated tend to be those types with greater impact, which produce smaller audiences per prime time program.

Some new efforts to examine the links, if any, between behavior (that is, uses) and evaluation have begun to be reported in 1985 and 1986 by Collett and Lamb at Oxford University. The outcomes of a procedure in which a miniature camera and recorder had been installed within the television cabinet, revealing domestic audience behavior while the set itself was on, were first of all to disclose a wide variety of behavior other than attentive viewing. When, at this author's request, a two-scale evaluation diary was also introduced, it became possible to correlate measures of presence (merely in the room), viewing (that is, facing the set), enjoyment, and impact. Although the correlations are not large (0.3 at most), they are very significant; and it is clear that enjoyment relates better to viewing than to mere presence. Depending on the type of program (demanding, or less demanding), impact also relates at different levels of significance to viewing. This kind of study must be developed further, but it shows that there is great variety in the way in which screen materials are experienced and used; it also shows a limited though significant degree of convergence in the results from two methods of documenting this encounter.

Overall, the picture now emerges that at sociological and cognitive levels of analysis, program types can be discerned that have distinct and matching attributes. Both the motivational and behavioral perspectives can place these types in a rank order, but the rank orders produced in these particular ways do not correspond at all well. Evaluation of programs forming types based on arithmetic averages of appreciation (viewers do not know they are rating types, they know they are rating programs, which are then grouped on a basis of prior sociological or cognitive characterstics) does not correspond with the apprent desirability of types when these are conceived as types by viewers in public opinion studies.

This suggests that, at a level of images of program types, a forensic democratic or consumerist model of choice is not functioning perfectly, if at all. People do not use or appreciate types that they say they will prefer to use. However, within types there is contrary evidence that people do know what they like and pursue it in their actions. Such coherence is not overwhelming and tends to be found only within particular program types.

CONCEPTS EXPLORED IN THIS CHAPTER

Appreciation. Liking for programs, subjectively assessed, hence truly an example of rating and quite different from measures of audience size, wrongly called ratings; variants of appreciation, such as impact and "worthwhileness" ratings have also been explored.

Categorization. A process underlying the creation of order, whether intellectual or administrative.

Dropout. The proportion of an audience who quit viewing; an index which may hold promise for validating.

Program Hybrids. Creative attempts to make programs of a new kind different from any customary type; face strong pressures from administrative and perceptual sources encouraging resolution into an existing format.

Program Types. Also called genre; a set of taxonomies which can be arrived at from at least five different approaches, though these give a considerable measure of agreement about the broad nature of the types and their contents.

"Psychographics." Profiles of individuals based on dimensions of personality; an advertising industry term seeming to avoid what in the United States commercial world are regarded as the unfashionable pitfalls of personality differences, which are admittedly problematic to measure and to use for sampling and other analytic purposes.

Reach. The number or percentage of people who have had some experience of a program, or a series, or a channel within a given time period.

Take-up Percentage. The number of programs viewed, per person, per program type, per week, for each 100 programs available within that type.

TV's Multiple Heritage. TV genres are developments of existing traditions in the theater, folk art, and print.

"Uses and Gratifications." A body of theory and research implying a marked degree of viewer autonomy and self-control, in distinction to theories of the hapless viewer subject to unsought influences and effects; since *use* is a construct of a different kind to that of *gratification*, this must at least be recognized and perhaps better lead to relabeling as *"needs* and gratifications."

CHAPTER 4

Challengers: Opponents of the Screen Itself or of Its Contents

INTRODUCTION: THREE PERSPECTIVES ON THE VALUE OF TELEVISION

There seem to be three very different standpoints from which to evaluate television as a social phenomenon. These three standpoints can be arranged quite convincingly in a line, with one end characterized by pessimism and a desire to oppose television grounded in a morally toned fervor; the other extreme is lit by an optimism, which is often attributable simply to the self-interest of those who find a prosperous livelihood in the industry. The explicit opponents of television, termed challengers, are many. It is not easy to find among them pure scientists or even many of those who doff their metaphorical white coats of objectivity to pursue the outcome of their findings as active citizens.

The advocates of television tend to be within the industry itself, or others such as politicians or scholars who hope to use it. Again, few of these champions are communications scientists, but they do refer to evidence developed by scientists to support the benefits they wish to attribute to television or to refute the arguments put forward by the challengers.

In a morally neutral position between the prophets of doom and the priesthood of the message systems of the screen are a host of communications scientists. This community develops the information (and in significant instances misinformation) on which the challengers and the champions nearly all seem to base their positions. Again, there is a further segregation of roles. Very few of the scientists charting the territory fought over by the challengers and the champions themselves take to one side or the other of the rhetorical lists. The implication is that if a communications scientist took one or another political position, this would undermine the credibility of the scientific findings on offer.

This expectation that scientists are dispassionate and detached from social action is set aside increasingly in other fields. In particular, nuclear and medical scientists now argue their political positions strongly without fear of losing professional esteem even among their political opponents. Evidently, these other fields recognize that the findings of science and their applications are separate functions, neither of which necessarily impedes the other. It may, or may not, be unfortunate that as yet most communications scientists have remained politically neutral.

It may be a symptom of the inability to make a sharp distinction between finding facts and deciding what to do with them that there is much talk about technology as though this refers principally to the hardware and physical entities involved. Yet the word technology should mean the knowledge about a technical field and not the mere contents of the field itself. Thus, if discussion among challengers, chartists, and champions alike all too often blurs the distinction between knowledge of a technical field and the technical contents themselves, it is not surprising that a distinction between evidence and how it should be applied is not acknowledged clearly either. The result of this may be that chartists keep to their charting for fear of being suspected of faulty instrumentation if they stray into advocacy based on their findings; correspondingly, the challengers and champions may not be as well informed as they might otherwise have been with many politically active scientists among them. We shall see evidence of this in due course.

A second point problem concerns primarily the challengers, though it also concerns the scientists: To whom do the groups address themselves? The metaphor of challengers and champions suggests a physical contest between the two, which the former might win. The outcome would be a new order in which new views would prevail. However, the metaphor usually falls short of reality so that challengers can air their rhetoric and listeners may be impressed, but nothing need change as a result. Television, with all its alleged terrors, would simply continue as before. The scientists likewise can chart their observations in cautious detail; however, what we have demonstrated with certainty is relatively scant, whereas what has been covered more copiously tends to be established only at more uncertain levels admitting of alternative interpretations. The output of the social science of admunications systems ironically tends to be poorly communicated outside the expert community. To be sure, nuggets of information are seized by challengers and by champions; these are sometimes used correctly and sometimes not, but they are seldom deployed in ways that imply a full grasp of their context.

The lay public is inclined to act in ways that suit the champions of television, using the facilities as they are provided. We have seen how people place a great value on having screen message systems and are broadly willing to pay substantial sums to acquire and to defend such possession; we have also seen how extensively screens are used. The public is not inclined to side with the challengers for several reasons. One reason is that most lay people realize they are not as well equipped (as chartists might be) to adjudicate the claims between challengers and champions, and here is the nub of one crucial difficulty for the former. If challengers hope to convince the lay public of their view point, they have to educate their readers (they are unlikely to use screen message systems for a self-destructive purpose), and by so doing, imply that viewers have not been sufficiently competent managers of their use of televison so far. If challengers were to succeed in such an enterprise, they would in some sense become controllers of public behavior; however, much of the philosophy that underlies the spirit of challenge hopes to convince the lay public that they should be autonomous and competent practitioners of self-control in a complex and tempting situation. Indeed, this is not just a goal but is also a prior assumption of the democratic ideology espoused by many challengers. However, if users already had such powers of discretion, there would be much less reason to press for social concern and control in challenging the institutions of television. The options for challengers are to press for external social control, as well as to work for more effective self-control among users. In some societies, such as those in Europe, both avenues until recently have been considered acceptable. The United States is almost the only place in which the social control of television is unacceptable except in extremely subtle or indirect ways.

Another reason why the lay public may be disinclined to side with the challengers has been suggested by the French philosopher sociologist Jacques Ellul (1980) who sees the technical system ("systeme technicien" mistranslated as technological system) as being the works of scientists and engineers translated into physical form. The public is dazzled by the new products of this system (which admiration is fanned by the works of champions, very appealingly in the case of medical science) and not only lay people but those who are scientists of the process of technical and social change have come to consider that "technical progress" is an irresistible flow in which new products simply have to be accepted; such progress is not just inevitable; it is also assumed to be beneficial. To treat the technical system (which after all is only propelled by human brains) as effectively supernatural is to give it some of the characteristics of a false religion.

Only by distinguishing true from this false religion can the ordinary person come to master the technical system rather than being mastered by it. Ellul's position refers not only to message systems using screens, but also to all advanced technical artefacts, including television. If television has become a false implicit religion, this is an obstacle to establishing self- or social control which goes beyond the difficulty just discussed. The false religion thesis is unprovable, farfetched perhaps, but also sufficiently serious and plausible to have to be given consideration. It is also different from another case, which we shall soon consider, that "television is a new religion" and a harmful one (at least in the United States).

CHALLENGERS:
IMPORTANT OBJECTORS TO TELEVISION

In assembling the cases of challengers and trying to give them a fair hearing, it will be useful to decide whether challengers believe the message system of television in itself is harmful or whether it is the contents, as they have come to be developed, which are harmful. This distinction between the message system itself and its contents connects with another important distinction. On the one hand, a reformist position can see some hope in applying controls to content and/or to the ways in which contents are distributed between channels or at different parts of the day, and possibly within different systems of availability and of payment. On the other hand, if the challengers insist that the features of the system itself are harmful for users, then there is little point in seeking controls over content to render television beneficial rather than harmful.

Two of the best known American challengers of television are Marie Winn (1978) and Jerry Mander (1978). Both attribute a wide range of problems to American television, and while Winn advocates greatly limiting its use and is considerably concerned with children, Mander sees equally important harms for adults and advocates abolishing television altogether. We shall also encounter Fred and Merrelyn Emery in Australia and Neil Postman in the United States, who have mounted serious challenges aimed at totally discrediting, and by implication, dismantling television. Finally, we have to pay substantial attention to George Gerbner, as a scientist-challenger. He differs from the group of Winn, Mander, Postman, and their supporters in that he has, with colleagues, accomplished a major body of research work in the field which he fights; the others have not.

Jerry Mander's four fronts of attack on television include two which are mainly sociopolitical and two which are psychophysiological. The macro-level arguments include the observation that American television has been in the hands of a very few major corporations and that it provides prepacked and ersatz "experience" by which real people (viewers) are insulated from real knowledge about the physical and social worlds, which is only provided second hand through a new priesthood of experts. These two contentions may have applied more markedly to American television in the mid-1970s than they do in the late 1980s or than they ever did in Europe. Mander is the first, but not the last, challenger who has tilted at television in the round, arguing that the entire message system is faulty or harmful, when it is at least possible that the arguments principally concerned television as it was then organized in the United States. Certainly British television has separated the commercial program makers from the publisher and other European systems have all devised various ways of avoiding a nexus developing between one (commercial) sector of society and the main channels of political information and discussion.

Mander's psychophysiological grounds of criticism include arguments that only when the screen is used to display text can it be an effective source of information; the nature of the pictures and their sequencing results in methods of viewing that involve passivity and lead to poor health. These charges would apply more clearly to television in whatever manner it is socially organized or its contents regulated and these are the grounds on which Mander has been joined by Winn (1978) and Postman (1982, p.278).

Winn insists that harms arise because "it's not what they watch" that is so important but the process of watching itself. Postman amplifies this with "people *watch* television. They do not read it. Nor do they much listen to it . . . One of the more naive delusions about television is that there can be great variability in the conceptual level of programs" (p.78). Here, Postman is also relaying a tenet of Goodhardt et al. (1975), that is, that people do not view selectively according to types of program. We have seen in the previous chapter, however, that there is much evidence from Great Britain for selectivity of viewing of programs by type, which strongly suggests that the greater number of viewers opt for the most part for less demanding material. However, the same research also shows that large amounts of more demanding material are provided and do reach the great majority of viewers. It must be acknowledged straight away though, that the British evidence concerns adults, while the concerns of Winn and Postman focus largely on children.

To illustrate the far-reaching appeal of Winn's and Mander's arguments one may recount the events in Gloucestershire, England, where a TV Action Group was set up by some concerned people, one of whom, Martin Large, (1980), wrote a book to advise families how to break the television habit. Reasons why one should not watch were detailed beginning with evidence from audience measurement sources asserting that children watch on average for over 3 hours per day (in Great Britain and more in the United States). If this was true in the magnetically passive image portrayed by these authors, it would seriously support their case that such a one-sided or supply-led pastime detracted from time and energy that should be devoted to a range of other more creative activities.

It is a pity, therefore, that these authors do not know that the amount of children's viewing varies in Great Britain from something nearer 2 hours per day in summer to about 4 hours per day in winter. Although the latter figure reveals a possibly regrettable degree of winter immobility, it also shows that to a great extent children are not trapped as automatons by the screen but view it when it is convenient. It is also clear from in-home observation that the "couch potato" model of the child viewer is often mistaken. Bechtel, Achelpohl and Akers (1972), and Anderson and Lorch (1979), in the United States, and Collett and Lamb (1985) in Great Britain and WCCO (the Minneapolis station which studied five families before and after they gave up their sets for a month) all have evidence that much of the "presence-in-the-room-with-the-set-switched-on" occurs in free movement. The set is treated for much of the time as just another person in the room. It has been convenient for the television advertisers, especially in the United States, to use and refer to this clumsy definition as specifying "viewing." Concerned observers then treat the whole 3 hours as "viewing;" writers such as Large (1980, p.36) state "the bulk of television is watched in a darkened room, with closed curtains. . . . After watching perhaps more consciously for a while, the viewers' mind is absorbed into the powerful electronically stimulated imagery as if in a trance."

This fear of loss of autonomy is expressed in several forms. One is the likening of television to a drug, as expressed in the title of Winn's book, *The Plug in Drug* (1978). An extreme form of this fear is shown in Large's chapter on the light emitted by the cathode ray tube and its alleged effects, not just on eyesight but on health more broadly. Relying on a book by Ott (1976, p.53) a theory is put forward that television "light rays permeate . . . the pineal and pituitary glands;" these rays are "artificial" and therefore considered not as healthy as natural light. Ott placed vegetables and mice in front of television sets and reported distorted growth in plants and cancers among the mice. In humans, Large (who, like Ott is a doctor) considers that "mal-illumination . . . may contribute to aggressive behaviour, heart illness and cancer" (p.56). Although these allegations are very serious, little further work has been done to look further into the possible effects of television light on health.

SCREENS, SPEAKERS, AND WAVES IN THE BRAIN

A second fear linked with the idea of loss of autonomy is developed through reference to electroencephalographic (EEG) studies of television viewers. The literature here has much empirical information to offer, some theory and a good deal of rhetoric. The first report is probably that of the American Krugman (1970, 1971) who started by recording a single subjects' EEGs for the occipital area (rear of skull, where visual information goes) while the subject was reading and while she was watching screened commercials. Krugman, who worked in advertising, deduced that television is a medium of low involvement and yielded brain-wave patterns different from those stimulated by print. This result was put forward as evidence to support Marshall McLuhan's aphorism that "the medium is the message," in this case taken to mean that it is the message system rather than the content that affects the brain. Two major flaws in this study included the fact that the subject at first did not even look at a television but at a rear slide projector; further, she may simply have been bored with the particular commercial. Krugman, however, repeated the procedure with true TV viewing reporting similar results. In later work Krugman (1979) expanded his evidence with commercials shown on a cathode ray screen, portraying Thomas Edison, this time reporting that varying contents also produced different EEG responses.

Two further studies (Appel, Weinstein and Weinstein, 1979; Weinstein, Appel and Weinstein, 1980) involved groups of 30 women who again saw commercials on television; more familiar commercials were associated with lower alpha activity; magazine advertisement reading yielded more beta wave activity, with its location more in the left brain than that evoked by television viewing. It should be pointed out that alpha waves are twitches on the EEG needle, which tend to occur at lower frequencies and are thought of as revealing a relaxed pattern of brain activity; beta waves have a somewhat higher frequency and are considered to correspond with a busy brain. An American group, Featherman et al. (1979), presented results based on 20 subjects, which partially supported the evolving picture; significantly less beta activity was recorded with television viewing than with reading. The comparison between the two message systems' evocation of alpha waves was more ambiguous and appeared to relate also to the contents being encountered. At the same time Walker (1980) asked 18 people to look at television, read, and relax mentally as well as work mentally (by imagining and counting). Again, reading evoked more beta activity than did television viewing, though not to a significant degree, and television yielded more alpha waves.

It is useful to present the work of Appel et al., Featherman et al., Walker, and Weinstein et al. as the scientific exercises of chartists; for although they are all aware of why their studies may be so important, they do not present them in the role of challengers. The same is not true for Emery and Emery (1975, 1980) who noted that Krugman's evidence of slow alpha wave activity with TV appeared to resemble what had been reported in the aftermath of sensory deprivation experiments. Television, with its scanner speeding across 500 or 600 lines 50 or 60 times a second, is described as though it pokes this terrible overload directly into the brain, which responds by switching off ("habituation"). This "direct" light is considered much more difficult to deal with than all other light people see, which is reflected light. The Emerys, like their cochallengers Winn, Mander, and Large, who write both for public and institutional attention, took their case to the Australian Senate Standing Committee on Education and the Arts, whose report gave the allegations serious weight. The Australian Broadcasting Tribunal (ABT) in turn commissioned further research on the topic.

Before examining what was found by Silberstein, Agardy, Ong and

Heath (1983) for the ABT it can be pointed out that the Emerys' analysis appears to have overlooked the physiology of the retina, whose numerous receptors would seem ideally designed to cope with the dot-activation basis of the television screen display. The eye itself takes from "normal" light a pixillated scan, which the brain is accustomed to composing into an experience of continuous objective existence. Second, it must be noted that in their discussions, the EEG investigators deal somewhat ambiguously with what the word "medium" entails. Mostly, they take medium to mean message system, so that the television screen with pictures is considered as a medium; variously, printed pictures are considered a different medium (Krugman) or televised text (presumably in silence) and television interview (sight and sound) are treated as the same medium (Silberstein et al.).

We shall deal with the distinctions appropriate in this field more fully in the next chapter, but it is useful to point out here that another way of making distinctions about media is to note what senses they address. Thus, silent pictures, whether in print or on screen use the same medium (vision) as printed text, whether on paper or screen; but the addition of sound means that television and cinema are multi-media message systems. The EEG studies gave very little attention to the role of the ear and to what "brain waves" are appropriate to track auditory information processing, let alone to the more complex matter of how programs may use visual and auditory information either in an interfering or in a complementary fashion.

The Silberstein project (1983) involved 24 12-year-olds. Four presentation methods were used: back slide projected text, televised (silent?) text, a television interview, and a documentary. Considerable technical care was taken with the statistical and physical procedures of the experiment. Paradoxically, it is one of the latter meticulous steps that may even undercut some of the study's value, for, in realizing that muscular activity of head and eye movement produces its own electrical signs, Silberstein et al. threw away those EEG (electroencephalographic) segments in which evidence existed of electromyographic (EMG) activity. Yet, it can be argued that it is part of the "couch potato" viewing syndrome that in some cases bodily and eye movement is minimized, which in turn diminishes the more active brain functioning (beta and theta wave forms) produced by print. Eye movement would be stimulated to some extent by scanning lines of text on screen, though probably not as much as by reading print on paper. The reason for less eye movement with television is that the screen subtends a smaller angle at the eye than does a page of print. Nevertheless, eye movement is more likely to occur in an examination of print than in response to a "talking head."

The results of Silberstein's experiments were that differences between slide projected text and televised text were not found in any of four kinds of brain activity waves (alpha, beta, delta, theta). This is presented as a test of the difference between "media" and is taken to refute the Emerys' conclusions. Perhaps a more sensible version of the concern about the "medium" is to treat the slide projected and televised texts as essentially similar in the sensory task they present, both engaging only the eye and discouraging a variety of coordinating arm, eye, and head movements. In this new view, the Silberstein et al. test of "medium" differences is not what it claims to be. Next, they report strong "content" differences, which they consider to lie within one "medium" of television. These involve differences in theta and alpha activity for both cerebral hemispheres between televised text and interview. The direction of these differences actually supports Krugman, the Emerys, and those who treat print, whether on paper or screen as more alerting than "television" (programming), which is less alerting. A useful feature of the Australian work was that, although the sample was very homogeneous and there was little variety of content within each of the display conditions, the degree of interest in the contents was measured and found not to be significantly correlated with any EEG measure. The same was true for vocabulary test scores and a measure of average amount of habitual television viewing.

The only content difference investigated in the realm of programs was between an interview and a documentary. Whereas the text and the interview yielded significant brain wave differences for both left and right hemispheres, the comparison between the interview and the documentary (here a real contrast of content rather than of "medium") produced less significant differences in excitation and were found for the right hemisphere only. This distinction fits in well with the theories of those who hold that the left hemisphere deals preferentially with "verbal" processing (that is, of words, whether read by eye or heard by ear). Stated another way, when the term "medium" is taken to mean the sensory pathways by which information is conveyed, the Silberstein et al. research does show differences in an expected direction associated with the medium in use.

Further complications involving sensory pathways, the content they carry, and the locations in which such information is dealt with in the brain are reported by Reeves and Lang (1986). Starting from the assumption that positive emotions are processed in the left hemisphere of the brain, and negative emotions on the right (Davidson, 1984), Reeves and Lang suggest that "negative television material" may be processed more in terms of spatial configurations (e.g., how close I am to trouble . . . (while the) left brain . . . is continually trying to provide conscious explanations . . ." (p.11); various segments of screen content were shown to 16 subjects and EEG records were taken. They did find greater arousal for negative than for positive scenes, but while the latter were only nonsignificantly more effective on left than on right brain activity, the negative scenes were significantly more effective on the right side of the brain. Reeves and Lang state that "the processing of emotion on television is lateralized" (p.16); but they have nowhere mentioned the role of music. As we have noted that television is a message system using the media in sight and sound, it should also be recalled that music is reported to be preferentially dealt with in the right part of the brain.

The value of Reeves and Lang's results is that they reinforce the case that television is not "a medium" that acts in one particular way upon the brain, but its varied contents act in different ways. The details of the prominence of music and visual components are of less importance to the argument than is the single result of differentiation by content. A similar result was reported by Kaneko, Yoshida, Shinod and Hitoshi (1986) who showed that Japanese viewers on seeing documentary screen material produced greater alpha activity (were bored and tranquilized), and less alpha activity when they were shown sexually stimulating scenes.

American researchers seem eager to use EEG traces to tap the effectiveness of television commercials. Rothschild, Thorson, Reeves, Hirsch and Goldstein (1986) had 26 women view 18 commercials while EEGs were recorded. Having established that recognition and recall of commercials were related to reduced alpha activity, the researchers focused microscopically on what they call "epochs" (the intervals from one sudden drop in alpha, i.e., attention point, to the next) and explored what was happening on the screen to define attention getting. Since the commercials included some rather humdrum cases, it was not the thematic content which was in focus but simply what are called "formal elements." Epochs were found to occur shortly after (visual) scene changes "or the appearance of a superimposed verbal message" (again a visual sign). Nothing was indicated in this analysis of the role of music and other noises that also feature as attention signals. These researchers are aware that unless alpha goes up (habituation), it can not be brought down again (new attention); and they want to be able to advise advertisers how to continue to hold attention. However, since viewers are continually seeking relaxation (higher alpha activity), the battle is for "figure" over "ground". Since no broadcaster is willing for their product to be the background, abhorring silence and insisting on filling in every available space (for fear the viewer will use the gaps to defect to another channel), the result is potentially self-defeating for all. In a party where everyone is shouting equally no one person can be heard; the answer lies with the metaphor near the start of the first chapter—but who will take the part of the potter's wheel?

It remains a matter of concern then that the typical experience of television viewing, with much being seen and heard that is of moderate or less impact, may be unduly relaxing. That is, it may provide not just a socially tranquil experience but may damp down brain activity. This may not only detract from any lasting value in the viewing, but it may also provide a basis for contrast when the set is switched off, inviting a need to restore brain activity that becomes manifest in behavioral hyperactivity. All this is, as yet, quite conjectural, although television challengers, such as Martin Large ("Television closes down the human nervous system", 1980, p.68), write as though they accept such processes as proven. The practical application of any definitive findings would be that if providing words by vision (reading) whether off a screen or a printed page is more mentally stimulating than the picture-vision and auditory-words mixture of most television, then it supports the idea of some challengers that the sheer amount of viewing (other than of pages of teletext) should be cut down. However, if there is no such primacy of print (though it looks as though there is), then benefits might best be achieved by control over television's content, with the hope that enough can be devised, which is stimulating to the brain while not totally eliminating the relaxation function.

FROM MOMENTS TO AGES: THE FIGHT FOR BOUNDARIES

Concern about the possible effects of technically sophisticated message systems goes back much further than opposition to television. Neil Postman (1982) has built a case that print was a message system that created the social category of childhood; by contrast, electric systems, starting with the telegraph but culminating in television, have operated so as to dissolve the separated phase of childhood. Postman provides evidence that not only is childhood becoming adulterated, but that adults are becoming what was previously considered childlike. Television is suited to presenting personalities and images rather than ideas; television reveals everything regarding "incest, promiscuity, homosexuality, sadomasochism, terminal illness, and other secrets of adult life" (p.81). Although much that Postman says proclaims his certainty that it is the fundamental structure of the message system that turns the clock back on childhood, in one place the option of control through management of content peeks through the dark curtain of his pessimism. Mentioning a quotation in horror from a television compere who sought to bind his viewers over the commercial break with "don't go away, We'll be back with a marvelous new diet and, then, a quick look at incest," Postman himself writes "as long as the present system of competitive, commercial broadcasting exists, this situation will persist" (pp.81–83). In a footnote he makes a rather crude distinction between "government intervention to control . . . the kind of information it will make accessible . . . but whenever television programming is free of rigid government restrictions, the American pattern is followed" (p.159).

An important notion in Postman's case is that with total disclosure offered by television "the idea of shame is diluted and demystified;" further "shame cannot exert any influence as a means of social control or role differentiation in a society that cannot keep secrets" (pp.85–86). What is lost, says Postman, is manners and he goes on to explore a possible explanation for the more popular contention that television has been a gateway to violence and aggression. If children see a violent and unprincipled world on the screen, they may not develop a clear conception of right and wrong, and the methods by which the former should be conserved. Here, Postman is concerned less with the fictional violence, which he considers is "clearly marked as . . . pseudo-fairy tales" than with "the daily examples of violence and moral degeneracy that are the staple of TV news shows," which may "undermine a child's belief in adult rationality, in the possibility of an ordered world, in a hopeful future" (pp.94–95).

Television is said to erode the dividing line between childhood and adulthood in three ways: by requiring no instruction to grasp its form, by making no complex demands on either mind or behavior, and by not segregating its audience. It is "the *idea* of childhood" that is disappearing (p.xii) at dazzling speed. This restriction of his thesis is employed by Postman to attempt to deal with a critique of his theory that he expects to emerge from the followers of Piaget, who holds that the human mind does not, on average, reach a functionally mature form of being able to deal conceptually with the world until around the age of 13. Indeed (though Postman seems unaware of this) much of the cross-cultural evidence (Dasen, 1972) suggests that if the phase of cognitive immaturity is taken as one important determinant of childhood, it is actually print which shortens this stage. Again, Postman has recourse to a concept rather than to a probable fact; he writes in his own italics that "*the idea of childhood as a social structure* did not exist in the Middle Ages, it arose in the sixteenth century, and is now disappearing" (p.144). Indeed, Postman acknowledges that "if Piaget is right, then . . . the new information environment is not 'disappearing' but only suppressing" childhood.

To conclude Postman's challenge, two final points are worth mentioning. First, he sees the issues of individual competitive and technical and political control as fully intertwined. In establishing the U.S. Constitution "James Madison . . . assumed that mature citizenship necessarily implied a fairly high level of literacy and its concomitant skills" (p.107); quoting de Tocqueville, the politics of America were the politics of the printed page. In this book this literate condition has been referred to as underlying a "forensic" model of control; a society of insightful adults regulates its affairs knowingly and their own domestic conduct with competence. If this ideal is sufficiently true in fact, then society can run harmoniously with a sufficient mastery over its functional institutions such as its message systems. Postman is saying that television is eroding this mastery by creating the "adult-child"; these are the conditions in which European models of control have not only anticipated but also have perhaps forestalled the alleged American collapse of child and adult differentiation, for in Europe while the forensic model has pervaded the rhetoric of regulations, it is the clinical model that has shaped their contents. Ironically, by treating adults as potential children and by placing controls of content and quantity upon television, one may have helped to conserve the arrival of more children into the realm of the social adulthood.

The second observation about Postman's challenge is to contrast its rhetorical boldness with its political mildness. To abolish childhood, if it is true, is no small misdeed, and Postman clearly regrets its possible passing. Although not addressing them directly, in writing his book, he says there are only two institutions with an interest in protecting childhood, the family and the school. However, in spite of their interest Postman portrays these institutions as emasculated. Is the individual powerless to resist "progress" he finally asks? He retains some hope in the individual, paradoxically, who may rebel against American culture. "Most rebellious of all is the attempt to control the media's access to one's children" (p.153). Postman admits that parents who have the will and resources to resist the corrosion of electronic culture are in a minority, but he looks with some hope to the small elite who "will contribute to . . . the Monastery Effect . . . to keep alive a humane tradition". So Postman is a challenger; he sees television as a destroyer of childhood and of the traditions of print, which was a message system responsible for a civilizing process. His target is not legislators or bureaucrats who might alter the rules by which the message system operates but an elite minority of individuals who might bear a torch for the future in the way in which samizdat writers are thought to do so in the Soviet Union.

Although Postman has impressed a number of critics and readers, others have reacted more coolly to his case or have provided evidence which by no means supports it. Wober (1984d) pointed out that Postman had not established that both the idea and the existence of a category of childhood were unavailable other than in societies characterized by mass literacy. Other societies without literacy both before the advent of print in the Western world and in our own time have the phenomenon of childhood. Thus in biblical Israel the book of Leviticus (Chapter 27) explains the significance of vows made by different people and gives values according to sex and age; the age bands run from a month to 5 years old, from 5 until 20, and from 20 until 60. The second age band denotes childhood as the subsequent chapter (Numbers,1) qualifies "those who are able to go forth to war" as aged 20 and over. Some time ago Wober (1971) pointed out that in many preliterate societies there were and are systems akin to boarding schools in which youngsters received formal education in adult lore outside their family circles. A portrayal of one such school was seen by millions of television viewers in the first episode of Roots. From Australia, Factor (1985) reports that Aboriginals signal the end of childhood by a circumcision rite at the onset of puberty. Not only this ritual undercuts Postman's case; another of his concerns, that television has supplanted childhood practices of play with ancient rhymes and games, is also refuted by Factor who reports that Australian children, who are no light television viewers, still conserve these atavistic ways.

Using sample survey methods in England, Wober (1984d) asked adults nationwide at what ages they considered a person was no longer a toddler, no longer a child, and had reached adulthood. On average, the toddler stage was thought to end at 5 and childhood at just under 15. A phase of teenagedness was implied in the result that adulthood was seen as beginning at just under 19. Thus, the span of perceived childhood corresponds closely to the definition implied by the ages across which compulsory schooling is required and provided. Although there was a significant negative correlation between the amount of television viewed in a week and the perceived onset of old age, there were no significant links between amounts of viewing and the perceived positions at which the milestones of childhood were set. Thus, while television may have some effect on perceptions of aging there is no sign of any influence from viewing British television on the idea of the existence of childhood, which Postman alleges in the United States is dissipated by the influence of this message system. It seems likely that this absence of a relationship has at least something to do with the way in which television has been organized for its first half century in Great Britain; considerable differences exist between the four channels both in ethos and in program types aired at any given time, the outcome being a culturally varied output and resulting viewing diet.

FROM AGES TO ETERNITY:
IS TELEVISION A RELIGION?

One common feature of the three great network channels in the United States is the ubiquity of advertisements. Starting from McLuhan's aphorism that not all television news is bad, as the good news is there in the commercials, Postman (1982, p.108–109) springs to what we will recognize is a common conclusion reached by different challengers via different routes—television constitutes a religion. Postman sees the principal TV commercials as "religious parables organised around a common theology." They "put forward a concept of sin, intimations of the way to redemption, and a vision of Heaven. They also suggest what are the roots of evil and what are the obligations of the holy." Amusing examples are provided of the parables of the ring around the collar, the person with rotten breath, and the stupid investor. As in the parable of the man who runs through airports, heaven is portrayed as a condition of ecstasy which is encountered "where you have joined your soul with the Deity - being Technology". There is much substance to add to the skill of this analysis; however, its validity lies in the extent to which viewers do fully and explicitly come to see technology as an autonomously willful deity as a measure of the extent to which they live with television, and at the same time quit any adherence they have to one of the recognized religions (among which some might include narcissism). This test is a much more rigorous one to pass than is applied by most analysts who like to label television a religion, and it is to be doubted that any one has convincingly shown that such a criterion is fulfilled, even in the United States.

Although Postman remembers to provide television the alleged religion with a deity identified as technology, other writers have bothered less with the latter detail in their observations. Thus, carried away at a conference in Aspen, a critic Michael Novak (1975) declared that "television shapes the soul." It does this because "the mythic structure of prime time news and programming is homogeneous, presenting good and evil conflicting in classic forms of moral heroism." Although Novak claims that "television . . . has vested interests in new moralities," it is a system of social control and it is not clear whether this control is being wielded in the service of "classic" forms, in effect, that fortify older religions, or whether something new is being propagated. In England Bakewell and Garnham (1970) had previously labeled broadcasters as "The New Priesthood;" the supernatural origin of the supposed priestly authority was not fully or convincingly set out, but one implication was that television housed a religion as rival to the Church which is the "established" religion of the monarch and his or her subjects in England.

Against the view of the entire message system as a religion, it is perhaps necessary to provide two views that these writers seem not to have considered. One perspective is illustrated by the fact that the Catholic Church has, through the journeys of Pope Paul II, very skilfully used television as a means of making its view of itself as the universal religion widely known; and Catholicism is certainly not involved in providing a new religion with "mythic structure" for its own new purposes. Analyzing 128 newscasts on Italian television in which five journeys of Pope John Paul II were described, Guizzardi (1986) lists a number of narrative and emotive elements, which reinforce the Catholic message. Six elements are singled out, including an initial setting of decadence requiring salvation, the arrival of a hero, the trial the hero endures (including danger to his own life, which has been all to too true for Pope John Paul), the voyage, the repetition (in which an end of one journey implies that another is needed), and an Apotheosis which is "the great enthusiastic celebration of the charismatic hero . . . who is going on a sort of pilgrimage to the end of the world, on behalf of, and together with TV audiences" (p.4). Very clearly also, this triumph is not a vindication of television, or of the Pope personally, but of Catholicism.

Another analysis, provided by Shils and Young (1975), describes the British Monarchy and the televisation of ceremonies such as the coronation and the wedding of Prince Charles and Lady Diana Spencer, as well as the annual Christmas message of the Queen (modeled on the radio fireside chats of FDR), as integrated new institutional forms of fortifying the established strength of the Church of England. These considerations go far to suggest that television may neither mediate nor actually itself be a new religion; instead, in sevral ways it may serve existing religions.

TELEVISION THE CULTIVATOR: UNCULTURED ITSELF OR CONTROLLED?

Before we examine the complex and extensive case put forward by the chartist challenger George Gerbner, who also thinks that "our chief instrument of enculturation and social control, television may function as the established religion of the industrial order" (Gerbner and Gross, 1976, p.196), it is useful to mention a category of opponent that is preoccupied with reform of the message system (seeing the user as an integral part of the system together with the sender) rather than its abandonment or destruction. Whereas in the United States Peggy Charren heads Action for Children's Television (ACT), now taken root also in Australia, her counterpart in Great Britain is Mary Whitehouse, President of the National Viewers and Listeners' Association (NVALA). Charren may focus more on the user's need to be more discriminating, whereas Whitehouse may place the burden to some extent more upon the broadcasting control authorities. To these we may add Thomas Radecki, Director of the National Coalition on Television Violence (NCTV).

These individuals and organizations challenge television in several ways. They assemble evidence to support their view that violence and its incessant depiction is socially dysfunctional; through their newsletters and use of the press and of television itself, by personal appearances and statements, they urge individuals to campaign for counteradvertising, backed by legislation; and they try to educate the public that by providing a viewing market for violence, we are promoting harm among ourselves. NCTV indexes and describes violence levels in particular programs or movies and presses advertisers to shun proximity with violent material. An international dimension is given to NCTV by ICAVE (International Coalition Against Violent Entertainment). In spite of energetic activity and a position earned in which television pays attention to the existence of such pressure, however, little success can be claimed, as message systems such as cable channels, video cassettes and rock video actually proliferate in the cultivation of a market for aggression (e.g., see Sherman and Dominick, 1986).

The pathway along which NCTV hopes to achieve its goals is of particular relevance to its American context. By holding its first national conference in October 1983, NCTV sought a place on the stage of the nation's business; by pressing for legislation to mandate one free advertisement for every three that air in promotion of violent programs, they serve several incidental purposes. They show that they feel they have no option but to press for legislative and thus central control over a feature of the admunication system; by implication it is futile to expect the individual (and every individual) to live clean by his or her own efforts. They place in contrast the difference between what they ask for, which is literally free speech on the one hand, and that which their statements would oppose, which would more appropriately be called expensive speech. By making this contrast they show that the First Amendment, which supposedly safeguards free speech, so far does little to enable it to occur in the mass admunications system, while many in entrenched positions use the rhetoric of the defense of free speech effectively to ensure that expensive speech has the final word.

An intriguing incidental implication of the necessity for, and the mode of challenge to, unfettered commercial television mounted by NCTV is that the open market in its address to violence, horror, and harsh sexual display reveals mechanisms of demand and supply based on the darker side of human nature, what Freudians might call the forces of the id, or, as some religious doctrines see it, the propensity to respond to evil that lies just below the surface in human nature. In this view it is likely to be those analysts whose upbringing has sensitized them to doctrines of the fall of man and to the need for salvation from this aspect of human nature, who tend to see television as a form of malign religion needing centralized control. There are observers who find it imperative to challenge television as an institution that will need measures of superordinate rather than users' self-control. One would expect such observers to refer outright to false religion or to metaphors from the realm of witchcraft rather than to find them discussing television as religion as though it was just another benevolent system for quelling evil, explaining the ends of human existence, and uplifting human nature. A contrary process of personal grounding in optimism may help generate hope among those who see innovation in the techniques of communications as usually welcome, who enthusiastically use network television for the extraordinary reach it provides, and who see it as bringing benefit rather than harm.

This positive tone is hard to detect in the work of George Gerbner of Philadelphia. During the later 1960s, Gerbner's content analyses displayed the ways in which violence permeated American television, apparently signifying those groups who were more and others who were less privileged in society. In 1972, Gerbner was one of those whose research formed part of the U.S. Surgeon General's report and Gerbner has on many occasions testified to legislative committees and to the public via television saying that this message system has functioned harmfully. Close reading of Gerbner's work with his colleagues delivers two impressions. One concerns the scientific function of establishing the nature of the harms attributed to television; the other consists of the unmistakable condemnation of these claimed harms. However, it is also worth noting what is absent, as well as what is present, namely, a cure to go with the diagnosis of the disease. Gerbner's articles call calamity, but they do little to provide a program for remedying the state of affairs.

The Gerbner team provided a theory of television's effects, which took a different direction from that of the main theories that had preoccupied the first 25 years of research on this message system. It is not unfair to see the period from 1950 to 1975 as marking the swift establishment of television accompanied by numerous studies of the possible imitative effects of viewing violence and aggression. In the laboratory (eg., Liebert and Baron, 1972) as well as in the field (Eron, Huesmann, Lefkowitz and Walder, 1972; Leyens, Parke, Camino and Berkowitz, 1975) a majority of researchers reported what we may call a "forward" effect of television. The screen displays some theme, and this points the way for individual actions, which tend to follow. A minority of researchers did suggest that viewing violence drained off violent impulses (eg., Feshbach and Singer,

1971) and some (Klapper, 1960) saw viewers as active takers of what they wanted from the screen, rather than as hapless passives who were mechanically led by what they saw; however, the prevailing view marked by the concerns expressed in the Surgeon General's Scientific Advisory Committee on Television and Social Behavior report (1972) was endorsed in a National Institute of Mental Health Report (Pearl, Bouthilet and Lazar, 1982, p.6), which declared "violence on television does lead to aggressive behaviour by children and teenagers who watch the programs."

Gerbner and his associates do not deny that this "forward" imitative effect occurs. What they do is to add that there is an equally or more important reactive or "backward" effect of televised violence. This is exerted upon peacable people who, on seeing violence, become afraid. In putting forward this case Gerbner and Gross (1976) tried to get away from an "atomistic" theory in which identifiable pieces of meaning produced replica effects; instead, they saw television's contents as a thorough expression of a form of culture, the whole of which would have a wide series of effects on viewers. Thus, although their theory started with assertions about violence, it soon produced a large number of supporting demonstrations. All of these cases were described by the Gerbner team as harmful (although it is quite easy to see that others might evaluate some of the claimed effects as beneficial).

The strong implication of Gerbner's descriptions is to censure television, and although he himself seems not to have an explicit program of reform, his case has been directly used by others. Thus the American Psychological Association's Board of Social and Ethical Responsibility released a statement in 1985 citing Gerbner's findings to the effect that that children's TV programs contain about 20 violent acts each hour and that youngsters who watch a lot of television are more likely to feel that the world is a mean and dangerous place. The AMA leaflet makes its appeal not to legislators as does the NCTV, but to parents who are asked to view with their children, to discuss the meaning of what they see in the family, and to direct their children's viewing by positive choices of prosocial material as well as by banning "some programs they find too violent or offensive." It is in this sense in which Gerbner has sought demonstrations of his thesis' truth and has seen them placed where prestigious agencies call for social or private action that we can call him a challenger. It does not matter that in this particular instance supporters of centralized public service controls would point out that appeals to parents would fall on deaf ears in precisely those cases where discipline is most needed and appeal most strongly to those families who already understand the need for and who practice some discriminative viewing. It is the goal rather than the method which defines the challenger. It does not detract from this analysis that at a convention in 1986 Gerbner answered a questioner by saying that he was concerned merely to report facts and that in doing so he pointed to no particular remedies. The rehetoric of his presentation makes very clear, however, that there is a need for change. We can now examine some of the platforms on which Gerbner's challenge stands.

The first campaign (Gerbner et al., 1977) compared light and heavy television viewers' perceptions of the incidence of violence in American society. Those who viewed more television did tend to a small but consistent extent to overestimate the occurrence of violence in society, even after interrelated measures of sex, age, education, and in the case of one adolescent group, IQ had been controlled. Not only were perceptions of crime linked with television viewing, so too was the fear of violent crime (Gerbner et al., 1978). It was claimed that the process of reaction to fear of crime was completed by heavy viewers being inclined to perform different kinds of behavior than were light viewers; specifically, heavier viewers said they had taken anti-crime precautions (keeping a dog, a gun, installing locks, avoiding certain areas) more so than did lighter viewers. Amongst children, heavier viewers were more likely to say it was justified to hit someone if one was angry with them, than were lighter viewers (Gerbner, Gross, Signorielli, Morgan, Jackson-Beeck, 1979).

This picture of the alleged effects of viewing television violence has been contested in several ways. Hughes (1980) and Hirsch (1980b) looked further into Gerbner's analyses of his data, most of which were obtained from national omnibus surveys, ill-fitted to the diagnostic use to which they were put. Further, these critics alleged that Gerbner's reports selectively omitted some counter-hypothesis results, and in any case defined the groups of heavy and light viewers so as to deal inappropriately with extremely heavy and with nonviewers whose behavior and attitudes proved not to be extensions of a supposedly linear relationship between weight of viewing and the assimilation of messages from the culture of television.

A different kind of criticism was made by Doob and MacDonald (1979) who implied that the heavy viewing fear of crime syndrome was likely to be an urban phenomenon distinct from rural lighter viewing and lower anxiety over crime (American urban markets tend to have more channels and view more television than do people in rural locations). Doob and MacDonald analyzed results separately from high and low crime areas in Toronto and found that fear of crime was related more to actual levels of local crime than to amounts of television watching. In Britain Wober (1978b) had sought, unlike Gerbner, to dismiss response set as a possible explanation for some who might endorse high values both on viewing claims and on crime estimates, whereas others would tend to mark both low; the crime questions were devised in positive (safer . . .) and negative formats (more dangerous . . .), and only that pair of questions where consistency was observed in the meaning of answers in both formats was used for further analysis. This done, no relationship was observed between television viewing and perceptions or fears of crime. Wober (1980d) further reported that a personality attribute, Rotter's Locus of Control construct, probably underpinned both the amount of television viewing and answers on crime; for when fear of crime was held constant the link between amount of viewing recorded on a week's diary and locus of control scores remained significant and positive, but when locus of control was held constant, the relationship hitherto evident between viewing and fear of crime collapsed into nonsignificance.

Research on this "mean world" hypothesis outside the United States and the United Kingdom has been problematic for simple support of Gerbner's claims. Working in Perth, Australia, Pingree and Hawkins (1980) reported that among over 1,200 school children, even when multiple controls for demographic characteristics and the perceived reality of TV were calculated, strong significant relationships between amounts of viewing of crime-adventure, cartoon and game shows and perceptions of the incidence of violence in society remained. Feelings that the environment is hostile related significantly, though less strongly, to viewing crime-adventure material. What was puzzling about this research was that children's ideas about Australian society related more strongly to the amount of viewing of imported American programs than to viewing locally made material, and that viewing American programs did not thus affect perceptions of the United States. This last result suggests that had controls also been applied for a personality measure, such as locus of control, the apparently causal relationships between foreign television viewing and domestic social perceptions may have disappeared.

From Sweden, Hedinsson (1981) reported a study in which involvement in the "reality" of television was a new measure, alongside amounts of viewing and several items on perceptions of social reality. Time spent viewing was weakly related to some of these perceptions, but not to the index of the amount of serious crime thought to occur. The strongest relationship was between amount of viewing and a retribution index (the size of penalty that respondents would like to see visited upon offenders, across seven different types of crime). Since there is actually very little violent programming on Swedish television, this suggests that people with a stronger sense of punitive violence (of which there is but little to be seen) produces fear and suspicion. In the Netherlands Bouwman (1984) examined 19 items on fears and perceptions relating to crime. Five correlations between these items and amounts of television viewing were significant, only one of which dealt with an affective "mean world" item ("you can never be too careful in dealing with people" - which is a lesson for researchers as well perhaps, in their approach to the scientific theories of others). Bouwman concluded that "cultivation of fear by television drama does not seem to be a real phenomenon in the Netherlands" (p.418). Among the reasons for this neutral result, Bouwman thought, were that Netherlands broadcasting is organized under a complex system of social control; often, when violence is featured it is explicitly to demonstrate its unacceptability so that a pure content count of injuries and deaths is unlikely to point to the meanings that such measures are said by Gerbner to imply in the United States.

A similar observation was made by Hawkins and Pingree (1980) who pointed out that, on Wober's evidence (1978b), it was likely that British heavy viewers (who see over 4 hours a day) may see less television violence than do many American light viewers (who see up to 2 hours a day, but where violence is much more common on the screen). This state of affairs arises directly from the control of schedules by public service authorities who ensure that the two pairs of channels (BBC 1 and BBC 2, and ITV and Channel 4) for the most part carry complementary program types, in which action drama constitutes only a small proportion (see Chapter 3) and in which most viewers find a correspondingly varied viewing environment in which stereotypes that might possibly be built up with experience of one program type are diversified by encounter with other types.

The varied nature of British viewing is demonstrated in Table 9. The data are drawn from 10 weeks' diary records made during 1983. The smallest number of diarists in one week was 438, but the average weekly number of diarists was 617. These people recorded an appreciation rating for each program viewed, and it was possible thereby also to count the number of programs viewed in each of seven program types per week. The figures shown are average correlation coefficients, having simultaneously partialed out sex, age, and class, relating amounts of viewing across program types.

Every one of these coefficients is significant at the 0.01 level even if the number of diarists in the smallest of the 10 weeks' samples was applied to all of them. Thus, people who view more adventure-action also tend to see more single movies and brief drama series; they also see more news, general interest, and sport material than do lighter viewers of adventure action. In effect there is a dilution of the viewing experience of adventure action series with soap opera, comedy, nonseries drama, and much else. The correlation across weeks but within program types reported in the previous chapter does suggest that certain people are more habitual viewers of adventure-action than of other program types, and it points to a possible localized effect of viewing this particular kind of material. However, the additional broad range of viewing experience, which even

TABLE 9
Links Between Amounts of Viewing in Seven Program Types

	Films Drama	Adventure Action	Comedy Lt. Ent.	Soap Opera	General Interest	News	Sport
Films, drama	1.0	.48	.43	.31	.28	.19	.17
Action adventure		1.0	.41	.33	.18	.20	.21
Comedy, light entertainment			1.0	.45	.43	.32	.31
Soap opera				1.0	.24	.30	.21
General interest, information					1.0	.47	.26
News						1.0	.33

patrons of particular program types will encounter, will serve to diversify impressions that might otherwise accrue from familiarity with each single genre.

The outcome of this particular arm of Gerbner's challenge is that in the United States his case is widely, though not uniformly, accepted that television cultivates fear and the desire for strong law enforcement measures. The thesis has also been reported as true by British journalists, although it is not widely accepted among admunications scientists outside the United States, certainly with regard to the functioning of broadcasting systems regulated by public service control institutions. Indeed, European researchers are not widely convinced of the validity of this particular challenge in the American context either, although the case is more plausible there. An intriguing turning point in the debate on Gerbner's cultivation thesis occurred at a seminar in Vienna in 1982 during which I was arguing with the professor. For a start, and in the habit of academic disputation, Gerbner was pressed with the proposition that his contentions were unconvincing even about the United States; he defended his point resolutely and I enjoyed the agility of his argument. A solution then occurred to me in which I put it to him that I would cease from doubting his validity, as far as the United States was concerned; indeed, I might even be willing to be convinced. Instead, I would concentrate on the better evidence that in European research there had generally been little or no support for his case. This failure to confirm a scientific hypothesis pointed, instead, to a success that could likely be attributable to European policies of broadcasting administration. The issue was one of control. In the United States, argued Gerbner, television controlled society; in several European countries, at least through the 1980s, society controlled television, undercutting and forestalling the opposite process.

All these arguments were about the portrayal of violence and its possible role in molding the public mind. Indeed, the argument continued in other forms so that at another convention in Philadelphia, the professor's own ground, it was put to him that the interpretations he and his colleagues alleged were attached to certain portrayed scenes (in this case, the striking down of a gay policeman, showing, they argued, that gays were to be seen as victims in society) were not necessarily, if ever, perceived by viewers in the ways that cultivation theory supposed. Violence, reiterated the professor, was power, and its portrayal showed which were the powerful and which were the weak groups in society; on the contrary, I suggested, violence was not always power but at least sometimes betokened weakness, both moral and intellectual weakness. Quite often it was the purpose of a plot or scenario to bring out just such a point. The matter has not yet been researched in these terms—to detect whether or to what extent and in what circumstances viewers perceive displays of violence as lessons of power, or as lessons of weakness; but plans exist to carry out such a survey.

The general case applied by Gerbner has been that the sheer amount of portrayal of particular ingredients (certain groups as victims, or as socially subordinate) will have had an effect on audiences. Bradley Greenberg (1986a) who has not argued so conspicuously as a "cultivation" theorist alongside the Gerbner camp, but who had provided much substance for the Gerbnerist case by accumulating numerous content analyses documenting the disparities in portrayals of various segments of society, has more recently made a significant interpretative departure from a position which he could have been implied to have held. "Let us urge . . . a diversion away from counting heads or bodies . . . and a concentration on the question of whether there may be more impact from what can be termed "critical portrayals" than from the acreage of portrayals" (p.11). The way to determine what is a critical (crucial) portrayal must reside in finding it through the eyes and the minds of viewers. Clearly, even the most insistent cognitive psychologist would not wish to ignore the role of actual content; but what Greenberg here calls a "provocative thought" is indeed a significant complexification for those who are traditionally behaviorists and whose substance of study is preferably that of observable "stimuli" and observable "actions" (even if these are often only attitude replies to survey questions).

Apart from the problem of violence and its latent messages, however, Gerbner has several other challenges, which he has laid at the door of American television. One of the most important of his allegations (Gerbner et al., 1982) bridges the "mean world" hypothesis with the claim that heavy viewing cultivates a "mainstream" of support for what people feel is a centralist political ideology. Heavy viewers were more likely than lighter ones to place themselves towards the middle of a seven point scale running from "extremely liberal" to "extremely conservative," regardless of the actual parties to which people said they belonged or which they said they supported. Looking at detailed policies, with issues such as ethnic integration and individual freedoms (on homosexuality, drugs and abortion), self-claimed conservatives and liberals who were light viewers differed markedly, but if they were heavy viewers, it made less difference if they also identified themselves as conservative or liberal as regards their attitudes towards policy propositions of this kind. An opposite tendency was observed with regard to seven economic propositions advocating government spending on various fields; here, self-professed conservatives, when heavier television viewers, tended to support more liberal (or possibly self-serving) propositions, just as self-professed liberals did if they were also heavy viewers.

Although the accuracy of these results need not be questioned (with some minor reservations about the use of personal interviews as the data source, in comparison to self-completion measures, which might have been preferable), the explanations attached to them and the consequent challenge they are required by Gerbner to carry do require some further testing. One departure from the previous "cultivation theory" work on fear of crime is that this alleged demonstration of the effects of television does not rest on detailed content analysis of the political notions carried in programs. These are merely inferred from the results of heavy viewers' opinions, and it is possible that the latter spring mainly from other underlying causes, which jointly also determine heavy viewing. Although Gerbner writes "television provides . . . a shared daily ritual of highly compelling and informative content . . . its drama, commercials, news and other programs bring a relatively coherent world of common images and messages into every viewing home" (1982, p.102) this blanket statement about what television is supposed to be conveying fails to satisfy two crucial questions. One concerns the improbability that there is a coherent ideology anywhere of centrist politics that senses populist opinion both to reflect its apparent desire for illiberal moral measures (anti-ethnic integration, antiabortion, etc.), as well as for indulgent economic procedures (support for government spending on health, environment, welfare, etc.) in which heavy viewing conservatives espouse more liberal opinions. The second question is whether such a package really is expressed in the content both of day time serials and prime time entertainment and information. A further problem is whether, even if television did portray such messages, viewers register much impact from them. Larson and Kubey (1983) have shown in the United States, as has been reported in the previous chapter with British evidence, that television is a message system with low overall impact, whose contents are thus likely only to impinge superficially on, or even to bounce off, most viewers.

Two studies outside the United States also have sought parallels to this Gerbnerist challenge, but both have drawn blanks. In Israel, Adoni, Cohen and Mane (1984) showed over 400 twelfth grade students three specially made television news items and asked questions about them as well as about realities with which they dealt. The amount of real life news viewing was measured and was found to have no relationship with the extent to which people differentiated in their knowledge between the real world issues and the ways in which these were reported on television. In other words, weight of normal viewing, unlike Gerbner's contention and corresponding more with the low-impact model, had little to do with formation of outlook, which corresponded more with personal proximity to some field of concern.

The second relevant study was carried out in London during the Falklands conflict between Britain and Argentina in 1982 (Wober, 1982b). A panel completed a week's viewing diary and answered questions measuring personal authoritarianism, as well as disclosing party identification and attitudes concerning how the conflict should be, and how it was being, covered by television. The authoritarianism items, while regarded as providing a reasonably stable personality measure arising from childhood rather than present television influences, corresponded reasonably well with Gerbner's items on resisting racial integration, intolerance of deviants, welfare spending, and so on. As with Gerbner, the study initially found that among Conservative viewers authoritiarianism varied little with the amount of viewing within each of three program types, but among Labour viewers (akin to the American designation of liberal) authoritarianism was greater among heavier viewers. This occurred not only for viewing news and current affairs on ITV (but not on BBC) but also for viewing soap opera. When, however, age, sex and amount of viewing to program types other than the one under scrutiny were partialed out, no significant links were found, with two exceptions: Conservative identifiers who viewed more action adventure were less authoritarian; and among those whose political allegiance was uncommitted or unknown those seeing more information on BBC channels were more authoritarian. BBC coverage of the Falklands conflict was identified by the same sample as being more liberal (or at least fair to the Argentinian side) than was ITV coverage. So any patterns linking viewers' attitudes or personality scores with amounts of viewing were more likely either to be spurious or evidence of selective viewing practices.

THE PLIGHT OF WOMANKIND ON SCREEN: NOT THEIR BIG APPLE?

A major challenge not just to television but to most message systems in western countries has been mounted by the women's movement. The challenge takes more than one form, and this may confuse some onlookers as well as possibly comforting defenders of the status quo. One contributor, Mandy Merck believed that media operations contributed to the materiality of (women's) subordination; she described how the editor of the American magazine *Ms* resigned from her post saying that its policy of presenting positive role models was a fantasy, misrepresented as feminism, which played into the hands of those who oppose any real change. Merck recognized a problem also in fiction, which reflects present facts, taking the view that "if this is 'how women really are' how can their oppression ever change?"

In the United States, the Annenberg group under Gerbner considers that the pattern of television's contents, both in terms of the numbers of people of certain kinds and of what happens to them, is taken by the viewing public not only as a fictionalized portrayal of reality but also of what real life ideally should be. Tuchman (1978) has referred to the small number of women in important parts in action drama as the "symbolic annihilation of women; "this is certainly one message that can be inferred from this undoubted fact of content. Another message could be that women are more sensible and humane than to be involved in such largely aggressive activities and their relative absence from this kind of screen fare suggests their superior nature. There is little sign of any search for such alternative interpretations among viewers. Instead, the content analysts have built a powerful case that presentation of women in much of American telefiction has been demeaning in its content and harmful in fact.

Tuchman (1978) reported that women were either ignored or, if present, were shown in subordinate roles of less initiative than those played by men. Gerbner et al. (1977) showed that, when involved in violence, women were generally the victims. Even soap operas in which women are present more than men are interpreted by researchers (eg., Greenberg, Richards and Henderson, 1980) as suggesting feminine subordination because they are shown in home-based roles. Signorielli (1984) found that even in situation comedies across two decades of television, men outnumbered women by about two to one. A number of American studies have shown that advertisements also place women in a narrow range of roles. Dominick and Rauch (1972) found 38% of the female characters shown in 1,000 advertisements were in the home, as against 14% of men. Men were more often in authority roles. In a comparable study Schneider (1979) monitored 300 commercials and found such sex stereotyping still prevalent. Knill, Pesch, Pursey, Gilpin and Perloff (1981) noticed that female product representatives in daytime commercials outnumbered males, but over 90% of voice over messages were by males. In Great Britain Manstead and McCulloch (1981) and Livingstone and Greene (1986) discovered that, as in the United States, British television advertisements tended to show women more often than men at home, and using the products being advertised, but again men tended to supply the voice-over arguments or advice in favor of the commodities.

More subtle content analyses have examined the implications which are to be read into the patterns of intersex relationships shown on the screen. Manes and Melnyk (1974) reported that only women who were low in occupational achievement were depicted as having successful relationships with men. The next questions are whether such messages, which researchers say are carried by television's content, are seen as such, on television, and as implying that that is how the sexes really are in life, and as implying that that is how people also should be in real life. These questions have been studied both among adults and children.

A final question is what is to become of the results of all this research? For the most part, in the United States and Great Britain, the lessons existing in or even taken for granted in this work are ventilated in books and articles, even in resolutions such as those passed by international conferences in communication sciences or of the women's movement. However, in Great Britain another institutional response was the creation of a new television channel, Channel 4, in whose management a parity of executive roles between the sexes was sought, and where positive efforts were made to contract with program making companies run by or employing women, and those who made programs embodying a liberated world view.

The concern had been that among adults (as shown by Gerbner and Signorielli, 1979) people who reported heavy viewing habits also more markedly endorsed items expressing sexist attitudes. This was interpreted as a causal effect of viewing experience (rather than that particular attitudes brought about certain viewing behavior). More to the point were studies among children in which area Gerbner's colleague Michael Morgan (1980) contributed a notable longitudinal study spanning 2 years. Heavier (female) viewers in the first wave of study proved more than lighter viewers to have traditional sex role opinions at the later wave. Among boys a reverse effect was found; those with more sexist attitudes at the outset were likely to be heavier viewers later on. From Canada a study reported by Tannis Macbeth Williams (1985) described developments at Notel a small town, which initially had no television but where people were tested before getting it, and 2 years later, in comparison with Unitel and Multitel, towns with progressively more television. As far as sex role perceptions were concerned, an apparent effect of the arrival of television was to make youngsters more strongly affirm more traditional attitudes.

Somewhat undercutting the edge of the challenge that television disserves women was one of Morgan's results, as well as several from Great Britain. Although traditional sex role opinions seemed to be fortified among heavier viewing girls, these were also more likely to develop higher educational and occupational aspirations. In Great Britain a mass of viewing behavioral (e.g., see Chapter 3) and parallel appreciation data show that, for all that some critics say that programs tend to do ill justice to women, women tend to view more heavily than do men and, what is more, also appreciate what they see more than do men. The reply one might anticipate from radical feminists would be that it is not surprising that the existing generation of women like what they see because they have been conditioned by a sexist culture, in effect, to like what harms them. There may be no empirical escape from this kind of criticism. However, one attempt to detect and distinguish between ideals and actuality was made by Wober (1981a) who posed three kinds of questions to respondents who also completed a week's appreciation diary. Three kinds of programming were held in focus—comedy, drama and actuality—and people were asked to say within each, to what extent they thought women were shown as having various attributes (e.g., want to be mothers, seek careers, etc). The second question took the same attributes and asked to what extent people thought women in real life were like that. The third question asked to what extent women should ideally have such characteristics. The method of analysis was to examine relationships between amounts of viewing of particular program types and perceptions of women's nature in real life.

Four such relationships were found, but this was not all; next, parallel relationships were sought between amount of actual viewing within program types, recorded on the diary, and perceptions of women's portrayal in those same types. Only two such parallels were found, and they suggested that, inasmuch as people who saw more soap operas also saw in them more markedly an interest in maternal as well as career fulfillment, since heavier viewing of soap operas also related to thinking that these two attributes were true of women in real life, then the experience of seeing soap operas fortified those views of real life. Where there were no correlations both between viewing and program content perceptions and at the same time between viewing and real life perceptions, it was held that viewing experience did not fortify attitudes. In this way it was deduced that viewing might reinforce one traditional attribute, maternal inclinations, but equally so one liberated characteristic, occupational aspirations.

The challenge, therefore, has been made by feminists (of both sexes) that television both in the United States and in Great Britain slows the attainment of equal opportunity for women by the lessons it incidentally inculcates in children and the attitudes it reinforces in adults. As mentioned, however, the application of the challenge has been somewhat blunted by a variety of directions it has taken. Gerbner's method seems to be by telling legislative committees to put pressure on the networks to devise more sex egalitarian programming. There may have been some success in this direction in at least a few cases—Superman has been followed by Superwoman; Conan the Barbarian has an equally potent female opponent; on television *Remington Steele* in the United States and Juliet Bravo in Great Britain feature women detectives, and others follow suit. Yet a massive market remains, or even thrives, in reaction for portrayals of unabashed male indulgence in violence as witnessed in *Indiana Jones, Rocky,* and *Rambo* movies. Elsewhere, some of the most organized and deeply felt pressure groups such as ACT and NVALA (previously mentioned) while pressing for the reduction of violence and sexual sadism and brazenness, to some extent move against other feminists who appear to condone or even invite sexual explicitness and on occasions imply the need for forceful behavior by women to parallel that among men. Thus, the challenge to television stemming from feminist-humane concerns is divided both in the United States and in Great Britain because of equivocal findings, goals, and methods.

In such a division, egalitarianism has to overcome experimental findings, which are themselves challenging: They are difficult to explain and to use as examples of the kinds of television contents that might achieve the effects desired by egalitarians. In a series of publications Durkin (e.g., 1985b) examined how American and British television portrays the sexes and concluded that the general pattern is to present males as dominant and females as nurturant and complementary. Although he is cautious about making conclusions from correlational studies of amount of viewing and its inferred effects on sex role stereotypes Durkin (1984) has taken a general view that the culture portrayed on television and that functioning among children are linked, so that attempts at devising counter-stereotyping programming might be effective and should be explored.

The results of such attempts have been problematic. In one small experiment with the first female weather forecaster on British television Durkin (1985a) reported that female viewers were less generous than men in their ratings of her competence attributes. This may have reflected a long-standing conditioning among women to expect such a task to be performed effectively by men, or it may just have been that the pioneer was nervous or simply not as good as her followers would turn out to be, with early male assessments influenced by traditional standards of gallantry rather than of objective scrutiny. Further discouragement was anticipated since O'Bryant and Corder-Bolz (1978) had shown that commercials depicting women in nonstereotyped occupational roles did not change children's beliefs about the sex of those who take up jobs such as welder, butcher, and so on. Durkin and Hutchins (1984) showed adolescents short programs of contrived careers educational material in three experimental forms—traditional, implicit, and explicit counterstereotyping. No expected experimental effects were found and paradoxically girls who saw the explicit counterstereotyping program were more likely than those in other conditions to reject the idea that there should be more female doctors, which had been the intended meaning of the message.

Durkin (1985b, p.113) functions not just as a chartist but as a challenger in that, faced with findings counter to those expected or (one may be correct to say) desired, he goes on to argue that "effective intervention strategies must be longitudinal." Johnson and Ettema (1982) had shown in the United States that it requires professionally made long-running material to accomplish useful effects in this realm, and moreover, that these are most effective when combined with teacher initiated discussions. From a British survey of 5,000 children under 13 Cullingford (1984) drew the conclusions that there would be little point in attempting to clear a children's viewing space by "quarantining" supposedly adult-only material into post-9 p.m. times, as more than one third of his sample already regularly watched their favorite material after that time. This, of course, leaves only two thirds who do not regularly transgress such informal limits, restrained to some extent by norms of family behavior.

Cullingford deduces that children pay superficial attention to the programs at large, resisting startling modeling effects from them. He believes that the part television plays is a minor if pervasive one which thus provides a key to two possible levels of imitative or reactive behavior, beliefs, or attitudes. One level, he says, is that of immediate phenomena, effects of imitative or reactive behavior, beliefs, or attitudes. This is the level at which many investigators look for effects and so often fail to find them. On the other hand, a deeper level exists to which television's messages, together with many others, filter down early in childhood and lay the foundation of personality, which is what determines behavior, beliefs, and attitudes in adolescence and in later life.

If this multilevel model of television's relationships with viewers is true, it would not only help to explain many of the no effects results of investigators such as Cullingford; the unsought effects results, such as reported by Durkin; or the no-effects verdicts offered by analysts, such as Hughes, Hirsch, and myself upon the profound effects claims made by challengers such as Gerbner. The multilevel model of television's relationships suggests that substantial effects be sought in the early years of life and viewing; this opens up questions of methods of control should there be a need for concern.

In the United States, Palmer (1983) certainly considers there to be such a need. He cites the findings of a 1979 FCC task force on children's television (subsequently shelved) as a

> scrupulously documented indictment of programming and scheduling practices in commercial children's television. The two key task force findings are that children are 'dramatically underserved' by commercial television, and that no industry self regulation for improvement occurred in the five years between 1974, when the industry had been charged by the FCC to act, and the time of the task force report, five years later. (p.15)

Indeed, in a 1983 speech, the FCC chairman Mark Fowler had dismissed any imposed minimum schedule for children as a violation of the First Amendment. He looked ahead to pay cable to deal with a part of the problem; but though pay cable (through channels such as Nickelodeon) may provide wholesome programming, it does so only for those who choose or who are able to buy it. Those without view the commercial networks and are subject there to the disservice these challengers believe prevails. In comparison Palmer states

> we learn from the cases of Japan, England and Sweden what is possible for children through television where national policy setting is prominent in establishing the children's portion. The needs of the populace take precedence . . . parents have a role and a responsibility to look after their children's interests. But parents need help. Their skills go only so far . . . (p.21)

In many cases, he should have added, parents neither see nor intend to combat any threat to their children's welfare. Palmer's challenge goes out here, sadly, from an American author but from an Australian address, destined to have little chance for effect other than upon an international scholarly community. The American networks locked in desperate competition with the new message systems of cable and VCR will seek to reach child audiences with what they will most readily view, rather than with what certain educators consider is good for them; and there are but weak institutional frameworks in the United States by which the threatening forces inherent in this purely economic system of control can be modified.

THE MODELING OF WAR
AND MANAGING ITS OUTCOME

There have been few major wars in which television has shown the proceedings to one or both the participants. Vietnam is by far the greatest and most painful case. In 1982 television was kept away from the hostilities in the Falklands, news from which was provided by military press conferences and by accreditation of a limited number of press and radio correspondents. There was little or no allegation that the nature of its portrayal had affected either this conflict, or that in Grenada when the United States invaded. In contrast, many television correspondents brought the Israeli invasion of Lebanon to Israeli and to Western screens, generating widespread hostility. Whatever the rights or wrongs of their actions, the Israelis had many complaints that television had altered, some say extended, hostilities by encouraging the PLO leadership to prolong its resistance. The Afghanistan War is not brought to Soviet screens and does not directly involve combatants on Western ones. The same is true in the war between Ethiopia and Somalia, while other African conflicts such as in Angola, Uganda, and Chad elicit sparse reporting that hardly feeds back upon the combatants. Where, as in South Africa, scenes in the near civil war were affecting the political climate in which South Africa's economic system survives internationally, television was banned.

MacDonald (1985, p.vii) has accepted the Gerbnerist standpoint having approached the role of television as an historian; "from its beginnings in the late 1940s, video fed the nation a powerful menu of propagandized, persuasive programming. In informational and escapist TV Americans were presented an interpretation of life in which a good 'us' was forever defeating, in 30 or 60 minutes, an evil 'them' . . . . Even into the 1960s, when the . . . . government was waging undeclared war in Vietnam, the political persuasion continued" (p.200). MacDonald refers interchangeably to "video" and to TV, presumably to include the cinema by the former. He is right to cite the fictional and mythical structure of much of the content, but this is emphasized to the exclusion of several important matters.

MacDonald makes little or no mention of print, in the 1950s still relatively more important than it became in the 1970s and later. Here, one should consider the *Reader's Digest* and other periodicals, which served to alert the nation to the very real threat of communism as a missionary creed, more serious in many ways than Nazism; the former is based on true enough ideals while the latter was a psychotic disorder. Much of MacDonald's analysis appears to condone communism by suggesting that American portrayals were distorting "the enemy" so it does come as a small surprise to read that in "the late 1950s the Cold War had changed. Josef Stalin was dead and the brutality of his regime loosened greatly at home and abroad" (p.90) (this was not the feeling in Czechoslovakia, 1968; Poland, 1982; and Afghanistan).

There is also an unquestioned belief that

> more than any medium of communication before it, television had the power to inform and persuade mass audiences. Where other media required efforts of reading and concentrated listening, TV was easy to experience . . . through an alluring amalgam of pictures, words, music, personalities, body gestures and captivating ambiance. It entered private homes during times of relaxation, there to spread its well crafted messages". (p.86)

Yet others have argued (e.g., see Salomon, later) that the relaxed ambiance is a poor one in which to make any serious impact, whereas the more demanding system of print is where serious reflection and remodeling of the foundations of belief systems systems can occur.

It is therefore quite possible that the torrent of images passed over by television have largely all washed away. The test would have been to see, if the hatred of communism had been portrayed mainly on the screen but not relayed in print, whether public sentiment reflected that of the screen. This test can not be made, as print and screen concurred. While MacDonald is undoubtedly right in his account of how the entertainment industry thrived, as did the armaments industry on the enterprise of opposing communism, the case is made too wholistically and without alertness to severely problematic other considerations. Thus, the United States was indeed the principal champion of what really is the free world in its stand against communism in Korea, and at least two nations—the Republic of Korea and Austria—remain grateful for the firmness of that stance. The blots on the U.S. record of support for Duvalier in Haiti and other unsavory Central and South American regimes occurred through policies generated by administrative and commercial interests and perspectives sustained by little or no public pressure. Likewise, MacDonald's analysis is aware that the Vietnam War was not the outcome of a popular desire, let alone pressure for such an initiative; on the contrary, it began by degrees, almost hidden from the public and so an explanation for a TV effect in promoting the war would really have to show that the climate of television impacted upon professionals in the military, diplomatic, and political elites, rather than on the public at large.

MacDonald devotes a lengthy and entertaining section to portraying "the TV Western As Political Propaganda" (pp. 134 to 145). The thesis is that the hero is the individual (American) defending the helpless right (women, children, traders) against the malevolent wrong (outgroups, often Mexicans, Indians). "For many seeking to comprehend the complexity of world and national politics in the 1950s and 1960s, television Westerns offered a straightforward answer: strong action unencumbered by legal sophistry - the political equivalent of the quick draw or the night in jail" (p. 141). Applied to the Cold War, this is a persuasive image. To take up the banner of sophistry, however, it is feasible to offer another analysis of the popularity of the Western as a glorification of the themes of growth, progress, and individual striving in an age when industry and bureaucratization were increasingly changing the reality of American life. The western represented a sanitized nostalgia for a yearned-for past, a root-in-the-branches phenomenon where the spaces of the Wild West led naturally to the orthodox idealism of Kennedy's New Frontier, Peace Corps, and space exploration, as well as to the unorthodox nirvanas of Kerouac's road to the peaks of Castaneda and the Californian heights of Ashbury. To be sure, MacDonald's account of the western presents one possibility about the role of the screen, but it is not the only nor even the most convincing possibility.

Nevertheless, it is true that TV crucially helped to precipitate the

United States into a false defense in Vietnam of Western free world democratic principles; for this reason one must see MacDonald as a challenger and discount his final turnaround

> the Smothers brothers' show . . . in the 1960s . . . was an oasis of liberal commentary. In the years since . . . Johnson plunged the nation into an Asian land war (early 1965) . . . where the medium had been the principal means of persuading the nation to accept unquestioningly a conflict against communism . . . it began now to pay attention to political voices critical of the government in general . . . unfortunately, it took a costly war in Asia for television to recognize its responsibility to American society and to perform with integrity, independence, balance and relative thoroughness its function as the most important medium of communication in the nation. (pp.247–248)

This ends the book and in so doing says not that television formed life and reality, but that death and delusion formed television, bringing it to its senses. The denoument is not convincing, and the sincerity of MacDonald's thrust is as a persuasive challenger of mainstream television.

THE MELTING SCREEN
AS A THREAT TO ETHNIC MINORITIES?

The final case we will examine against Anglophone television (there are several other charges, still) is that it supports the entrenched interests of the majority White Anglo-Saxon Protestant (WASP) communities in the United States and Great Britain; and in so doing it restrains ethnic minorities from expressing their own interests to themselves as well as to the majority. The WASP-centered television system is also considered to restrain ethnic minorities from their right to powers in the economic and political realms proportional to their numbers in the state.

In the United States there are three substantial ethnic minorities: blacks (12%—Poindexter and Stroman, 1981), Asians (6%—Hur, 1981) and Hispanics (8%—Valenzuela, 1981). In Great Britain there are not more than 2 million from Asia (50% Muslim, 25% Hindu, and 25% Sikh) and a similar number from the Caribbean (8% in all, compared to over 25% in the United States). The relative concentration of such communities makes them appropriate users of new message systems of "narrowcasting." Thus SIN (the Spanish International Network) reaches Hispanics in the American South and cable systems both in the United States and Great Britain carry minority interest programming. In London and Leicester, British Asians extensively use VCR tapes of Asian language movies for entertainment and the reinforcement of ethnic identity. The development of narrowcasting services at least raises questions about the extent to which nationally networked screen services, hitherto thought of as catering for and even developing a unified homogeneous culture, should simultaneously try to cultivate plural national identities. Britain's Channel 4 has sought, and to a considerable extent has developed, an audience of diverse parts. By screening programs privately targeted to ethnic (among other interest-defined) minorities Channel 4 has reached parts of the population that other channels have not similarly reached, with material of special interest to them.

Apart, however, from narrowcasting structures, which carry the possible drawback of promoting an unequal cultural pluralism, ethnic minority members view much mainstream network material. This poses a "catch-22" problem. Either this viewing in unfruitful, like the sower's seed on stony ground, having no enculturating effects on minority viewers and thus proving tangential to their existence, if not exactly a waste of time; or it has enculturating effects, with the consequent erosion of older identifications. Paradoxically, the culture of which the program *Roots* was just a coincidental part may in effect be deracinating. Howard, Rothbart and Sloan, (1978, p.258) reported that after *Roots* "an overwhelming percentage of both races indicated an inclination to discuss the program with members of the opposite race" and it appears that over 80% of male respondents actually did so. If then viewing *Roots* catalyzes interethnic communication it may help to develop increased feelings of common rather than of separate identity. Desired by some, this is unwelcome for others.

This describes part of the problem for ethnic minorities. For majority viewers there is another "catch - 22." Either they see a screen world with fewer minority characters than exist in the real world and television thus symbolically lessens the standing they accord such communities; or they see a screen world reminding them of the ethnic and cultural multiplicity of the real world, an experience possibly so challenging that minority citizens come to be further resented because the majority culture may have to make unwanted changes. In the earliest days of television in America, Fife (1981) reported that "Black Americans simply did not exist outside of their highly stereotyped occupations as shoeshine boys, maids or tap dancers." By 1953 however, the *Amos 'n' Andy* show had been canceled and such Uncle Tom type representations were no longer seen after the civil rights movement. The institutional mechanisms for effecting change have included the work of bodies such as the U.S. Commission on Civil Rights, the National Association for the Advancement of Colored People, and more recently the National Mexican-American Anti-Defamation Committee. Together with the purchasing power of minority viewers this coalition has achieved for ethnic minority portrayals a basic level of representative decency that has not yet been matched by parallel campaigning for dignified portrayals of women.

In spite of improvement in portrayals of blacks documented by Baptista-Fernandez and Greenberg (1982) Gerbner et al. (1982) insist that heavy viewing of television changes viewers' attitudes harmfully. Thus, not only did one in five of their survey sample say they would not vote for a black for president or that they would object if a black were brought to dinner, but the proportions of people with such anti-integrationist opinions were higher if they were heavy viewers. The correlations are firmly interpreted as effects of television viewing, and Gross (1984) has emphasized this view with evidence that such positions appear to have intensified over time. In Great Britain, without having attempted to relate such phenomena to television, Airey (1984) states that "race and class prejudice and discrimination . . . exist in large measures . . . (and) . . . younger people, who are less likely than older people to express prejudice themselves are particularly pessimistic about the growth of race prejudice in Britain" (p.121). Although Airey had no television viewing measures, the younger groups can be seen as a television generation in that they have been familiar with it all their lives, compared with those over 35, among whom progressively fewer had familiarity with television in their formative years. In this perspective it may be encouraging and help to clear the reputation of British television that younger people themselves have less prejudice than do their elders.

The possibility also exists that the advent of Britain's new Channel 4 in late 1982, with its specific responsibility to provide for the interests of ethnic and other minorities, may have contributed to an increased awareness of the existence and problems of prejudice. A BBC (1973) report had much earlier examined whether the comedy *Till Death Do Us Part* (whose format and chief character was later familiar as Archie Bunker in the United States) might be strengthening prejudice. Over 700 people were questioned after seeing the show and it was concluded that the experience of viewing probably provided "some reinforcement of existing views, both liberal and illiberal." This implies polarization with at least some intensification of a sector in which prejudice is found. A subsequent comedy *Love Thy Neighbour* used a similar approach of presenting a bigot to draw ridicule to his views; there is no known research exploring its possible effects among white viewers, but among a sample of blacks (IBA, 1975) the educated minority reported the show was distasteful. There followed a succession of comedies of interethnic harmony (*Benson, Mixed Blessings*) but, as an exercise seemingly in nostalgia, the Alf Garnett (Archie Bunker) portrayal was resuscitated in 1985.

To explore whether television portrayals might influence nonminority viewers' perceptions of reality, Wober and Fazal (1984) devised a study in two British regions - the North West, where census data disclosed that larger numbers of ethnic minority citizens were living, and the East, where there were fewer. Survey subsamples made estimates of the numbers of minority citizens visible in real life regionally, seen on television, and considered to be living in the community at large. The final entity, which is known by mediated rather than by direct impressions was closer to the regional estimates in the North West where there actually are more minority inhabitants, but closer to the television estimates in the East where the numbers considered to be seen on television were more than those estimated to be living locally. Television information of an

incidental kind may thus play some part in forming a view of the structure of society, even before it influences attitudes, especially if personal
knowledge or immediate evidence is not available (see Adoni et al., 1984).
An earlier study (Wober, 1981c) had shown that in Yorkshire, respondents had quite different attitudes to the quality and prospects of life in
Northern Ireland than were reported by a sample in that province, who
were clearly more optimistic. The Irish had the evidence both of mediated
and of direct knowledge, whereas the Yorkshire sample relied on mediated information, which evidently must have been responsible for different attitudes as well as perceptions.

THE SLIPPERY SCREEN:
A WORTHY TARGET FOR CONTROL?

Research shows that in the area of interethnic relations television and
other mass message systems have a potential for informing people either
accurately or wrongly and for influencing their attitudes. Several ide-
ologies, which thrive on their own within the majority and minority
communities, variously seek to foster cultural homogeneity or plurality
and are correspondingly pleased or irritated by messages they consider
explicit or even implied in television news and entertainment. The challenges are several, that television should either take a hand in social
engineering, or that it should remain strictly neutral. All that can be said
is that research has suggested that it may be very difficult for television
to manage an inert role, so that the ways in which it may set out to, and
may achieve effects can be of considerable functional or dysfunctional
importance to society. There is, therefore, an option either to "manage"
television either by mechanisms of open market control as are more
characteristic of the U.S. situation, albeit with elements of effective influence by pressure groups, or by mechanisms of social control as are more
common in most other societies. What should be clearly recognized is
that the idea of "deregulation" by which some argue that mechanisms of
social control should be dismantled, to be replaced by noncontrol or
freedom, is a chimera. By turning away from centralized controls equally
forceful but different systems of market-force control come into action
and regulation of one kind is merely replaced by another mechanism of
equally effective regulation, albeit one which serves different purposes.
The appropriate term for this process is thus reregulation.

The changing screen, moreover, has radically altered what certain
forces in society may wish to control. As Greenberg (1986a) has pointed
out over 40% of U.S. households had cable by the mid-1980s or were able
to receive satellite or pay channels. This number is expected to exceed
50% by the end of the decade. One black and two Hispanic satellite
channels already exist and are cabled in communities with suitable viewing markets. Viewing with approval the fact that objective content analyt-

ic studies had increased in sophistication, attending not only to gross measures of quantity but to ways in which minority portrayals are grouped within rather than spread across programs, and to ways in which the different ethnic groups relate (or more often do not relate) together, Greenberg nevertheless acknowledges two major kinds of difficulty for research in this field, to which a third can be added.

Greenberg's two challenges to research comprise one that realises that there is now increasingly no easily identified package called television whose content can eventually be described. Viewers increasingly do not have to take from a homogeneous display chunks of experience that are assayed as though by the analyses printed on the sides of cola cans; with nonhomogeneous products available, users can choose their experience that cuts across the overall array in any of a variety of ways that will yield very different profiles of content. Greenberg accordingly refers to a "gulf between what content projects and what viewers perceive, observe and learn" (1986a, p.182). This is the reason why the British studies cited opt for a subjective approach to a description of perception of content, rather than by undertaking inventories of objective definitions of events. Leading from this, Greenberg's second difficulty is that effects studies can no longer subsume the hypodermic model of pinpoint sources of effect, or the cultivation model of wholistic milieu sources of influence, both of which rely considerably on thorough specification of contents as a first step to identifying effects, be they malign or otherwise. Instead, viewers to an increasing extent, by being able to choose the kind of material they view, can influence themselves rather than merely be influenced. Their predicament increasingly returns to that which Klapper (1960) understood when he advised that it was less important to note what television did with viewers than to note what viewers did with television.

Yet even in the new ecology of message systems it can still be detrimental to an individual's rights in society if viewing choices remain between fewer, less varied, and less luxuriously appointed minority channels on the one hand, and more opulent but, possibly because they are freed now from apparent monopoly responsibilities, increasingly mainstream culture majority channels on the other hand. Here lies the third difficulty identified for challengers of television in the ethnic minority field. There is little point to appeal to individual viewers to modify the ethnic content of what they see. It is absurd to address the white community to ask them to spend some time looking at a Hispanic or black channel even if there is reason to believe that otherwise they dwell in an illusory white world as their more usual viewing experience. Conversely, it is a brave challenger who would know how to advise ethnic minority viewers to apportion their viewing between mainstream and minority programming. Consequently, the challengers' pressure has to be applied to broadcasters. As Greenberg writes (1986a, p.184) "it is prudent for programmers to be sensitized to just what kinds of imprints (these) portrayals have for both white and black viewers, especially young people." To support his strategy of persuasion Greenberg cites research showing that white viewers do not reject black characters or shows in which they appear. Conversely, black viewers are attracted to shows including blacks, and identify with such portrayals, especially if they are at all favorable. Thus, programmers have nothing to lose and something to gain by casting minority characters, perhaps even in pairs, rather than as singletons or in large groups.

Here is a gently persuasive yet important challenge. Whether it can be effective may depend on at least three difficulties. One is that the research indicating black viewer choice of programs featuring black characters was based in an ecosystem of largely white network programming. It is less sure whether such ethnically mixed material will remain equally appealing for this particular reason once fully ethnic minority channels become available. A second difficulty is that program makers may increasingly think in terms of the new apartened ecosystem of multi-channel cable in which white and black environments call for and increasingly get representations of their own differing worldviews. Third, the ideological climate in the United States has always been against coercion or restraints placed on freedom of expression; programmers can not be ordered what to do, or what not to do. They have to be asked and persuaded and this is a daunting challenge for researchers to accept who normally prefer an objective or motivationally neutral stance. Little will happen, therefore, unless there is an institutional mechanism of social control over the broad parameters of screen contents, similar to that arranged by European societies; or an array of vigorous campaigning pressure bodies who take the researchers' conclusions via the public conscience (and, probably, purse) to affect the actions of program makers and network managers.

DIRECTIONS AND MECHANISMS OF CHALLENGE: AN OVERVIEW

There is no lack of challengers to the phenomenon of television, alleging its harm outweighs its good. This reaction is not simply due to the speed and extent of the spread of television. Postal services, road transport, and other innovations have been developed and have attracted very widespread use but have not brought with them an array of enemies such as have sprung up opposite the camp of television. An important reason for this is because such other services seem to exist as peripheral externals to human consciousness, to be used as and when they are needed; but television seems to reach into the mind and the soul of the user, many of the most aware of whom feel that they may not simply be users, but are simultaneously used. An element of guilt or shame is probably not absent from many of the challengers' standpoints, and rational as well as irrational anxieties are brought to bear against this message system.

In forming a perspective on all these challengers it is useful to bear some distinctions in mind. One concerns the ways that the society in which the challenges are being made actually controls television. In a totalitarian society, the challenges have to be covert and are likely to be concerned with ideological rigidity. In more open societies, the challenges are more vociferous and probably also more varied. Those who want affairs to be altered have to direct their appeals in ways that have some chance of having an effect, given the structure of the society in which they operate. In the United States the appeals tend to be to individuals as consumers, or to individuals as producers rather than to a central authority as legislator. In Europe appeals can be both to individuals and to rule makers.

The second kind of distinction differentiates between those worries that consider the very mechanism of the message system to be harmful at a psychophysiological level and that concentrate on trying to lessen the simple amount of hours of use devoted to it, and other concerns that focus more on contents and imply that increased viewing would not of itself be harmful but might even do good if contents were suitably altered. To the group of those who consider the message system itself faulty can be added those who consider the content of the messages so distorting and unamenable to change that simple reduction of viewing could be a useful therapeutic goal.

Television has been accused of harming children's health (Winn, Large), of destroying the very idea and experience of childhood (Post man), and of reducing the level of literacy (Singer, Morgan, Williams). Television has been accused of promoting violence and aggression among children and their elders (Belson, 1978), as well as of promoting fear and unreasonable perceptions of the world as a mean place that requires harsher levels of institutional and political control than would really be required to tame objectively true levels of such hazards (Gerbner).

The flickering screen, prompting some observers to be more obsessed with its visual than its auditory aspect, has convinced the Emerys that the brain is narcotized by diligent viewing. Not only is this considered bad in itself, but it is said to be harmful when viewing stops because individuals become hyperactive in an attempt to replace the flow of external stimulus. These are the kinds of concern that suggest that it would have been better if the universal screen had never existed (Mander, Large).

Belson is an extremely experienced Australian researcher who has pursued the implications of his findings with all the vigor at his command. Belson has pointed at particular kinds of violence-containing programming saying that they are the more likely prompters of real life aggression. Though funded by CBS, his message has been addressed directly to the broadcasting authorities in Great Britain and, by implication, to any who are in a position to control the content of programming anywhere. Belson has not tried to influence parents and children directly, implying that those who could be reached by and would be amenable to persuasion probably already operated ways of warding off harmful influences, and those who would neither hear him nor follow his advice if they did were the ones who were in most need of it.

Although Gerbner has sometimes written as if there was no point in advocating control of screen contents in the United States, the implication of his work is that a less biased and copious provision would produce less harm. Reflecting Gerbner's concerns that American television strengthens sexism, ageism, intolerance of weakness and of diversity it follows that if portrayals were more egalitarian and held the weaker segments of society in greater esteem, then the message content would be altogether more harmonious in any effects it might produce. The difficulty for Gerbner's position is that it seems useless to appeal to a vast public to decimate its viewing, and almost equally unpropitious without adequate statutory mechanisms of control, to appeal to the networks to mend their ways. The result seems to be a clarion vioce of dissent poured out on stony ground. A perception of pointlessness of critical analysis in a society where the powers under criticism control the most important systems of message dispersion (communication is precisely the wrong word here) and oppose the challenges being offered was voiced by the keynote speaker at the thirteenth annual conference on policy analysis, intended to connect scientists with legislators, at Arlie, Virginia (Gandy, 1985).

What might be called a small-scale constructivist alternative is seen in the work of the Singers and the advocacy of Greenberg. These top rank researchers are primarily scientist-chartists by training, and professional tradition and their low profile of a persuasive approach to reforms raises the question of whether they should validly be considered as challengers. An opposite view has some merit, but the position taken here is that since these investigators have gone further to indicate that television as it exists can be and too often is used in a way that entails harm, and since they have both suggested remedial action, they are certainly challengers. The Singers have worked to teach young people in schools about how television functions, and they have thereby promoted a more aware and healthier mode of viewing. Greenberg has raised awareness among producers that the nature and effects of their unbalanced representations of minorities may be harmful and that different profiles of casting would provide equally, if not more commercially, attractive television and probably less risk of social disharmony.

Three further grounds of challenge to television can be noted. A major one concerns the alleged distortion of news. In the United States Altheide (1976), McCombs and Shaw (1972), Gandy (1985), and others have suggested that television news services tend to set a particular agenda of what constitutes news, which has to fit certain dramatic and structural criteria. In Great Britain, a similar case has been led by the Glasgow Media Group (1976, 1980) who, in a succession of books, have insisted that there is a right wing political bias to television news. This has been said to hamper left wing led actions such as the strike by miners in 1984.

The agenda-setting function of the news services is complemented by a less widely recognized phenomenon that can be termed "agenda-cutting." An example of this in an American context would include the blind eye turned to the war in Vietnam in its earliest stages and to the predicament of the native Americans; in Great Britain the neglect of constitutional developments involving the European Community provides another example of agenda cutting. As yet, however, there has not been a serious challenger who has taken screen services to task for any shortcomings in the area of agenda cutting.

The second challenge concerns the sin of avarice and alleges that television stimulates greed. This is said to be prompted directly by advertisements but also indirectly by training people to expect a never-ending flow of attractive stimuli so that when away from the set, people constantly need and seek gratifications, often through eating or by wanting to acquire material things. The British symbol of the potters wheel (see Chapter 1) is recalled by those who feel that intermissions are valuable in themselves and that "visual silence" helps to encapsulate and protect the experience offered by programs; it may also help to fix or localize that experience and discourage it from generalizing itself to expectations of constant gratification through other senses. This whole allegation has not often been investigated but Wober (1980d) has reported two studies, which show that there are no significant correlations between measures of viewing programs of various types and an index of personal dissatisfaction with the material rewards of life.

Finally, there is the allegation that television can infringe the privacy of nonprofessional participants quite often in ways they do not expect, or welcome when they encounter them. Thus, some take part either voluntarily or coincidentally because they find themselves at the scene of a "news" event; and many cases of trauma have resulted from interventions by television that have often been made in the most well intentioned manner (Wober, 1985d). In the United States the route to minimizing traumas of this kind includes establishing standards in the course of professional training; an Association of Media Psychologists has thorough codes of practice for those who offer any kind of counseling in public on radio or television. In Europe, protection against human rights abuses of privacy is generally in the care of those state or parastatal bodies that have responsibility for the control of broadcasting. What television may do to individuals it can also do to institutions. For example, American football is now sometimes played with intermissions for television advertising breaks, and Olympic and other sporting contests are scheduled at times often inconvenient to the athletes but suited to the networks and their audiences. Thus, the people and institutions that television portrays can be disturbed in various ways by the experience. This challenge to privacy exists largely without a famous challenger, but several journalistic commentators have dealt with the effects of television on institutions, albeit without generating much focus on the matter.

Most of the alleged harms chronicled here can be avoided or minimized by viewing less, or by suitable controls of content. There seems to be no convincing case by any of the major challengers that the message system in itself is radically corrupting or harmful for viewers or for participants in programs. It is principally the way the system is used, by program makers, as well as by viewers, that may lead on occasions to harm. Thus, societies where controls are well devised, and where personal hours of viewing (helpfully kept in check by modest availability and perhaps a pricing structure devised to deliver quality rather than quantity of channels and programming) are moderate are unlikely to suffer harm from television.

CONCEPTS EXPLORED IN THIS CHAPTER

Agenda Cutting.   The exclusion of certain topics or events from news or documentary examination—a complementary phenomenon to agenda setting.

Apartened TV.   A "climate" of a combination of channels in which certain channels serve particular sectors of the population and are unlikely to be used by viewers in general.

Crucial Portrayals.   Acknowledges the role of viewers' perception in recognizing which, out of a range of contents on the screen, are experienced as important; the concept links the research approach of "behaviorist" content analysis with the "cognitive" view that effective contents are what viewers say that they see as prominent.

Cultivation.   A process said to differ from pinpoint ideas of TV effects, in which a mass of ingredients on a broad front have a formative influence on viewers' perceptions and attitudes.

Deregulation.   A misnomer suggesting that by dismantling systems of obvious centralised "social" control, screen systems would function freely and "without control"; in effect, a less obvious but market-force system of equally marked control, but for different goals, would come into being. The term should be replaced by "reregulation".

Medium.   The term is used here, as in biology and physics, to refer to that continuum by or across which information reaches each sense receptor system. Thus, light is one medium, air/sound another, molecules in air/smell a third. What is colloquially called a medium—television, the press etc.—is here called a *message system.*

Religion.   A system of ethics depending on a supernatural source of authority—hence outreaching television, which may, however, serve religion (or undercut it).

Separate Roles for Scientists.   Can include investigation and social action; these roles need not harm each other.

Symbolic Annihilation. The idea that by *not* showing some social group on the screen the message is that that social group has no significance or influence or power in society.

Technical Determinism. The belief that the discovery of new technical possibilities of its own accord. and irresistibly sees these options brought into existence—a belief opposed by Ellul.

Technology. Logos (knowledge) about techne (skills, art); thus, the word originally meant the *study* of industrial skills/arts - not the hardware itself.

CHAPTER 5

Champions:
The Prophets of the
Power of the Screen

INTRODUCTION:
THE NATURE OF DESCRIPTION AND PRESCRIPTION

Although the iceberg of research has a relatively small superstructure, which is visible and whose jagged profile can serve as a metaphor for the sharp divisions of controversy displayed in public, all this is sustained by a much larger body of work, which remains below the surface. The whole edifice is integrally related, however; the balance of the iceberg and the direction in which the peaks tilt is determined by the shape and position of the submerged structure and there are stresses and strains as new masses become frozen on or as other parts break off. We are not going to attempt to describe in any detail or even to label the various compartments and directions taken by such research. Much of it is especially concerned with broadcasting, though a great deal else which appears to have no such outward connection can prove to be importantly linked with matters being debated in the world of television.

Examples of pure research that easily become applied to problems concerning television include work on the mechanisms of interest, fatigue, distraction, and learning; work on social learning or role and behavior models, self-esteem, altruism, and aggression; studies of how the brain receives and processes information coming from the various senses, and of imagery articulation are all rooted in pure realms of research, but relate readily to that of television. Methodological matters, such as comparisons of telephone, diary or personal interview procedures for collecting data, spring more frequently from the applied field of market research but also have much to offer to investigators of television. It is sufficient here to note that where necessary some of this scientific literature has been and will be called upon in explaining the positions of challengers and of champions and in placing their claims in some context.

When all is said and done research goes little further than description and explanation of situations and processes. Even explanations which appear to beg for action or advocacy are often left unfollowed by those who have expounded them. As an example, a study of teenage suicide declared that an imitation effect following television portrayals had clearly been demonstrated; yet the authors refrained from suggesting any restraint be enjoined upon broadcasters (Gould and Shaffer, 1986). This is not a restraint obeyed by challengers; nor does it inhibit champions, of whom there are perhaps three kinds. One consists of leaders within the existing screen industries who benefit themselves from what they make or sell. Another kind is of systematic observers, scientists who genuinely believe in the benefit that screens can deliver, as they now are.

A third breed of champions advocates some new screen system or development in which the mode of use or content may be substantially different from that of "traditional" television but where an important ingredient is still the availability of pictures or printed words on a screen, probably accompanied by sound. Champions of the changing screen must be distinguished from those who are merely heralds. Heralds are legion, while champions are few, and the former are merely observers while the latter are advocates. By heralds we mean those who say that change is inevitable; they point backwards to history, see the unplanned and uncontrolled change, which they believe has been beneficial overall, and point forward expecting a similar situation to prevail. The only sort of change that they do not thereby acknowledge as feasible is that social science may have advanced sufficiently so as to display the likely outcomes of various pathways of technical change, thus opening the way for a society to try to determine the outcomes it prefers.

The technical term for heralds is "technological determinists," and it is worth pointing out something about the nature of their kind of thought, which is related to Marxist thinking, for this reason: Both systems of thought consider that the unfolding of history proceeds according to what amount to laws of the nature of human minds individually and in combination. Marxism believes in a quasisupernatural force of history that propels society, however unevenly, toward an eventual pattern of communism. Technological determinism believes that technical innovations, as the product of human imagination, will inevitably be produced and harnessed and that this application may have major and

unpredictable effects on society, but these must just be accepted, implying that technical innovation is the primary good, and must be served. In
effect, the machine is elevated to the position of the (false) god. This is
the only sense in which one may accept the claim that "television is a
religion;" rather, it is only the current technical form that attracts respect from those who adhere to the wider case that the next message
system must be better and ushered in as soon as it is invented, thus
killing the (false) god of today or pushing it into the background.

   Champions differ from heralds as they have reasons rooted in the
service of humankind and society to argue that the application of particular message systems whether television or new screen devices will be
beneficial. The goal here is not to clear a pathway for the convenience of
the technical artefact or system but to harness the system for the sake of
society.

CHAMPIONS: SCIENTIFIC
AND OTHER ADVOCATES OF TELEVISION

Not all champions are hostile to the challengers we have encountered
already; indeed, some champions are themselves challengers about some
aspect of television. Structurally, those who believe that television can
and does have important effects need not find it impossible to believe
that these effects can be helpful in some cases and harmful in others. It is
less likely that one may believe television has only good effects, though as
we have seen there is no shortage of those who think the role is overwhelmingly negative. We can perhaps now say more about the three
kinds of champions. One consists of those who make positive use of the
message system themselves to educate or entertain the public. Here, it is
worth making a distinction between outward champions and those who
simply find their employment within the institutions of television. Another kind of champion is the group of industry leaders, be they owners,
senior managers or in various ways responsible for the institution,
which they so often see attacked and which they want, therefore, to
defend and even to vaunt on the same grounds on which they are challenged. More subtle than these are the few chartists who have distilled a
positive view from their considerations; their analyses need not refute all
the accusations brought against television but at the same time point to
otherwise unsuspected benefits that can flow from the presence and use
of television.

   The positive riders of television's wavelengths include the evangelists
who simply find the screen an effective way of reaching huge audiences;
they include makers of prestige series explaining culture and science,
such as Britain's Lord Clark (*Civilisation*) and Jacob Bronowski (*The
Ascent of Man*) and in the United States, Carl Sagan (*Cosmos*). They also
include screen journalists going back to Edward R. Murrow, who tackled

the ascendant Senator McCarthy and less far back to those who deflated the Vietnam War and who led MacDonald (1985) (whom we have seen included as a challenger) to conclude his book by writing "it took a costly war in Asia for television to recognise its responsibility to American society and to perform with integrity, independence, balance and relative thoroughness its function as the most important medium of communication in the nation" (p. 248). The champions include entertainers such as Great Britain's Jimmy Saville who hosts a series called *Jim'll Fix It* in which their hearts' desires are contrived to be briefly realized for children who write in, while in the United States there is the family of Sesame Street programs, which set out to teach as well as to amuse and where in *Fat Albert* and the *Cosby Kids* positive social messages are carried in a framework of popular entertainment.

As a special phenomenon, television has helped shrink the world's size but expand its consciousness in alerting western nations to the famines in Africa and in mobilizing popular action as was done by Bob Geldof's Band Aid organization. In the late 1980s, Bill Cosby's show has topped the charts (British data on appreciation levels strongly indicate that the show must have an equally or higher appreciation in the United States, a distinction which is not automatically shared by all the most widely seen programs). Dr. Cosby (Dr. Huxtable in his show) has a Ph.D. in educational psychology and has set out to use television in a positive way, hoping or believing that influential and self-enhancing ideas can be transmitted to young (and old) black (and white) viewers. Dr. Gordon Berry (the researcher who worked on *Fat Albert*) reports that the Cosby show has proved unaccountably popular among white South African audiences. This might well be because in the Cosby/Huxtable family the apprehensive whites find reassurance that blacks inhabit the same humanity as whites.

What one may perhaps set aside here is the whole field of explicitly political broadcasting, since when one party or faction puts out programming or generates news this is heralded by itself as enlightening the viewers, even if by the same token opposing parties, feel that such material, however democratic it is to place choice before the public, is misguided and must be opposed.

A PROPHETIC MESSAGE
DELIVERED ON TELEVISION

Of the educators probably the most interesting has been Dr. Bronowski. Neil Postman (1982) has written derogatively of Bronowski's series, even if not quite so scathingly of him as of Sagan, of whose *Cosmos* series Postman says it is more about Sagan the star than about the universe; Postman says *The Ascent of Man* was "supposed to be about . . . a theory of cultural change" (p. 114); yet the very title of the series even apart from any of its contents (which may need only to sustain its name and thus its central conception) remain in the memory as an affirmation that the human condition has improved over the centuries and will continue to do so. Some who have seen the series or even just heard or read about it recall the image of Bronowski in the mire of Auschwitz, as though to convey that the human potential is but evil and dissolute at its core. However, the title and the rest of the work, as well as the images of Auschwitz itself, are there to insist that mankind has evolved to encounter a more complex existential challenge than that faced by other primates; and human efforts to make this challenge more explicit, including the broadcast of the television series demonstrate an awareness and concern that exemplify a superior condition that validates the claim implied in the series' title. It was not contended by Bronowski that man has ascended in moral condition (the intellectual achievements are there, but not really at the heart of Bronowski's concern and message) as a result of the advent and use of television. Television is merely the message system by which the tale could be most widely told.

This theme of *The Ascent of Man* (Bronowski, 1973) is symmetrically and, some might claim, ideologically opposed to that of the Fall of Man. No television series has yet been made under the latter title, one reason being that features producers like to be positive. Instead, the darker spirit of this theme is found in the work of so many of the challenger researchers whose witness seems to propose that science is a Pandora's box of debilitating novelities. Television is thus seen as corroding the human condition, which is generally too weak to resist such temptation. Some prophets, therefore, call out for individual resistance in the face of temptation, but more of them observe a Descent of the Viewer; the only effective retrieval from this decline is accomplished when a central authority harnesses the horses of television's apocalypse and causes them to be run in ordered tracks.

At the end of his course Bronowski (1973, who has attributed the idea for the series to the BBC executive Aubrey Singer, but who has obviously warmed to his theme) laments a "terrible loss of nerve, a retreat from knowledge into . . . Zen Buddhism" (p. 437); on the contrary, he asserts that "the ascent of man will go on" (p. 437) . . . "Every man, every civilisation has gone forward because of its engagement with what it has set itself to do" . . . "Knowledge is . . . a responsibility for . . . what we are, primarily . . . as ethical creatures" (p. 436). There is no explicit mention of religion here, and Bronowski seems keen to exclude a divine role in giving any direction or power to this human quest. This implicit denial seems to stand outside the evidence of Bronowski's much loved science inasmuch as he argues that there is an energy consuming process of distillation of a higher human order going on of its own accord, which is something that does not occur in the natural physical world. Thus, this seemingly self-propelled ascent of man, proclaimed on one of his most proficient recent artifacts, television, is a metaphor of one view of the potential of this message system as one part of the whole process. Unlike

Lord Clark who merely used television to celebrate the glories of western civilization, and Sagan, who described those of the Cosmos, Bronowski was not just a passenger on but a celebrant of the message system and thus an optimist making his series different in essence from all its other seemingly great parallels.

CHAMPIONS OF THEIR INDUSTRY, AND ALLIES

This metaphor of ascent characterises the theory of the last champion we shall discuss, but before that there are some simpler cases to consider. These are the industry spokespeople, particularly in the United States, who proclaim the merits of their system. To quote once more from Postman Leonard H. Goldenson, chairman of the board of ABC declared in 1981 that "as communicators . . . and as citizens . . . we require a new kind of literacy. It will be a visual literacy, an electronic literacy, and it will be as much an advance over the literacy of the written word we know today as that was over the purely oral tradition of man's early history" (p. 118). Postman notes the irony that it was science, brought about by print literacy, which gave birth to the message system over which Mr. Goldenson presided; by the same token the electronic message system might promote new competences (it would not be right to call them literacy) which would yet further (to parallel Bronowski's confidence) enhance the human condition.

A declaration on these lines was recently made by Derrick De Kerckhove (1985) who is far from being an industry spokesperson. Inheritor of the mantle of Marshall McLuhan in Toronto, de Kerckhove points out with the critics of television that "it turns the viewer into the product," but this appears to him as a source of optimism. He turns his back on Bronowski's view relegating to the world of print the notion that "as long as you can ignore the real impact of the environment upon you, you can cultivate the illusion of entertaining a coherent, permanent and improvable self by reading books which better your soul." De Kerckhove believes that through survey research and polls which "scan the audience as the tube's light beam scans the brain" television discovers and gives the public what it wants. One of these desires is to see television "absorb and replay the violence of our frustrations in an orderly fashion." To this cathartic function De Kerckhove gives credit for the fact that "we have not yet been blown out of existence in a third and final world war." He believes that telegraph and radio brought about two world wars among industrialized countries, but television by its distractive power is holding a third such conflict at bay.

Other claims of a cohesive function for television were voiced by CBS president Fred Friendly in a British series, *Television*. The appropriately named president noted that after President Kennedy's assassination, the nation was so shocked and destabilized that some feared a collapse of civil order might follow. Television, it was said, saved the day. In reality, it was probably President Kennedy himself who had ensured safety in disaster. For a mark of the good leader is to imbue his or her followers with a sufficient sense of purpose to carry on with confidence even if the leader becomes absent. Grief is not to be confused with chaos, but this does not detract from the good point (Greenberg, 1964) that television provided a focus around which people gathered to receive news and to confirm a feeling of solidarity. Other positive achievements of television had been the portrayal of racist violence against civil rights campaigns, which had undermined further support for segregationists; the live portrayal of Senate hearings of McCarthy's investigations, which eventually punctured that senator's credibility; and the showing of scenes of violence from Viet Nam, which turned American public opinion against any continued support for that war (see MacDonald, 1985).

Curiously, Mr. Friendly's colleague, Gene F. Jankowski (1985), denied much of this claim for television's powers. In an international colloquium Jankowski said "television has been accused of causing almost any number of things to happen, ranging from tooth decay to withdrawal in participation in the Vietnam war." Jankowski set hard tests by which to judge television's powers, asserting at the start of his speech that "no one has been able to establish a direct causal relationship between television . . . (and) . . . a range of behaviors generally considered to be undesirable;" later, he said "media are not the prime movers. I know of no country where television has either caused a revolution or stopped one." Aside from the problem that it would never be possible to show that a revolution would have occurred, but for television, Jankowski saw the glory of television in that it has little or no autonomous responsibility for evil effects (or for good ones) but that "it can enliven and enrich a culture," and that "its value comes from the degree of satisfaction the user derives from it." Although we have indicated in Chapter 3 that systematic measurement of viewer satisfaction has hardly been publicized in the United States, where behavior has generally been used as an index of the mental state, British experience has shown that television does indeed deliver widespread and reasonably high levels of appreciation. We have also seen that people would pay substantial sums in order not to be without screens affording access to fiction. It is less easy to gain widespread approval, however, for the idea that television enriches a culture unless it can effectively be shown that there is great breadth and depth in programming that stimulates new directions of fruitful expression beyond the screen (an effects proposition that Jankowski has denied it has been possible to verify) or that allowances are made in the definitions of the terms "enrich" and "culture" that will enable the assertion to seem true.

It is probably important to observe that the champions of new screen message systems are few and relatively difficult to discern. The entrepreneurs Ted Turner and Rupert Murdoch set up satellite channels to compete in a marketplace for their own gain; other entrepeneurs of videocassette or cable put forward their wares in a similar spirit. This is not to decry their enterprise but rather to point out that their cry is not a clarion in favor of a better society, merely to herald what they say will be a better served one. There is no confusion here between describing the popular idea of the prophet, as one who foretells, and the deeper understanding of the prophetic role in forthtelling; many of the stereotypical prophets of old had to forthtell unpopular messages but this does not obscure the fact that others proclaimed good news.

The new message systems involving the screen include VCR; satellite and cable channels, which supply much the same as terrestrial broadcast television (TBT); teletext in a one-directional or in an interactive two-dimensional mode; computers; and home printers. It might be too facile to dismiss satellite and cable as not essentially different from TBT, but it may serve for the time being to do this as these systems are all characterized by an admunicational provision of information and entertainment in various proportions. The VCR is different, for all that its use may be narrowing in experience, since it involves an essential act of autonomy: the user obtains the film (by recording off air, rent, or purchase) but then plays it in a self conscious act of independent initiative that makes the VCR appliance psychologically distinct from other television. Here is a place where one might have heard a prophet or champion extol the independence-enhancing feature of VCR, but no one has done so.

Teletext has won its few admiring adherents. Greenberg (1986b) has described British progress in this area with somewhat greater enthusiasm than have the British themselves. It is the computer, however, which has almost launched a few hesitant champions. Taking the computer to refer broadly to any reasonably complex calculator available to the user, a number of writers have described its actual or potential role with some enthusiasm. Turkle (1984) has told how within an institute of higher learning the detachment afforded by the message system has helped its users to be tolerant of each other('s messages). Hellerstein (1985) has described how people use a computer network, not just for calling up lists of academic reference, but also for lonely hearts advice and as a self-administered dating agency. These are cases where the "communication" afforded is primarily by the visual medium (one reads the messages on screen) but also what has been called "automodal" (Wober, 1985c). By automodal quasi-communication one means that the perceiver may provide, by his or her own imagery, a sound of a voice, a smell, or a touch to attach to the information received mostly visually from another person via a screen.

It is problematic as to whether automodal quasi-information is a good thing or not. It could be seen and dealt with as a more vivid means of encounter than what would occur if operators registered a sign in only one modality; on the other hand, there is the chance that much of what the user projects as characterizing the other may be false. It has to be asked whether, or if not why not, people have not used the telephone or the ansafone to strike up acquaintances in the same way as has occurred with the computer-aided bulletin boards of the screen. In fact cold telephone calls other than for conspicuously neutralized sales or survey purposes are regarded as threatening, both to the recipient and to the originator, and are not made less so by answering machines. The reasons for this are probably two. First, the message hung out on the computer network is rendered nonthreatening because it is in public territory, since many other users can read it, but a sound recorded message is private, having lodged itself in the territory of the receiver. The second reason, which is the point of all this analysis, is that a screen-carried message is entirely coded and conceptual, carrying information about the originator transformed into the neutral realm of print, from which the reader lifts meanings as the reader covertly wishes them to be. By contrast, a voice recorded message carries reality about the originator in one medium at least, that of sound. The print-based screen messages are, therefore, intriguing but, at least for social psychological purposes, problematic. There are thus the writers who describe events and say "this is what is happening" but few, if any of them, insist about facilities such as Bitnet "this is a magnificent prospect, this is what ought to be made to happen, not just within some hallowed precincts of higher learning but for the public at large, everywhere." There are no prophets to this prospect.

Looking further into the future there has been one prophet who appears to favor new message systems; but on further examination one may have to realize that he is really the champion of an older system. Addressing Britain's committee of enquiry convened to propose methods for financing public service broadcasting, Peter Jay, sometime telecaster and Great Britain's Ambassador in Washington, made a strong case for paving the way to a phenomenon he calls "electronic publishing." To attain this, all sets would have to be provided with descrambling equipment to count units received for which payment could be made; eventually, via multiple channels carried by satellite and cable, the user would have access to a very wide variety of materials. Jay did not examine the economics of generating picture programs, but it seems likely that they will always remain expensive, especially if reasonable or even high quality is desired. Efficient program makers would then grow up to command supply, and without any social form of interaction, the market would tend to take shape in containing expensively made picture programs of a limited range of the more popular types and categories, while the less popular types would be less elaborately made, or even provided essentially in text. The text could be available on screen or probably as well, with the marketing of cheap home printing equipment, in hard copy. The screen might thus be bypassed, other than as a testing or scanning device on the way to a different way of bringing print into homes. It is likely that a market in sumptious bindings would spring up so that users would compile their own books (like photograph albums). But the role of the screen in facilitating this eventual goal will probably be a minor one, and again this may underlie the dearth of prophecy in this regard.

THE SCREEN AS A RUNG
IN A LADDER OF SKILLS

Although Jankowski and similar industry champions generally seem to defend the way in which television is run in the United States, his parochialism is not a characteristic of a much more subtle thesis put forward by Patricia Greenfield (1984). Her analysis applies to the nature of the message system almost regardless of how it is commercially organized. Greenfield notes at the outset that although studies in television's early years had "recommended teaching children critical viewing skills . . . in the years since these early studies . . . little progress has been made in using (television) positively . . ." (p. 3). Since her book is called *Mind and Media*, Greenfield also makes it clear that what she means by the latter term is each whole institution of admunication such as television, print, and radio. We should bear in mind that these are not the senses in which the term media is applied in these pages. For example, television involves two media, not one, and these are the avenues by which messages reach the receiver's two separate senses of sight and of hearing. Nevertheless, Greenfield states clearly that television does require users to decode two parallel streams of information, and this gives a clue to her own account of what is possible in an ascending sequence of skills, which may begin with decoding and then go on to develop encoding proficiency. Briefly, Greenfield's theory is resonant with Bronowski's; she believes people can, and will with a modicum of the right encouragement, become more sophisticated and satisfied with what they do. Experience with television turns out to be a suitable starting point for such an ascent. Here, then, is a champion of television with a constructivist rather than a complacent view.

Quite contrary to Neil Postman's assertion that one does not have to learn how to decode television, Greenfield points out that children do not fully develop the skill of construing all the conventions by which meanings are conveyed on television until about the age of 10. Important evidence on this comes from Africa (Wober, 1976; Siceloff, 1983). Africa is a place where people who have rarely if even seen film can still be found; reporting from rural Tanzania, Siceloff noted "many were surprised by the way that films depicted the passage of time. One man told us he couldn't get over the kind of cotton they had in the pictures. One picture showed people planting cotton and in the next picture it was already sprouting! Where could he get a hold of some of that cotton seed?" (p. 203). While this exemplifies what may be called a semantic misunderstanding, there is also evidence of misconstruction at a perceptual level. In answer to a question "was the field at the end (of a zoom shot) the same as the beginning of the picture . . . half the viewers throught that the field at the beginning of a zoom was different than a field at the end of the zoom. . . . People had to learn the meaning of a zoom." Such learning is more likely to be found among younger people, but the African evidence does show that these conventions, sometimes thought to be self-evident, have to be learned. Among western populations viewing much screen fare this learning is accomplished, as is that of the spoken language, with very little or no explicit instruction.

A crucial next step in Greenfield's argument depends on evidence presented by Salomon (1979) from Israel that, among 7- to 9-year-old children, those who had watched more of *Sesame Street*, regardless of social class, did better on a number of tests designed to measure "skills related to the program's code of symbolic representation" (such as shifts of camera position). From this Greenfield concludes that "television literacy is indeed fostered by exposure to television itself" (p. 16). This may yet reassure Postman, for Greenfield affirms that while "children must be *taught* to read, they learn TV literacy on their own by simply watching television" (p. 17). Nevertheless, there is a danger that the complex codes of the screen "will be used automatically and without effort, that (it) will be processed passively rather than actively." This problem has to be combatted by appropriate social arrangements and institutions. Throughout Greenfield's book there is a dual approach in which, though it is emphasized that it is necessary to elicit "activity through forces outside the program itself . . . through the use of carefully chosen techniques television can, on its own, make the child an active participant" (p. 31).

A number of questions must be raised about this thesis. One concerns how generally it may be supported by other evidence. A second is whether the conditions that it suggests are best for a creative role of television are actually being met by institutions and practices in the United States or elsewhere. At least two widely different studies question the general validity of Salomon's findings. In Ghana, Gilbertson (Wober, 1976) tested children on their ability to infer three-dimensional meanings from simple pictures printed on two-dimensional paper. There was no sign that those with greater television experience had better interpretational skills than children who were unfamiliar with the screen. Several years later Williams (1985) failed to find any better performance on spatial skills among children in two towns with television in comparison to another without it, or in the latter town after it had acquired television. Salomon's results may have had another explanation, for example, that the kind of families who were early purchasers of television and whose children saw *Sesame Street* may also have had a different climate of motivation and of use of other educational toys and practices than were to be found where children were not so familiar with *Sesame Street*. Second, programs such as *Sesame Street, Mr. Rogers Neighborhood,* and *Freestyle,* a series produced for public television to teach equality in sex role expectations and cited as effective stimuli for cognitive and social development, may actually be less widespread in the United States (as E. Palmer laments) than is desirable, or than their equivalents in other countries.

Some of these drawbacks are faced by Greenfield who acknowledges that too much viewing can be associated with passivity and with a reduction of demand on the imagination. She says, therefore, that television's potential strengths should be acknowledged and maximized, and its weaknesses minimized, while at the same time applying the same approach to get the best of other message systems. Exactly the same spproach is taken by Brown (1986) who, while being cautious about some of the ways in which some message systems might be wasteful of time or effort, is nevertheless broadly optimistic that by explaining to parents and teachers the strengths of each message system, their combination in use will be very helpful overall.

This advocacy by Brown is very similar to that expressed by a colleague of Greenfield's, Aimee Dorr (1986). Dorr finishes one of her chapters by stating "one soon sees that both children and television are neither as good nor as bad as thinking would have them be and learns how to maximize the magic of television and the braininess of children using it" (p. 20). She ends her whole book on a similar note of considered championship "with the knowledge we have today we can do much to make the transaction between children and television a good one" (p. 148). The hinge on which this optimism really hangs, however, is the pronoun we; for while those who know how to harness television well can obviously benefit themselves and their children by it, there remains what is probably a majority who do not know, in spite of books about how to make good use of the screen by Brown and Dorr (and others, such as by the Australian, Patricia Palmer, 1986).

Both homes and schools can readily teach children to make positive use of the screen, and several projects for doing so are cited by Brown, Dorr, and Palmer. The potential for good is, therefore, not so much in doubt as is the question of its realization. The main point here is to demonstrate that a case has been put forward that is very different in its constructive optimism about television from so many of the worried challengers that have preceded it in this chapter.

Greenfield's optimism extends beyond the presence of the television screen. Again citing work from Israel (1984) it was found that when children were trained to watch the screen in a more active, careful way by asking penetrating questions about what they had seen, one effect was an increase in reading comprehension scores. Thus, viewing skills under suitable conditions could promote reading skills and make possible transfer across message systems (note, this does not yet mean transfer across media, in the sense in which the term is being used here). More often though, perhaps, television's pictures supplant explicit verbal treatment by commentators and actors, and Greenfield suspects that habituation to the pictorial message system has in practice led to unsophisticated or inadequate writing performance. By contrast "radio is like print in that it presents and therefore fosters an articulate verbal style of communication" (p. 75). In comparing message systems, Greenfield says explicitly "in defense of television, while the sense of hearing may be less important . . . than in listening to radio or tape, television does not result in any long-term reduction of the importance of auditory stimuli in general" (p. 87). Radio is stronger, however than television in stimulating the imagination. This is one of the reasons why Greenfield recommends, overall, that "parents should restrict the amount of television their children watch at home in order to use other media and experiences to foster reflection and imagination" (p. 84).

Turning to new screen devices, Greenfield rejects the scare that video games are addictive and analyses what makes these games attractive and what skills they use and foster. An initial sample of four suggested that those who were involved with games preferred them to television because they offered active control; goal presence also increases interest but these advantages are offset by the observation that playing violent video games raises the level of aggression in small children. However, two-player video games reduced levels of aggression. The suggestion, therefore, (which may apply to simple television viewing as well) is that aggressiveness may be stimulated by too much viewing that involves too little social interaction. This solitude may yet be a prospect for the future, however, for Greenfield quotes a computer programmer as saying excitedly that "video games are revolutionary; they are the beginnings of human interaction with artificial intelligence" (p. 110). Since humanity has had to grapple for eons with the problems of dealing with real or human intelligence, this new task can be seen as reactionary unless from the point of view of the machine. However, the point emerges that humans now will have to deal with artificial, as well as with real intelligences, and the competences in (and indeed the taste for) dealing with the former will be promoted by familiarity with screens from the simplest level upward.

Since "pictorial images . . . tend to elicit parallel processing . . . a child whose main media background was television, rather than print or radio could be more prepared for the parallel processing demanded by skillful video game playing" (p. 101). Not just parallel processing but spatial skills of the kind involved in "solving" the Rubik cube are likely to be promoted by screen viewing experience, so that the child is equipped with the basic skills to begin what Greenfield terms the ascent of "a ladder of challenges" (p. 110). Briefly, many games present increasing levels of complexity and players are enticed into tackling the next levels by achieving some success at the primary levels. Gagnon (1985) has reported that, at least among women subjects, practice with a videogame increased their scores on a test of visualization. Whether this represents the inculcation of a skill that had not been present, or the bringing into play of potential that had not hitherto been realized, it was also true that practice at videogames produced higher game performance among players in general. Better performance is motivating, and when players feel they have mastered one game they are likely to progress to another more complex game or activity. This takes children eventually from the world of video games to those of computers and word processors. A 1983 estimate was that 18% of children in California had computers available at home, and surveys generally affirm that these devices are most likely to be found in gadget-hungry homes where there tend to be many TV sets, video games, and (in Great Britain at least) more chance of teletext ownership and use.

A number of studies and examples are quoted to show that children enjoy word processing, can work together well to write projects and even books, and enjoy editing and revision much more than they are willing or able to do with the more private labor of script. Early evidence indicates that children working with word processors produced longer and better quality essays than did those without. Greenfield follows previous contentions based on evidence with newly literate people in Africa that the ability to rearrange and thus discover the relationships between propositions or abstract statements is fostered by literacy, and suggests that "as writing by computer becomes more widespread it will lead to better performance by a larger proportion of the population on the type of formal problem involving the mental manipulation of abstract propositions" (p. 134). In France, the same idea was realized and made the basis of a proposal that computer science become a compulsory subject in secondary school. Another French idea is to install the devices necessary to give all telephone users access to directory information by interrogating central computers. This was designed not merely for economic efficiency but as a means to make the population at large familiar with the new message systems of keyboard and screen.

In all, the championship expressed by Greenfield, even though problematic in several aspects, is unusual and usefully positive. It has sufficient cautions and realism to set alongside what may seem to be some of its unconventional and ambitious claims. Thus, in one place it is boldly stated that "television is, in certain respects, an intrinsically democratic medium. Within . . . developed countries it is democratic in that it reduces the advantage possessed by middle class people in the world of school and books. On a global scale it is democratic because it can help alleviate the problems of educational development in the Third World" (p. 61). These two assertions are perhaps better seen as expressions of potential rather than of performance. Too much literature on knowledge gaps (Gaziano 1983) suggests that with access to any message system, it is the information rich who get richer while the poor get left behind. This is not only because the more competent find the new systems just as motivating as anybody else does but because the former have better developed contexts into which new information can be and usually is integrated.

One of the crucial studies on which Greenfield's edifice is built, which saw the screen as an instrument of enhancing reading comprehension, may have another explanation: It may have been the penetrating questioning rather than the screen back up that was the main instigator of improved reading comprehension, which could have benefited by penetrating questions about anything else even such as the latest sports results. In brief, it may be that (as the Greeks knew well) to ask is to teach (rather than that to show is to teach); and it is an important and negative feature of television (though not of video games or computers) that it *never* stops to ask, or just leave a moment even for reflection when the viewer can ask himself or herself a question or digest what has been seen—again, not enough potters wheels.

Nevertheless, even with cautions and provisos, the merits of television and subsequent screen adaptations are skillfully detected by Greenfield and repeated by Brown, and the invitation is made to deploy these advantages to maximum effect. Many useful steps have already been taken in such a direction, for which the school is seen as perhaps the most important institutional facilitator of positive uses and behavior. Greenfield begins her section on "Guiding Home Viewing" by saying that teachers can have a strong influence on what children can watch in their homes. Parents, it is implied (and regrettably all too often true), have tended to allow lazy and unconstructive viewing practices to prevail. In schools, provided that screen experience is not misused as a way of allowing teachers to relax, a great deal can be done that uses one message system's strengths to complement others. Noting the widespread interest in fiction (and shrewdly realizing a good way to win viewers to its own programs) CBS has distributed millions of program scripts together with coordinated teachers' guides and student notebooks. This allows viewing to occur but to be something that is in itself an object of the viewer's scrutiny.

In a way, although Greenfield is a champion of television, defending its (potential) democratic value and seeing it as the first rung in a ladder of challenges that provides today's microcosm of the evolutionary ascent of man, she also directs a challenge not to the message system itself, but to the viewers.

It is for the population, which has in ancient biblical view been given the power of choice between the paths of good or of evil, to choose the creative and good way. Which parts of the population do take the high road and which take the low, and the proportions of the former and of the latter are in the first place the problem for researchers to discover; following this it is the province of policy makers and creators of institutions to devise structures that will encourage more people to realize the positive potentials of the various message systems that are now with us, and which are becoming ever more commonplace. A great merit of Greenfield's book, and the reason why we encounter it at the end of this chapter, is that it deals mainly with children. Through them it looks to the future role of the changing screen. Certainly, it is necessary to know how people have used television during the three developing decades during which it has held sway. This knowledge will provide the landmarks by which a future course can be detected that people are likely to follow. Equally, the extent to which children can change and accept new message systems and the ways in which they may even modify these message systems by making their interests and abilities known to the system engineers and marketers are the topics of Greenfield's concern and which the next two chapters will also try to examine.

SUMMARY:
CHAMPIONS OF THE SCREEN

Three kinds of positive advocates of the screen have been identified and discussed: current industry moguls, to whom one might add the champions of the changing screen, if one can find any; the creative passengers of existing airwaves who have sought to use the opportunities opened up by mass viewing for positive social purposes; and genuine scientists who start as dispassionate observers or at least investigators and who are open to influence upon their ideas and theories according to the results they discover in their research. Some of these, certainly, have been positive about the screen. Interestingly, several of the optimists are women whose research has been at least partly concerned with questions of formative effects of the screen on children. This observation is not intended to typecast women, for they are also to be found among the most emphatic challengers of the screen (Winn, Charren); it is harder, however, to find men among this particular group of champions.

In exploring the nature of championship of today's screen we have encountered a difference between those who are merely describers and others who are advocates. The former, when applied to the future in their approach to the changing screen have been termed heralds; they calmly observe that technical innovations will arrive and that these will cause major alterations in, even problems for, society. Quite often these heralds see no point in expecting any opposition to the changes ahead, just as there is little point in welcoming problems. This position is to forsake responsibility, which may be particularly regrettable among those who have become better informed than others; for if a lay person can be excused for having no opinion about an issue on which he or she is ill-informed, the one who knows something, indeed who is bothering to tell others, is in a better position to make a value judgment as well. They may feel, however, that their role is like that of the weather forecaster who informs the public that there are tornados ahead, with intervening periods of sunshine. In such a case the public is left to interpret this sort of information; the difference with major changes in the technical system, however, is that individuals are not in a position to make the major decisions and to put them into practice.

A fundamentally optimistic view of human potential has been expressed on television; in a series called *The Ascent of Man* the analysis is that humanity has improved in its grasp of the condition and of the possibilities facing us. It is clearly not the implication that humanity has reached a pinnacle of its quality from which there extends a plateau or a drop; instead, it is implied that, probably in unforeseeable ways, humanity will make the best of the changes in the technical systems that lie ahead.

A reflection of this ladder of moral condition is a theory of an ascent of mental skill, which holds that the domestic television has equipped children with abilities to visualize spatial relationships that lead in turn to a readiness to use extended and interactive devices involving screens. Curiously, this vision has screen users ultimately spending more time with script; another prospect of electronic publishing also thinks in terms of an eventual goal in which the experience of the picture screen may just have been the lowest point in a cycle from which reading and writing will recover a primacy over the picture as a mode of communication over admunication.

CONCEPTS EXPLORED IN THIS CHAPTER

Ascent And Fall.   Two opposing doctrines, rooted in depth of religious systems and belief, which affect ways of assessing the role of the screen. The view of ascent is optimistic, improving, confident; the view of fall is precautious, pessimistic, defensive.

Champions.   People who advocate the merits to society of the screen in the home—the screens which bring picture programs as in the first two decades of television, or in developed forms which will add text and interactive facilities. Champions proclaim their criticism within a moral context, either from a position of possession, operation, or knowledge of the effects of the message system they advocate.

Gadget Hunger.   An eagerness in certain homes, or among some people, to acquire the latest forms of message system (and probably other) hardware. The condition is opposite to that of "computerphobia" or "techno-stress" (see next chapter).

CHAPTER 6

The Changing Screen and a Changing Viewer

INTRODUCTION:
THE EMPIRES OF PRINT AND SCREEN

The empire of print has arisen and achieved its power over a period of 500 years. Many scholars have claimed to see the crumbling of this domain in the face of the alleged effects of various technical innovations from the telegraph to television. None of the new message systems, such as the phonogram (or gramophone, as it is known in Europe where evidently the imprinted trace of the music is accorded priority over the message sounds conveyed) or radio, was widely seen as the basis of its own empire, however, until the arrival of television. Now even this new order, which has hardly established itself over a course of 30 years, has numerous would-be heralds of its demise. Ironically, the great majority of these make their case in print, but they do not proclaim that television is dethroned to return to the supremacy of print. Instead, they point to "new media" still primarily involving the screen, such as teletext, videocassette, telepurchase and telebanking spread by cable, and entertainment spread by satellite. In short, they are inebriated by the profusion of devices for bringing information and other experience to the human receiver, and it is made to seem that these new devices will loosen the grip that television had supposedly begun to exert over the sentient lives of its enthralled populations in its few short years of power.

For the home user, the screen has been changing almost ceaselessly since its arrival. Over 30 years screens have typically become larger, clearer, and have acquired color. Supply systems have provided more channels and the instruments of immediate control; the switches have become more personalized in passing from their positions on the screen cabinet to a detached hand held device. To have the switch on the cabinet determines a relationship in which the set is an object of potential attention for the family as a unit. The user's movement to and operation of the switches or channel selectors when they are on the cabinet are conspicuous acts whose performance is either socially agreed, or a challenge, in either case involving collective response. In contrast, the remote selector switch is a personal weapon of whim and control. People still view jointly, but with a remote switch in one person's hands the social psychology of the room is now subtly altered. Power has been personalized and those who do not have the remote control device are confronted with the results of the controller's initiatives, rather than leaving the options open to inspection and negotiation. It is rare for users to install multiple remote control devices for a single screen, thus democratizing its use.

In several ways then the set and its immediate accessories have continued to change, affecting how the screen is used. Further changes concern how the signals are brought to the set and can be stored and the range of material that is involved, generated either by public broadcasters of whatever kind; by private corporations, such as banks or stores; or by individuals, as in the case of videotelephone. All these forthcoming changes raise questions about the empire of (network) television.

Where, if it exists at all, has the dominion of television held sway? Behind the screen it has involved large industries of production, hardware, and programming; it has produced effects on most institutions that have fed into it, such as the cinema and sport in the entertainment sector, and the machinery of law and of government in the realms of information and of social control. All this may change in the wake of altered ways of supplying the domestic screen. These economic and political consequences, while extremely important and interesting, are not, however, chosen as the focus of interest for this book.

The other territory of the empire of television lies in front of the screen, in the minds and lives of its individual and family users. We have looked at some of the research and controversy, which has seen television as a threat to society in a number of ways, whereas others have seen television as a benefit. What will the envisaged changes in technical systems entail to the existing balance of television's social roles? Will the claimed harms of mainstream television be alleviated? Will benefits be enhanced or new ones introduced? If no net benefits can be expected with any confidence are there any good reasons why progress in forms dictated by the needs of certain industrial complexes should heedlessly be adopted for populations worldwide? This last question is evaluative, involving certain assumptions and beliefs about human needs and nature, and an answer is not offered here. However, to help to pave the way for those who do wish to debate the question, we need to establish a credible description of what is actually happening when individuals send, receive, and process information. In making an analysis of these processes, it will be helpful to try to answer some of the important questions about the supposed achievements of the empire of television.

To understand what its vast audiences have done with television, we have so far examined evidence on audience behavior and satisfactions, as well as some of the arguments about supposed and more convincingly attested effects. In this chapter we will try to unravel and provide a useful system for naming the skills involved in operating message systems. With some of the framework that this systematization provides, we will then examine some of the very few efforts that have been made to explore Marshall McLuhan's extension of the Sapir-Whorf hypothesis, that the structure of the message systems that individuals have to use from birth onwards may have a particular role in the formation of individual sensibilities. By sensibility we mean here the profile of the senses according to which people perceive their surroundings and into which they deliver their own contributions of expression. Psychologically, the realm of sense and perception precedes that of meaning and social relationships. It has been easy to study attitudes and common to study actions in the wake of television experience; it has been less usual to inquire into the very organization of perception and how this may, or may not, be influenced by experience with television.

A TAXONOMY OF SKILLS INVOLVED IN SENDING AND RECEIVING INFORMATION

A good point of departure for the analysis that follows is to note that there are at least seven pathways for information to reach the brain where experience is composed, and these pathways involve the seven sense receptors, of which four (hearing, sight, smell, and taste) are located in the head and three (touch, proprioception, and the awareness of temperature) are diffused over and through the body. Each of these sensory gates allows access to a source from which messages can be sent. The nature of the energy, which moves from the transmitter to each of the sensory gates, is different for each of these senses. For this reason, it is important to signify this difference by a system of terms that reflects the individual quality of each sensory pathway. It will be most appropriate to use the word medium for the sense-feeding soups in which all individuals swim, and each medium is the soup through which signals come from their sources to the sense organs, which are the gateways for this information on its way to the brain.

This use of the word medium, which is different from the relatively imprecise purpose to which it is generally put, is drawn from the sciences of biology. It is unlikely that it will be possible to alter the somewhat shapeless course of the popular usage, but it may be that in the scientific domain some order can eventually be achieved so that the conceptual tools (definitions), with whose use knowledge can advance, are not the jellyish objects of common and careless speech but are more sharp and apt.

We can now begin to see why, throughout this book, television has not been referred to as a medium but as a message system. A medium is the ether through which light waves reach the eye. It is also the medium through which electromagnetic radiation reaches a receiver antenna from a television transmitter; the television set is thus both a receiver and a transmitter since it provides its picture as the signal with which the viewer is concerned. Another medium is air (or the molecules which constitute it, rather than the ether between them) and this carries sound. Television, therefore, requires two media with which to reach its perceivers; it is a message system and not a medium. The nature of the two media that television uses is of considerable importance in understanding the processes of perception, which underlie the rest of the psychology of television use. Television's two media engage the most important of the human senses, vision and hearing. Print engages vision and, therefore, is a different message system from television, though it is one that uses one of television's two media.

To highlight the ways in which television is perceived, it is also useful to examine other senses, not immediately involved, to see what can be and is done with them. The sense of smell records the presence of particular molecules and seems similar to hearing and even to temperature perception in its use of gas as a medium. However, hearing is by far the most sophisticated of these senses, by virtue of the accuracy of its physiology and the extent to which message systems can provide a corresponding accuracy of encoding the information they transmit. Dogs have a much more refined smell sense than humans do, but neither species has begun to develop devices with which accurate and sophisticated communication could be achieved by use of a medium to excite the sense of smell. Such devices are, however, conceivable. Analog systems would involve establishing a code in which certain smells and their combinations are given particular meanings that perceivers would learn; digital systems would involve establishing a different code in which a particular smell is presented and then canceled in precisely organized sequences whose conventions the perceivers would have to learn. The British press once played with the notion implied in the headline "Smelly Telly On The Way" (Daily Star, 16 May 1985) but the clumsiness of the encoding possibilities was readily apparent when it transpired that viewers had to be issued with "scratch cards," which they had to scrape and sniff when told to do so within a particular program. The instructions as to when to scratch which panel were spoken; thus the olfactory medium depended on the auditory one, which made the former even more limited. This shows us by contrast that with visual and auditory media the starts and ends of messages are signified in each medium itself, giving it a kind of autonomy of use, to add to its accuracy.

To construct a message system, an effective device is needed with which to transmit signals into a medium. It is worth settling upon a general term for such devices, apart from transmitter, which has already a fairly specific use. *Sign agent* is proposed as the name for any of these devices. For the visual medium, there are probably three important kinds of sign agents: screen systems, page systems, and the human body itself. Among screen systems are TV sets, cinema screens, and instrument dials. The theatrical stage should probably be included as an example since the proscenium frames the front surface of a space within which the messages are generated; however, the theatre is also an auditory sign agent. An element common to screen systems is that of sign mobility; that is, the elements can move. In contrast, page systems (which some screens occasionally mimic) do not carry moving elements. The presence or absence of visible movement and how it facilitates learning and then deciphering codes is a topic on which there has been much psychological research, generally suggesting that movement makes a difference depending on how skillfully it is used: It can help or hinder effective communication.

Page systems of visual sign agents include books, screens, posters, and paintings. Two characteristics are common to this group: two dimensionality and immobility. This means that they allow for inspection and reinspection at the user's pace. Two dimensionality is probably useful where script is involved, as attention is directed to the content of the signs rather than to a more complex structure which must be presumed is involved with three-dimensional signs. Two dimensionality also requires the perceiver to do some cognitive work to attribute three-dimensional depth where the sign is a picture; a considerable amount of research from the Third World (Wober, 1976) shows that what are assumed by some Westerners to be obvious pictures needing no interpretation do not always function that way in other cultures; this is true both for still (page) pictures and moving (screen) ones.

Television technologists have recently pursued a variety of goals in changing the screen (e.g., see Fujio, 1982); one of these goals is a three-dimensional display. Researchers at the Japanese Broadcasting Corporation (Nippon Hoso Kyokai—NHK) had pursued this by various methods including polarized spectacles and by using holography; "however, these methods have problems such as unsatisfactory picture quality, eye fatigue, and a very large volume of signal to be transmitted . . ." (p. 14). The NHK group fell back, therefore, on large screen high definition display as their aim. Yuyama (in Fujio, 1982) refers to the existence of the screen becoming less noticeable with increased size, "the contents of the picture do not appear flat but have depth . . . and the volume of picture information approaches a level acceptable to the vision process capacity, involving the viewer in what they see on the screen" (p. 15). In addition, wider screens begin to produce a "tilting effect on the sense of balance of the viewer;" this is in all probability what was termed the 'E' effect by Witkin (1967) in America, who had studied the interrelation of bodily processing of information that was both proprioceptive (from posture in relation to gravity) and visual (from the eyes on the world as seen).

Although there is little evidence that visual and olfactory senses are linked, this is not so with regard to proprioception (as discovered by Witkin and by the NHK researchers) or with the sense of touch (Waln, 1984). Waln points out that "touch dominates vision at birth . . . is the more elemental mode of communication that is the first language used in infancy . . . children aged 4–9 experience developmental changes in the dominance hierarchy from tactile to visual . . . tactile deprivation produces an increased desire for tactile data, and satiation in the tactile modality reduces the drive for visual data" (p. 2). This reminds us that the human body was listed as a visual sign agent—for sending messages about posture and gesture to others. The body was considered as different in important ways from page and screen sign agents; the most important reason is that the body signs internally or reflexively, with its encoding mechanism in close integration with its own decoding apparatus. In other words, the body is instructed to move or pay attention to its own state of touching and of temperature by the same brain that receives the information about these very conditions. The media for these sense modalities of pressure and position, touch, and temperature are the body's own tissues.

The overlaps or ambiguities that exist when a sign agent is a source for more than one medium must not be allowed to obscure the analytical distinctions being made, and that also correspond with neurological realities. The provision of posture and balance information makes use of internal media, but manifestations of posture and gesture are also visual sign agents for other people. However, when in turn one sees portrayals of others and their posture and movement and one has some sense of immediacy of or involvement with the portrayed reality, one's own system of balance and position is called into play and interacts in a complex way with what one encounters on a display such as wide screen television. With relatively small screens inside bulky cabinets giving them a securely located position in the room, television has relatively little proprioceptive quality of which viewers are aware; this may change with much wider screens and what was at first sight an audiovisual medium may be a sign system that uses these two media, but which also triggers the body's own internal proprioceptive (posture and pressure) and haptic (touch) media.

A SYSTEM FOR NAMING
DECODING SKILLS

The plan of analysis being built here has started with a decision that a crucial element in describing and understanding message systems must be that a person's sense organs are separate gateways for information that reaches each inner sensory pathway from its own medium. Each medium is supplied with information by sign agents that can only activate a single medium. Message systems can include agents, such as screens and speakers, that reach eyes and ears; but no serious attempts have been made to incorporate "olfactivators" or devices which engage the other distance sense—smell. There is value in noting and classifying what the various different sign agents can do; and at the receiver's end there is usefulness also in sorting out the skills involved in making sense of what is received from each medium and attending carefully to what is known about the neurology of how different kinds of information are dealt with in the brain.

The key word with which to enter and eventually to order this maze of skills is literacy. The origin of this word lies in its Latin roots which stand for letters (of two kinds—the actual ingredients of the alphabet, and by derivation, the world of book learning) and the ending -"ate" which relates to "-act" and refers to having made or done something. In short, literacy means the ability to decode messages encoded in writing, from page sign agents active in the visual medium. Without this, it may be unwise to extend the use of the term literacy to a grasp of the content of literature, which may well have existed among bards before the advent of widespread literacy (or ability to read and write). If literacy most sparsely means the ability to read and write, it will best serve scientific analysis if the word is not then buttered over other scenes of activity, as such imprecision can serve to hide or distract attention from what precisely is going on in the performance of other skills. We will need new terms for such skills, and some scholars have begun to experiment with such terms.

Examples are necessary to illustrate the inadvisability of misuse of the important word literacy. In 1975 at a British symposium in Manchester on "Audio-Visual Literacy" one speaker explained that "audio-visual literacy was the ability . . . to assess and evaluate . . . what they see and hear;" shortly after, the same speaker called the same idea just "visual literacy," thus implying no difference between the terms "visual literacy" and "audio-visual literacy." Another speaker said that visual literacy meant "literally, the improvement of children's literary style, taste or even vocabulary." A well-known television critic held that *Star Trek* was "actually a very audio-visual book . . . (because) . . . the first paragraph is printed in block capitals throughout." In 1976 a British historian of the screen explicitly distinguished literacy from visual literacy in saying that "if the battle for literacy is not yet over . . . the battle for visual literacy has not yet begun" (Briggs, 1976). This simply implies that literacy itself is somehow not visual, but visual literacy presumably is. We can now see clearly that the word visual is unnecessary, and likely to be confusing, when attached to the word literacy.

It might be thought that colloquialities affected only British authors not involved in systematic scientific work; however, such usage was also to be found in the American scientific community. An eminent psychologist explained about the brain that "visual presentations will engage the right hemisphere . . . verbal presentations will call for left hemisphere functions . . . it is suggested that television constitutes a primarily visual presentation . . . and that print is primarily a verbal stimulus" (Singer, 1977, p. 129).

Singer supposed that television will be dealt with in the right hemisphere of the brain. The explanation here, however, bears in mind that television carries both spoken words and pictures, and the spoken words are likely, as Singer says, to be processed in the left side of the brain. Singer's use of right and left as an opposition has stood parallel to visual and verbal, suggesting a similar opposition. However, visual and verbal are not exclusive opposites; what is uttered may be verbal, or not, if it is wordless melody or rhythm. What is visual may also be verbal if it is writing or other symbols of language. Visual information that is nonverbal (pictures, scenery, and the like) may be processed in the right side of the brain; visual information that is verbal, like auditory information that is verbal is dealt with primarily in the left side of the brain.

These examples are from the mid-1970s, but a short review of the literature over the next 10 years will show that such misunderstandings persist. An extremely competent study offers in its abstract the definition that "children's development of an understanding of TV as a medium, commonly referred to as TV literacy, is increasingly being recognised" (Dorr, Doubleday, Kovaric and Kunkel, 1983). Here, the deracinated term literacy is seemingly being used to mean "a grasp of how messages are encoded" and probably also "the social significance of TV messages" (such as, that TV violence is just entertainment, and not real). The damage that is possibly entailed with such uprooted terms is that they will mean one thing to some users and another thing to others. In short, they will lose meaningfulness and can even become so bland as to be "meaningempty," which is particularly ironic in a field where literacy also has an evaluative flavor, suggesting a sophisticated and shared depth of understanding encountered among well-educated people. This danger is recognized by Benjamin Compaine (1984) writing from Harvard on what he calls the "New Literacy." This is "the bundle of information skills that may be required to function in society . . . (following) the increasingly widespread use of . . . communications technology" (p. i).

Compaine acknowledges 22 scholars who aided his work and says that after thorough review "we are satisfied that . . . New Literacy (other labels are welcome) has both substance and significance . . . that is likely to come about from the increased use of digital electronic processes" (p. v). Compaine's openness to new labels is both welcome and wise. He realizes that before hard evidence is in, ideas and phenomena and processes must be recognized and named, and the identities of the emerging realities can not yet clearly be discerned; inappropriate names will lead to awkward management of discourse. The key term Compaine realizes is literacy, and he says the overarching meaning it has been invited to accommodate "both reinforces and muddies the concept . . . it reinforces because . . . literacy is not a simple commodity, but a dynamic bundle of skills that may encompass visual, auditory, mechanical and other abilities, with the mix varying . . . among cultures. The variety muddies the waters because it is hopeless to try to describe literacy if the term is extended to include proficiency in any particular skill" (p. 6).

Compaine is surely right in his diagnosis. A bundle of several skills is involved in deciphering meaning from messages that reach individuals; to call all of these skills literacy is confusing. Where Compaine stops is where we will now continue, which is to recognize and suggest names for the different skills each based on particular sense media. Before doing this we can draw support from Compaine for two of the proposals already discussed here. Compaine notes the distinction between sign agents and the messages they send and calls the former formats and the latter substance; then, following McLuhan, he says that "the message of the New Literacy notion is that changing processes and formats may have a long term effect on how users deal with substance" (p. 16).

Literacy is a term that should be reserved to refer to the skill of decoding messages presented visually by writing or other codes such as semaphore and also to the skill of encoding, or writing. For technical reasons, the use of the term literacy should stop here; it should not include the ability of dictating prose, composing spoken verse, or assessing the aesthetics or philosophy of one's own or others' literary works. Parallel to literacy, the British magazine *New Society* (21 February, 1985, p. 12) recently realized that as numeracy meant the ability to deal with the meanings inherent in numbers then one could identify a skill they called *graphicacy*, which is the ability to communicate "through maps, signs, plans, symbols and models." Here, one could accept the idea of the term graphicacy, although it could be strongly argued from empirical evidence that it should itself be subdivided into two or three separate skills for which separate terms are needed. However, it might be advisable and harmonious to seek a term from the Latin rather than the Greek roots, so as to keep on a level with literacy; thus, "picturacy" might be a better term. The distinction between this and the ability to decode semaphore, which involves an alphabetic code that has to be composed to yield words, is clear. There is also a problem with *New Society*'s reference to numeracy, for numbers can be dealt with if read from the page, or if heard by the ear; it is likely that numeracy as a higher order skill that is really mathematical proficiency is an entity based on two other lower order skills, which are abilities to make meanings of numbers encountered by eye and by ear.

It is known from Africa (Wober, 1976) that many people who have no difficulty with reading text do have considerable difficulty in interpreting pictures. This demonstrates first that what *New Society* calls graphicacy or we call picturacy is different from literacy, but it is further known that skills of inference from films are yet different again from those of decoding meaning in still pictures and diagrams. Therefore, it is worth listing three skills based on the visual medium; literacy, still picturacy, and moving picturacy. It will be remembered that it has often been maintained that there is a neurological basis, too, for distinguishing between literacy and picturacy skills; in the former, the information is processed preferably in the left part of the brain, in the latter two cases, in the right. It will now be realized that we are distinguishing and naming separate skills based on attention to the medium by which a sense is addressed and also by distinctions concerning the sign agents involved. Two other kinds of sign agents, therefore, require attention before we turn vision to another sense. One kind carries numbers; and it may not matter whether these are on a screen, a dial, or in print on a page, though it may make a difference if they move according to their own pace (as in meters or in such items as pages of teletext or travel information boards). The second sign agent here is the human body, which delivers messages of expression written on the face or in bodily posture and movement. Again, it may be taken for granted that viewers can accurately know meanings carried from these sources; however, simply to raise the possibility of different skills being involved, by applying the scope of a naming system, points to the greater likelihood that, especially across cultures, but even within them, not all perceivers are equally skilled in the practice of what we can call "expressionacy" and "gesturacy." Empirical work might show that movement in these matters, as with numbers or words, introduces a new element so that "motionacy" might be recognized as yet a different (although likely to be overlapping) skill.

The bodily origins of expressionacy, gesturacy and motionacy involve a reflexive mechanism, which is probably not called into play by most exercises of literacy or numeracy. Thus, when we see a facial expression, bodily gesture, or movement, we may relate it to our own assumption of such expressions or gestures; some signs might encourage imitation, such as smiling, but others, involved in aggression for example, might encourage opposite internal gestural responses. These, in turn, might interact with the extent to which one accurately decodes the signs one is seeing. Reeves and Lang (1986) have reported that screen scenes involving implied reactions of flight produced greater cortical arousal in the right hemisphere, but scenes that did not stimulate potential physical relocation produced greater arousal in the left hemisphere. Again, this is different when the sign agent is a real person with regard to whom one has to respond in a real manner, and when the sign agent is a representation on page picture or screen, when the viewer's real response system is not so easily engaged. The distinction can be illustrated with examples of children who, before they fully realize that the screen is not real, react kinetically to threats of danger such as posed by wild animals or phantoms, and similarly, from the cross-cultural literature where accounts are found of audiences who shout advice at the screen Tarzan to avoid the dangers he is unaware of behind him. In this case we would say that such audiences are 'gesturate' in that they properly interpret the menace of an attacker, but they are not fully 'moving picturate' in that they fail to some extent to take the screen contents as representations rather than as real. In any case, we grasp that at least two skills are involved in this case; they are both visual but one (gesturacy) more readily calls into play the internal medium of proprioception activating the right cortical hemisphere than does the other (moving picturacy), which also reportedly involves the right cortex.

It is useful to extend the taxonomy of coding skills across the remaining senses, before raising two major questions about the whole range of these skills. Audition is the next most important sense after vision, and this is reached by what can be called "softspeakers" (the human voice, telephone, and earphones) and loudspeakers such as nonpersonal radio, television, and paging systems (the distracting etymology of which takes us back to that medieval court player the page, whose meaning was not that of a human sign-bearer like a leaf of paper, but simply that of a pedo or child).

Through audition we deal with words processed, we are told, in the left side of the brain and with music, processed in the right. Whatever is meant by music may seem easily distinct from speech to the Western European language tradition, but many world languages from Africa to China are tonal in which the melodic aspect of the sounds is used to carry meaning in a far more complex and precise way than is the case with the extent of intonation found in English. This not only brings verbal language into interaction with the whole brain in a way that is apparently less the case with English, but in so doing it interacts in a different way with the visual medium which, psychoneurologists report, delivers its nonverbal material (plans, pictures, diagrams) to the right rather than to the left side of the brain for cognitive processing. To refer to the skills of decoding softspeaker messages, one might suggest the terms oracy, which has a connotation of person-to-person (rather than a shared, person-to-multitude) social context and musicacy. Oracy differs from literacy because of the medium and hence the primary sense involved and also because literacy involves the alphabetic subcode that is necessary to compose syllables (and thence words); in oracy the syllables are given as primary units. The distinction can be explored by examining anagrams. The words tear and rate involve the same letters, but they combine to yield different meanings; moreover, te-r is almost certain to be understood as tear, but r-te could be taken for rote or rite as well as rate; thus, letters each do a precise piece of work in a way that has no corresponding subunit in the skill of oracy, unless one wishes to argue that phonemes are equivalent to letters.

Moving from oracy and musicacy to the senses of olfaction and taste, the framework of comparison reveals that an important distinction between encoding and decoding skills can more readily be recognized here than, for example, with literacy. To make meaning of smells, one makes distinctions between the chemical attributes of complex molecules which suggests the term moleculacy. Moleculacy extends across a wide range from perfumes to unpleasant odors and tends to develop meanings at an affective rather than at a cognitive level. It is valuable to make the distinction between the perceiver, and the skills of getting the olfactory "message" right, and the sender, which is often inanimate, but where animate is often poorly organized. Bodily smells are an essential component of emotional stimulus and, to a considerable degree, are not under articulate control of the sender. The world of perfume attempts to tackle this, but many people say they buy and use what they themselves like, rather than attempt to control the olfactory messages that have particular meanings for those to whom one wishes to communicate. Decoding is thus very different from encoding in the world of olfaction and its skill of moleculacy and points to the need to be alert to similar distinctions in the cases of musicacy and literacy.

Among the bodily senses of touch, proprioception, and thermal awareness, only the first will be dealt with here. This sense has been developed among the blind to yield a skill that can be called tactile literacy and which is distinct from the ability to take meanings from bodily contact with the limbs and faces of others in a way that is analogous to the difference between visual literacy and picturacy. The messages in bodily contact, from handshakes to stroking, punches, nose rubbing in cultures where this is practiced, and kissing need skillful encoding and decoding and can both, for the present, be called tactacy. Proprioception and thermal awareness involve little encoding of cognitive meanings (though proprioception is eloquent in the experiences of sport and dance), but both are mainly cases of internal awareness rather than of communication between others.

LEARNING AND USING
DIFFERENT MEDIA SKILLS

Having examined the range of senses and the skills which their uses entail and offer opportunities for communication channels of different merits and drawbacks, we can put forward the two questions that are the keys to a satisfactory understanding of how new message systems may appeal in particular ways. The two questions are first, whether and how different message systems engage with ideas or emotions; and second, relating to complexity and ubiquity, by what age the skills involved in using message systems generally are, or indeed can be established.

It is tempting at first to suspect an interrelationship between the cognitive and affective components of communication skills. Music and musicacy are poorly developed vehicles for getting ideas across but have rich depth of emotional range; words and literacy, on the other hand, have a high capacity for carrying ideas which, may at first be thought to overshadow the emotional potential of the ideas. Pictures and picturacy are less agile than the written word at conveying ideas but are able to have marked and differentiated emotional content. Incidentally, as with olfactory communication, the difference between encoding and decoding skills is more easily recognized in picturacy than in writing and reading words. Of course, readers do develop a full range of emotional experience from what they read, but this does not arise directly from the letters or words themselves but rather from the internal ideas and associations that these words generate. The emotional scope of listening to poetry (or reading it into the mind's ear) is likely to be an outcome of a complex interplay between the tonal aspect of words and their music and the ideas they carry.

The chemical senses of smell and taste are not well developed routes for conveying ideas or facts between people, but they do connect well with feelings. The sense of taste is probably not explored very often to its limits, so that most people, in cultures where the economy delivers more than a simple subsistence, aim for a modest range of pleasant taste experience that happens to coincide with the basic needs to eat and drink. In some cultures, as in the United States, where people chew gum, or in the Third World, where they chew various mildly hallucinogenic vegetable concoctions, taste experience has been separated from nutrition and provides a means of personal experience; but this is correspondingly a very poor means of interpersonal communication.

To some extent taste may be a universal structure of human neurophysiology that reveals itself in verbal analogies (as in sweetness and bitterness), which correspond to survival-related realities. Thus, sweetness is experienced in the natural world from sugars, which are nearly always safe to consume and which give rapid energy; acid or bitterness are the tastes of gastric juices regurgitated or of berries and other vegetables of which many examples are unsafe to eat. Thorson and Reeves (1986) have cited evidence that young babies show cortical activity resembling that which accompanies pleasure when sugar is placed on the tongue, whereas mild acid produces the opposite effect; Harris and Booth (1986) reported that among 6-month-old babies, a significantly greater percentage accept high- rather than low-sodium cereal. This evidence suggests that responses to sweet and salt taste are likely to be biologically determined, at least among Western populations. The development of a sophisticated cuisine in which feelings rather than simple percepts or ideas are conveyed, of care for family or guests and the desire to bring about a differentiated welfare gives rise to a higher order skill that relates to moleculacy in the same way as being well read relates to mere mechanical literacy. Such a higher order skill is possessed by the gourmet but notably there is no particular name for it in English, although the somewhat tasteless construction alimentacy would be a suitable analog for the purpose.

The sense of smell seems to encounter a greater range of potential experience than is provided by taste. At the negative extreme are the smells of ordure and of putrefaction, clearly unsafe in proximity and therefore probably linked at a neurophysiological level to reactions of disgust and retreat. It may only be in a culture where death has come to be accommodated as a part of life and accepted as not final, but as a stage of spiritual evolution, that the smells of ordure and putrefaction can be unlearned as a source of dread. It is notable that most lists of "new media of mass communication" probably do not include tear gas, but it is a true member of the class of mass connecting sign agents nevertheless. Its cognitively simple but affectively powerful message is probably shared across all cultures. It is equally notable that Aldous Huxley's 'vision' (or sniff?) of soma notwithstanding, new technology has developed no pleasurable olfactory analog to tear gas. The nearest equivalents include one in the realm of vision, which is that of public displays of fireworks, a conceptually void but emotionally positive form of mass admmunication; and one in the realm of audition (and vision) which is the "pop" concert either in live performance or surrealized and taped or broadcast as pop video.

The second of our key questions about media and sensory skills concerns the ages at which they are commonly grasped and used. Here the gateway opens to the possibility of differences between cultures and of the notion that the available techniques of communication help slowly to construct the patterns of sensibilities that prevail in the members of each culture. It is easy to see that even in schooled cultures fully supplied with print, effective literacy is not established until the age of seven; by contrast, moving picturacy in cultures where television is widespread is established at a useful level by age two. Working in Israel, Salomon (1979) reported that watching television by its own agency, unaided by explicit instruction, was associated with enhanced skills of still picturacy; that is, children with television experience were able to make inferences about what simple line-drawn pictures showed, more so than were children without television experience. Greenfield (1984) suggested beyond this that decoding television pictures is a self-taught skill, which equips people to tackle video games which, in turn, pave the way to higher order skills involving computer and word processors. These observations of television's supposed formative influence do not imply anything about literacy, and they are recorded in societies in which an appreciable amount of viewing was taking place.

Where there is no schooling, literacy is exceedingly unlikely to occur, let alone to be widespread. The possibilities then arise that members of cultures without schooling either have one less skill than is developed elsewhere or that they acquire other skills in compensation or as expressions of their creative and communicative urges and powers, which we might suppose are at a similar level of potential throughout mankind, simply being expressed in individual ways in different contexts. Whether or not they have pictures or letters on page or screen, nearly all cultures have mechanical sign agents with which to make sounds, either for music or even, in a few cases, for lexical purposes. With the former, decoding skills are generally learned at an early age, say from 2 to 4 years of age so that simple tunes and rhythms can be detected and enjoyed. Notably, encoding skills are formed significantly later and, depending on the complexity of the sign agents or instruments involved, may be restricted to only a few members of the society. Language is, however, a cross-cultural universal, and it must be true that an adequate ability to decode and encode is developed from the age of two onwards, not reaching its full capacity until at least 10 years later. Here, the auditory skills of oracy (in its encoding and decoding versions) can be accelerated and deepened by formal instruction, possibly with the aid of parallel progress in literacy skills.

The ages at which the visual skills of expressionacy, gesturacy and motionacy are established are not as well defined, but it seems very likely that they begin to be organized at an early age, between one and two, and that they develop to quite an effective level without a great deal of explicit instruction. This places these visual skills at a developmental level alongside of those of oracy and musicacy. Oracy links more naturally with the world of literacy, whereas musicacy links with the less well recognized skills of mobilacy and posturacy, the ingredients of what is commonly called body language. Note, the skills of mobilacy and posturacy are those of interpreting the meaning or experience of one's own body movement and posture to oneself and do not involve vision and deciphering the acts of others. These sense data are said to be processed preferentially in the right side of the brain, where they would be available for integration with visual nonverbal information about the posture and movement of others. Thus, it is easy to suppose why body language can begin to be learned at an early age, coming well before literacy, and which may therefore earn the title of the "queen of communication skills."

Although it is now clear that communication skills are not all learned at the same ages, or with the same degree of self-tuition, and that for some important skills decoding probably comes before the ability to encode (though for some basic survival indicators needed to inform others of a baby's bodily discomfort which it wants rectified, encoding probably comes before decoding), it is tempting to suppose that there is some way in which all these skills are structurally equivalent. Thus, a word in print carries a meaning that reaches the brain via the eye; a complex sound made by the human voice carries a similar meaning brought to the brain by the ear. Neither sign needs in itself to be totally exact and restricted to a singular form; thus, type faces vary enormously in shape and size, and different colored inks can make one rendering of a written word extremely different from another. Similarly the timbre, pace, and volume of voices can make one sound rendering of a word extremely different from that of another rendering. Nevertheless, meanings are accurately attributed to an impressive degree, though a young child can grasp the essentials of speech by use of its skill of oracy while it does not begin to develop a command of literacy until much later because the alphabetic code adds a level of complexity to the visual task and the infant is given much more experience with spoken language, developed responsively to the baby's own utterances. Look-see methods of teaching reading try to avoid the complexity of the alphabet by treating words in effect as pictograms. Success with this method will rely on concentration on few signs and repetition and will remain tied to particular print forms until the child works out for itself (or with explicit help) that each letter has its particular identity, at which stage the new learning method becomes the same as the old.

A thorough review of the skills involved in personal and mass communication now reveals that the production of writing and its reading are probably the most complex of these skills. To learn to read and to write generally requires formal external aid; and although it is taken for granted in literate Western societies that the abilities to decode still and moving pictures are autonomously acquired, as is oracy, in some cultures these visual coding skills also require formal instruction so that people can become proficient all in the same way. Conventions of picture meaning have to be standardized; otherwise there is no basis for assuming that signs can be understood as intended.

MESSAGE SYSTEMS, MEDIA, AND MODES OF SENSIBILITY

The idea that message systems may have wide ranging effects on society reflects the thinking of many scholars over the last 50 years. Several have focused on the role of print, from Elias (1962) to Eisenstein (1979) and Postman (1982) past the great milestone of McLuhan (1962). These authors assert that widespread literacy following the arrival of print has caused people to think and feel differently than they would have done without such a development. Print users store and compare opinions and facts, develop individual viewpoints and a taste for privacy, and strive for intellectual mastery and control over others and over the environment. Antonius (1938) has told how the introduction of presses into Beirut by American missionaries in the mid 19th century "set in train a revival of the Arabic language and, with it, a movement of ideas which, in a short lifetime, was to leap from literature to politics" (p. 37). Later, observing the differences in individual sensibility and social organization between preprint culture, whether in Europe or in Africa, and print-served societies, McLuhan went on to assert that television would accomplish as radical a change again, reversing the developments associated with print. While "the phonetic alphabet translates man from the magical world of the ear to the neutral visual world" (p. 18) television was likened to the message systems of preprint served cultures in McLuhan's aphorism "the new electronic interdependence recreates the world in the image of a global village" (p. 31). It is merely ironic that an explicit awareness of this idea probably circulates up to now primarily among scholars who are the best available examples of print-dominated sensibilities. Those who populate the supposed global electronic village appear not to be very explicitly aware of the fact.

What kind of evidence is there that abilities and sensibilities have changed over the 30-year advent of television in western countries?

There is anecdotal evidence that standards of handwriting have deteriorated; there is better substantiated sign that scholastic performances have faltered if not actually fallen in the United States; correlational studies show, without thereby proving anything, that heavier television viewers are likely to be lower achievers on various cognitive tests. Gaddy (1986) has shown that distinct links between measures of overall television viewing and verbal and computational test scores mostly disappear when statistical controls are introduced for attributes, such as the educational capital in the home. In contrast to this, reading was positively related to verbal achievement (though not to computational) test scores.

Some of this evidence, and other studies discussed in the previous chapter, suggest to some that recent influences, possibly including television viewing experience, have produced changes attestable at an individual level. Cerulo (1984) has written of the "symbolic environment" at another level, in which television has "dramatically increased the diffusion of visual symbols . . . and generated a rise in the public's exposure to images" (p. 566). Here, she refers to visual images but neglects to observe that television provides as many and possibly as powerful acoustic images as it does visual ones. Arguing that the new visual ecology would affect the public, Cerulo showed that in the "crucial period of 1950 through 1960" while television ownership became practically universal in America, a parallel change occurred in the nature of illustrated magazine covers; they increasingly used visual symbols, with less use of labeling. Beniger (1983) had likewise just shown that political cartoons had come to use less verbal labeling, allowing the pictures to "speak" for themselves. These changes no doubt occurred in the style of printed artwork, but it is not possible to conclude that any corresponding change has been wrought in how skillfully people see, that is, in our new terms, that there has for this reason been an increase in picturacy. It may just be that editors and artists have come to present their material more nonverbally, reflecting an awareness of fashion shared at an elite professional level.

A more pervasive change has been claimed to have occurred by Volgy and Schwarz (1984) who note that "television's intense visual characteristic combined with its small picture . . . can create a sense of vicarious involvement and interaction with the characters and stories presented on the screen" (p. 761). Their evidence is that some people say they have participated in political activity, but other sources suggest that they have not done so (such as writing letters to, or telephoning officials). Volgy and Schwarz expected to find that undocumented activists watched more television and more news than did others, and this is what their results did show. Since Volgy and Schwarz's theorizing and evidence is at odds with that of Yuyama, mentioned earlier in this chapter, and also with the material on the subjective enjoyment and impact of various types of programs reported in Chapter 3, it is probably advisable to hold judgment of their claim in abeyance. However, it remains of interest because it points to a structural, or what some have called a formal, rather than a content-related effect of television on behavior and in their own words is "an element richly deserving further investigation" (p. 761).

How, then, might one open up the question of television's potential structural effects? One study was reported by Wilkus, Woelfel, Barnett and Fontes (1972) of the State University of New York at Buffalo, who noted Marshall McLuhan's assertions that the introduction of 'new media' have affected "the way in which individuals organize experience and fix perceptions." After mentioning the speculation about the balance in the use of the five senses, which should have provided them with their test quarry for study, Wilkus and his group chose for investigation another idea of McLuhan's, that message systems differ in the extent to which they are 'hot' or 'cool.' A hot medium is one that "extends one single sense in 'high definition.' A cartoon is 'low definition' simply because very little visual information is provided." McLuhan argued that print and certain associated "technologies" have been "hot, fragmented and exclusive, but in the age of television we see a return to cool values and the inclusive in-depth involvement and participation they engender" (McLuhan, 1964, p. 3). Taking a further cue from McLuhan that "a culture in which television is the dominant medium will produce a person characteristically different than will a culture based upon print," Wilkus and his colleagues assumed that the more that individuals are "exposed to cool media, like television, the greater should be their capability for recognizing patterns based on limited information."

It is possible to produce photographic prints of exposures with the amount of detail either enhanced or held back, so a test consisting of 36 pictures of ordinary household objects was prepared, with some pictures more detailed and full of information than others. Undergraduate subjects indicated their extent of use of six media (newspapers, radio, magazines, television, movies, and records and tapes). The upshot of this was that the measure of television use was not related to any other variable, be it the extent of use of some other medium or, more important, the pattern recognition performance on which the McLuhan argument would seem to predict a significant positive correlation. Wilkus et al. tried several other statistical procedures to combine data and in other ways to allow every chance for the expected effect to arise, but no such result appeared. Therefore they concluded that they "clearly fail to confirm the central hypothesis underlying the work of McLuhan" (p. 6).

Unfortunately, this is possibly too stringent a condemnation to utter. For the hot and cool hypothesis is probably the least well argued and supported (largely from literary critical analysis, of the kind referred to in our first two chapters) of McLuhan's ideas. It certainly remains to test McLuhan's other notion that a major change in the media environment (that is, the pathways used for information transfer, which call upon the "bundle of skills" referred to by Compaine) will promote a change in the balance in which each of these sense-based skills is developed. There are two particular ways in which this contention can be examined. One is to look for some effect associated with the arrival of literacy and the use of print, either by comparing cultures with and without print, or by contrasting people within a culture who differ in the extent of their familiarity with print; the other option is to look for some effect associated with the use of television.

On the trail of print, working in Africa Wober (1976) following Biesheuvel and others observed that Africans appeared to excel at skills involving integration of visual, auditory, and kinaesthetic sense data together with feedback from motor performance. Not only were test data reported suggesting that Africans equalled or excelled over other groups in certain tasks involving processing of mixed sensory inputs, evidence was also available that Africans lagged in performances requiring decoding and encoding of symbols of certain kinds presented and detected only visually. It was suggested that the absence or recency of print and a developed tradition of picturacy, together with an alternative development of systems of auditory symbols in tonal language and music, and heightened use of body languages involving what we may call mobilacy and posturacy, might have been partly responsible for the patterns of test results obtained. The term sensotypes was suggested for the particular structures of individual sensibility and competence in decoding and encoding that would result in any one sensory environment that was substantially different from another.

Returning from Africa to work in the field of television, it was then asked (Wober, 1983b) whether television viewing might constitute a sufficiently new sensory ecosystem with an impact on individuals' information processing practices that might be reflected in the kinds of imagery they reported using and preferring. It was known from Sheehan's work in the United States (1971) that people differed in the extent to which they reported clarity of imagery based in the different sensory modes. Sheehan minimized the possibility of different sensory styles characterizing different individuals, but his results did clearly indicate that his sample as a whole could be termed visual rather than auditory in preferred style, and they certainly reported much weaker olfactory imagery. At that stage it did not appear to Sheehan that there might be culturally linked differences in the extent to which people possessed the attributes he had measured.

Self-reports of imagery practices at first sight seem unlikely to be a source of reliable evidence about how people really do process information; however, from Australia Richardson (1977, p. 38) has reported that self-reported imagery vividness "remains relatively stable over time" even when measured with different tests, and Kieras (1978) in an extensive review judged that "imagery is one of the most powerful factors influencing memory for verbal materials" (p. 551). A reasonable argument therefore exists for using measures of imagery style as a possible key to the exploration of effects that might be associated with major alterations in the sensory ecosystem of a culture, such as appear to be presented by the arrival of television.

Wober (1983b) pointed out that in Great Britain, a person born in 1950, would have been likely to have been familiar with television from the age of five; anyone born later would have been increasingly likely to have been thoroughly familiar with television. The age band 16 to 34, currently identified as young adults in British public opinion survey practice therefore correspond with a "television generation;" the next age band of, 35 to 54, was one whose members had lived until 10 years of age without the experience of television. Those aged 55 and over were definitely of a pretelevision generation. Thus, survey questions on imagery experience in visual and auditory sense fields could conveniently be analyzed to examine whether differences might exist that would correspond with changes in the sensorium that one might associate with television. Developmental theorists generally claim that cognitive styles are established before adulthood, so imagery preferences for particular senses would be laid down in the context of the media environment experienced in childhood and should not be altered greatly by an altered environment encountered as an adult.

Interestingly, two contrary theories predict what might happen to sensory preferences or practices with the arrival of a major change in the sensory environment of a culture. The first and more obvious theory, which one may associate with the arguments put forward above by Cerulo and Beniger, is that television greatly adds to the stock of visual information requiring to be processed, and much of it is not totally matched by the spoken words that accompany it. Therefore, well-trained viewers might come to think more in visual terms, and this could be reflected in the extent to which they report the use of visual imagery. An opposite theory can be drawn from the work of McLuhan and Postman, and this leans to some extent on displacement of print. If television viewing means that people read less, then for all the visual processing done, it is not very complex because it is to a considerable extent self-evident, whereas print presents the challenge of decoding the alphabetic level symbols, as well as the mere shapes of letters which, in themselves, are meaningless. Moreover, television is not just visual because it carries essential spoken content, and much that is learned from the research on how people watch television (see Chapter 3) implies that people do to some extent select what they want to see and "make meaning" of it (rather than just sit back passively to be painted upon by the beams emanating from the set). This means that the sound content of television is important. In all, then, with the displacement of print and the substitution of a message system in which the sounds may be more taxing than the pictures, television might be expected to promote the development of auditory imagery.

Wober (1983b) devised several items designed to explore imagery practices (such as: "when reading something in print does it seem as if a voice is reading out what is written, inside your head?"), and analysis of these suggested that there may be three kinds of such imagery. One can be called *crossmodal*, as in the example quoted, in which an internal image is generated in a sense other than the one by which the information was originally supplied. In *Intramodal* imagery a percept is internally repeated in the same sense mode as that in which it was first encountered. *Automodal* imagery refers to the production of an image by choice, in whatever sense mode is preferred. Thus, in adding numbers some prefer to see visual symbols such as dots or scales, while others hear voices (their own, or others') speaking the calculations.

The results of several surveys were that younger adults were generally more likely to report auditory automodal imagery than were older people. This would fit in with a substitutional rather than a formatively visual explanation of television's effects: however, the situation is more complicated than this. It was also possible to obtain correlations between reports of imagery practices and the amounts of television viewing, overall, or within various program types. The outcome of these observations was that people reporting more or preferred auditory imagery actually tended in some ways to be lighter users of television; in contrast, those with stronger visual imagery tended not only to use, but also to appreciate, their viewing more. This correlational evidence, albeit weakly, tended to support the first, direct, rather than the second, substitutional, possible explanation of an influence of television.

To help settle this conflict, it was necessary to find a population in which the youngest adult age group was not a "television generation." Until recently, the white and colored population of South Africa who are, moreover, like the British population, also literate, constitute such a group. If television's presence was actually causing the increased auditory imagery reported among British younger adults, the imagery should not be observed in South Africa. The result (Wober, 1985c) was that South African adults not only showed higher auditory imagery claims in the younger age groups but did so to a greater extent than did the British adult samples. This goes a long way to setting aside any possible explanation that television is causing an increase in reported auditory imagery, so the second part of the substitutional theory is discounted. It is still possible that the first part of the substitution theory, that suggests that print familiarity is reduced by the advent of television, and that this has more powerful consequences for shaping the sensibility, remains plausible. The South African sample, at all ages, was more likely to report auditory imagery than were the British groups, but the same was true to a greater extent with regard to visual imagery. Overall, the highest visual imagery claims were found among the South Africans, and the lowest auditory imagery reports were in Great Britain. These results may support a hypothesis that the prominence of print in peoples' lives is linked with increased visual imagery. It was not possible to have the South African results correlated with amounts of television viewing, although that had now begun and indeed the questions had been put to a television viewing sample.

Supporting Gaddy's (1986) results from the United States, two further projects in Great Britain add weight to the possibility that print has some formative effect on some of the structures of mental life. In one, over 300 schoolchildren provided evidence on how much they watched television, read books, went to the cinema, and listened to music; they also indicated the extent to which their feelings were stirred by experiences with each different message system (Wober, 1985b). These schoolchildren also indicated the extent to which they experienced or used seven kinds of imagery, and several correlations were found between these imagery items and the extent to which the children either read themselves, or were read to by their parents. Only one correlation emerged with television use, and that was negative, showing heavier viewers were less likely to report one of the auditory imagery experiences. Sensitivity to information encountered through different message systems again showed positive links with print familiarity and, to a lesser extent, with the use of music; again, those who used television more extensively tended also to acknowledge lower levels of sensitivity to messages encountered from music and from books.

A second study used a sample of children, aged from 5 to 12, who filled in, or had parents fill in for them television appreciation diaries showing what programs the children saw and how much they liked them. An additional questionnaire included measures of the familiarity with other message systems (how much they read, were read to, heard music on radio, and so on) and of the occurrence of imagery, again with seven items. Factor analysis revealed five factors or clusters of message system use and familiarity, including an auditory one, film and video, computers, television, and print. Regression analyses showed that only one factor, print, had positive relationships with the extent of reports of imagery, involving experience of reading or being read to. Television use had a less significant but negative link with the imagery scores where adult programs were concerned; however, children who saw more children's programming did not have any negative link with reported imagery experience. These results tend to fit in with the previous ones from adolescents and adults and suggest that, as McLuhan and his predecessors had claimed, print may indeed have a formative effect not just on the content of people's thinking but also with the very machinery of thought, that is, the sense modes at least and the ability to repeat mentally or even to generate images not just visually but also auditorally. On the other hand, the further McLuhan contention that television may have as marked a structural effect as print is not supported by these results.

If television does have a structural effect, at least on the kinds of measure investigated here, the mechanism is likely to be an indirect one. It may work if by watching television more people thereby use print less than they otherwise would have done. The common argument that the level of aesthetic quality of mass readership in the days before the arrival of television was no better (or worse) than the aesthetic level of what is viewed on the screen does not touch the substance of the issue being discussed here, which deals with the mechanism rather than the content of messages. The question arises whether the same results would occur if the screen comes increasingly to carry text and the skills demanded by viewers come to include literacy as well as picturacy. Much that Greenfield (1984) has reported about the use of word processing in schools and by children at home suggests that what we may call CADS (Coding And Decoding Skills) may not depend on the precise nature of the sign agent being used by the message system (paper pages or screen text) or even on the medium (the sensory channel, such as audition, in being read to, or vision, used in reading), but rather on the level of coded complexity of the message.

Is there any evidence to support this view that moving picturacy may be a skill that has little structural consequence for the development of other skills? Using a method in which they are almost the only practitioners, Larson and Kubey (1983) supplied 75 students with electronic pagers, which were called up at irregular intervals, when participants had to fill out self-reports indicating what they were doing and how they felt. The information allowed television to be compared with music listening in a number of ways. Although viewing was recorded as a primary activity nearly five times as often as was music listening unaccompanied by the screen (it is not clear how much "viewing" was absorbed as essentially a musical experience), the latter was characterized by much more positive mood states. Larson and Kubey state that "music is more involving . . . because it speaks to adolescent concerns . . ." (p. 25); the words of rock music tell of turbulent feelings and it is supposed therefore that this kind of music functions importantly at a verbal level. Note, that oracy and musicacy have been tentatively identified (though not by Larson and Kubey) as separate skills, but these researchers suggest that teenagers are adept at both.

Curiously, and well against the pontifications of McLuhan and his followers, Larson and Kubey conclude that if young people have been "socialised by the electronic medium of adult culture—television—we might expect greater social continuity in the transition between generations" (p. 28). Socialization by "youth music" points to a greater possibility of change across the generations. Thus, television is seen by no means as a message system that is revolutionary in its structure (let alone content), but music of certain kinds, because of the content which is supplied to it by its largely adult creators, is considered more influential. While Larson and Kubey's material suggests that influences associated with particular message systems arise from the kind of attention given to the range of meanings they carry, it was a parallel hypothesis but one working at a structural level that was put forward to try to explain why the younger adults in both Great Britain and South Africa had the more frequent claims of auditory imagery; regardless of the presence or absence of television, the last 30 years have witnessed a great expansion in the availability of music. This is evident from the spread of medium and long-play discs to the multiplication of radios and "Walkmen." The younger generation have had more occasion to encounter acoustic (nonverbal) images in both South Africa and Great Britain; and sounds present more of a challenge to the perceiver than do pictures, as a source from which to realize some meaning. In McLuhan' terms nonverbal sounds are "cool" while pictures are "hot."

Here it is worth mentioning the work of Milton Sherman (1985) who has commercially protected "Earsight," a word he devised to refer to the crossmodal visual images evoked by radio. In fact Sherman refers to radio as a "visual medium." He does not make a clear distinction between the verbal and nonverbal content of radio, but his examples in a "presentation" included a number of sound effects, which complement and extend the images suggested, at least to some listeners, by the spoken text. Sherman cites support for his contention that "the eye of the ear can be as effective as the ear of the eye" (p. 127) from experiments with children reported by Greenfield (1984) in which radio was found to be, in some circumstances, a stronger stimulus to (visual) imagination than was television. As a matter of fact, neither Greenfield nor Sherman appear to have shown evidence about auditory images evoked by sights. The power of sound is likely to arise because the perceiver has to produce his or her own visual images upon which one may project and elaborate added meanings. These suggestions may be given by radio, which does not fully provide filled in detail (McLuhan's "cool" definition), whereas the screen more nearly does this task for the perceiver, undercutting any need for him or her to develop much Amount of Invested Mental Effort ("AIME" referred to by Salomon [1979] who showed that this was an important precondition for learning). Paradoxically, this reveals wordless television as a more difficult message system than is radio, as it may be easier to evoke one's own pictures to complement sounds that are heard, than it is to supply words and hence ideas to pictures one encounters on the screen. Word-filled television has to be skillfully devised so that the words match the pictures in both their superficial content and the associations they evoke, if they are to work with and not against each other.

NEW INSIGHTS SHED LIGHT
ON THE CHANGING SCREEN

We are now armed with new ways of thinking about sign agents that reach particular senses via their corresponding media and about the skills required to decode and encode such messages. Do we have anything to say about the ways in which people will adapt to new sign agents, which tell us anything more than what other scientists are saying without the particular analytic structure developed here? First, in the jargon being used here, there are not really any new media; the media being used by new sign agents are the ones that connect with the seven senses and which always have done. What is changing are the ratios relating the uses of each of the media to each other; and more particularly, the levels of coding complexity that are being used across each medium. Let us now ask these questions: What are the new sign agents about which people are getting most excited, and why? Do these new agents present users with heightened demands to process messages arriving by particular pathways? Finally, how might users respond to new task demands, if indeed they are much different from old ones?

The first question will be dealt with in a limited perspective. We are not concerned here with the proprioceptive revolution brought about by widespread automobilacy or even with the advance by Suzuki training methods in inculcating performance and interpretational (hence also perceptual) skills in young musicians. We have decided to concentrate on the changing screen, consisting of videocassette recorders, TV games, and home computers and word processors, as well as teletext. Consistent with our attention to words, as tools of science, and to sharpening the meanings that terms are going to be expected to carry, we may applaud the clarifications supplied by Paisley and Chen (1984) who pointed out that "the terms 'videotex', 'videotext' and 'teletext' have been used inconsistently" (p. 109). They explain that "videotext" means words conveyed by broadcast or wired methods, whereas teletext refers to words (or crude diagrams) carried in the crevices of the orthodox television picture signal. Videotext (with the terminal t) apparently "refers to text transmitted by cable, telephone, or other non broadcast channels" (p. 111).

Amidst a host of contemporary writings, one by Wilson (1986) deals with "videotex" as all these things, so he has disregarded Paisley and Chen's distinction or advice. The position taken here is rigorously concerned with the viewpoint of the viewer. Those who drop the terminal t from videotext merely reveal their laziness or insensitivity to language, or both, particularly regrettable from any writer raising the banner of literacy, and the solecism is of little operational importance. It does, of course, provide a warning that the users may not be thinking clearly so that the reader can be vigilant to spot other implied misconceptions. The distinction between videotext and teletext may also be of little importance for the psychology of decoding processes. These distinctions, of course, do matter for the sociology and technology of production and distribution. What matters for the viewer, however, is whether the words or pictures are presented on a screen and whether the viewer has any control over the pace and position of the displays. Control is important as it enables the user to take in information at a rate at which it can be digested.

The new message systems about which there is such excitement first include various means of delivering entertainment to the screen, where the viewer has no control. It may matter little whether the technique is to pass electric current through cable, laser beams through glass, or radiation from transmitter to aerial with or without a satellite in between. The result is a picture or a screenful of words available according to the design of the sender. The skills needed to decode these images are mostly those of moving picturacy, oracy, musicacy, and literacy; and these skills have been in play with orthodox television. As we surmise from indirect evidence, the first three skills dominate, and literacy is least called upon or developed by the experience. It is true that capacity of cable systems is such that room is created for the supply of texts, but the economics of production allied with the nature of viewer demand means that the tendency has been for multiplication to provide for the first three skills to the continuing disadvantage of literacy. Music video is said to be a radically new phenomenon of the late 1970s and 1980s, and it is certainly new; however, the skills it engages are those of moving picturacy and musicacy. Literacy is not involved at all, and oracy is at a disadvantage for two related reasons. First, the beat and volume of the music are often so insistent that these nonverbal elements dominate the attention to the exclusion of words being sung; second, both the cascade of visual images (which rapid cuts, dissolves inversions, rotations, and other tricks emphasize) and the torrent of sounds are information that preoccupies the right side of the cerebral cortex. Words are said to be dealt with preferentially in the left side of the brain, and the process of transfer and attention to this aspect of the information is quite likely to be impeded by the other content of music video.

The next family of new sign systems gives the viewer control over when the orthodox broadcast messages will be used. Here we have videocassettes and videodiscs, which allow programs to be descheduled (the term "time shift" suggests that time is being shifted, which it can not be), entered at any point, repeated, held still, and, with sufficient apparatus and determination, recombined in different sequences with additions and omissions. All the evidence is that a public rapidly acquires these devices and that they are used principally for entertainment. A Swedish report (Monten, 1985) indicates that 18% of households there had videocassette recorders, but only 3% had home computers. The summary text explains that "Sweden is on the threshold of the new era in the areas of Cable-TV, satellites and personal computers;" this is a common enough shorthand way of heralding a time of change, but the detail is more precisely that VCR, unmentioned in the preceding summary, is the really widespread innovation, whereas the other devices are still at the stage of a shallow threshold at least in Sweden. A British study (Wober, 1985a) reported that 25% of British homes had VCRs; soon after, Greenberg, Gunter, Wober and Fazal (1986) found that among a sample of British children (weighted to be nationally representative) 53% said they had a VCR at home. Watkins and Brim (1985) said that 15% of households in a Michigan sample had VCRs, while 7% had computers. Levy and Fink (1984) had already noted that 6 million American households had VCRs and projected conservatively that at least one fourth of the nation's homes were likely to be so equipped by 1990.

Three reasons why that total had already been surpassed in Great Britain, where Hannah (1982) confidently expected "three quarters of all households to have a VCR by the end of the decade" (p. 296), illustrate the ways in which diffusion of these devices relate to economic elements and to others of needs and gratifications. Such reasons have little to do with effects that might be wrought upon the structure of thought; instead, they pose problems in the field of social control of content, since it is difficult for a society, or for responsible members of a family to hide materials they do not wish to reach more immature members of the society or of a family. One reason for British enthusiasm over VCR is likely to be the high appeal of existing broadcast services. Viewers' desires to see competing programming lead them to preserve through the VCR the chance to see what they have missed. This short-term hoarding is different from a library use of VCR, which exists as well but which is perhaps less extensively pursued. A second reason for the difference between American and British rates of diffusion of VCR is that the American alternative to a limited array of network broadcast choice had been to pay for extra cable channels, the strategy being to expand, rather than to conserve, the basic array of available ingredients. A third reason for different rates of expansion is likely to relate to marketing campaign decisions; for some years, the Sony manufacturers of VCRs had been in litigation with a U.S. program maker and until that action was settled it was clearly a dubious climate in which to press ahead with marketing the machines in the United States. In Europe, without such litigation in progress, Great Britain presented a market with good broadcasting worth copying onto machines, a public very willing to buy imported hardware, and a contrast with neighboring countries with less praised broadcast networks and more resistance to imported hardware. Great Britain, therefore, presented an excellent point of entry for the Japanese VCRs, which were energetically marketed. Apart from this market with its high quality software, another fertile territory for rapid diffusion is a society where there is much wealth accompanied by poor or censored broadcast services. Certain mid-Eastern countries fit this pattern and have a very high penetration with VCRs, on which people view imported and illicit programming (Boyd, 1985).

Levy and Fink (1984) report that in the United States, about half of all recordings will be played within 3 days, but that two out of five tapes are likely never to be replayed. The more frequent purpose was to deschedule material (they do not elaborate whether off air or from cable channels) but certain video materials such as how-to-do-it instructional programs had reasonable prospects as library ingredients. In a brief reference to "the old debate concerning television viewing and literacy" Levy and Fink consider this may become more salient as stored TV programs provide new competition to reading; this competition is likely to come most markedly from television's better quality material, such as adaptations of classic fiction. There is evidence (Wober, 1980b; Taylor and Mullan, 1986) that people who have both read a book and seen the screen adaptation just as often prefer the quality of the latter as that of the former. By the mid-1980s, a number of specialist video journalists were writing of the prospects of harnessing pairs of VCRs for home editing purposes. Here one meets the distinction between the coding and decoding skills of moving picturacy; yet there has been very little reported use of VCRs for such a creative purpose. If people have access to two VCRs, they much more readily use them privately for duplicating tapes than for editing them. It is only institutional groups that make much headway with encoding exercises, and the end of the 1980s are likely to see some progress with the marketing to private owners of easily used and affordable videocameras. These would clearly replace celluloid home movies and even much of the "family archives" market using still photography, just as film cameras in their time supplanted the longhand diary and scrapbooks of the 19th century as a means of recording personal milestones and of storing family history.

The overall indications from experience with videorecorders is that they have spread quickly in response to different combinations of needs and existing marketplace factors. Apparatus, which requires decoding skills already comfortably in place, far exceeds the availability and use of devices that call upon and perhaps develop new encoding skills. Nevertheless, there are signs that there will be a prosperous minority of people who respond to these opportunities. Significantly, their interests have been called by the bookish label "library" uses, both with regard to collecting published classics of the screen and also for family records. Equally significant, the physical videocassette box is sometimes made to resemble a bound volume, and there is as yet no appropriate term in use by which to call a "cassettary" as a cultural resource equivalent to the collection of books in the library. These library uses share one aspect of their primarily pictorial materials with print: They defy time, as semipermanent records, and involve that aspect of order, which McLuhan called "linearity" and associated particularly with print.

This characteristic of "linearity" is well examplified in the first nationwide videodisc project launched anywhere, the appropriately named *Domesday Disc*, produced in Great Britain by the BBC in 1986. To commemorate the 900th anniversary of the Domesday Book, the catalog of the nation's assets compiled in detail for King William the Conqueror, the Disc project constitutes an invention that is more brilliant for its social than for its hardware arrangements. Thousands of schools across the nation contributed basic geographic and social data on their area; and this collection, together with significant contemporary documents (probably including one by myself, a survey of attitudes during the Falklands War), forms the equivalent of nearly 1,000 print volumes but is all stored on two discs. The disc player, discs, linking minicomputer (to facilitate control of precise search and access) and screen cost less than £5,000, within range of affordability for the participating schools. Most who will buy the sets have contributed their own data and have a vanity-related motive to "bring home" this piece of themselves in today's history. Diffusion of this information system could thereby reach most of tomorrow's population, aided by a neat piece of "marketing." There have been, and will no doubt continue to be, hardware problems, but the motive to overcome these will be increased when other databank providers realize that a market for a new form of their wares has been created. For the users, no transformation of consciousness will have occurred; simply a new and deft way of accessing information including both print and pictures on the screen (both of which could be detained in hard copy as well) will have become available.

Apart from library and descheduling uses enjoyed by those who consider themselves responsible adults, the VCR (unlike the videodisc) gives an opportunity to young or irresponsible people in societies where broadcast content is under some control to evade that restraint. Others who consider themselves as hyperresponsible and who challenge the structure of the state can use VCR to view and to show material the state might wish to suppress. In Sweden, Roe (1985) reports that there was a panic over the finding that teenagers were viewing sadistically violent movies, otherwise certainly unavailable off air, on VCR. In Great Britain there was a similar concern about the spread of "videonasties," in particular just over 50 titles on a list including such items as *The Texas Chainsaw Massacre* and *Night of the Evil Dead*, the sales of which were prohibited by a fresh act of Parliament. Some controversy existed over the extent to which such items were being seen; one survey (Barlow and Hill, 1985) estimated that nearly half of youngsters below independent cinema-going age had seen at least one such movie, and 22% had seen four or more. This challenged the notion that such viewing was merely a passing fashion among teenagers to "prove their adulthood;" an ingenious survey (Cumberbatch, 1985) suggested that the extent of use may have been exaggerated by researchers presenting lists of titles whose plausibility produced false-positive responses. A less known survey, however, (Hartshorn, 1983) asked schoolchildren to write in their own titles; this method still yielded a high rate of encounter with such movies. Even when the 1985 legislation had been enacted, the sales and rental statistics from cassette shops showed that horror and macabre thrillers remained the most extensively used genre. This indicates to the broadcasters that there is a demand as yet unsatisfied on the public service airwaves, one which is being supplied in the United States by cable and more recently by cassette and in Great Britain by the latter. In Great Britain restraint continues in the mid-1980s over what is available for the 98% of the population who use broadcast television, and a concern that the advent of a deregulated market would gravely threaten the economics and mode of operation of the public broadcasting systems.

These studies give little indication that the new message systems of videorecording on tape or disc have done much to change the sensory environment of the using public, from what they have been accustomed to on television. Without introducing any interesting changes of sensory structure, however, they have posed problems for certain societies involving the content transmitted, the implications of which will be explored more fully in the final chapter. To some extent, content has also been an issue raised by initial users of video or "television" games. Most of these games are not "tele" (coming from afar, sent from a very few sources to very many users), not are they entirely video, but they are audio-visual-motor systems generally set up by individual users for themselves. For a time, and perhaps more in the United States than in Europe, critics were worried that gaming arcades were harmful for two reasons: habituation and loss in gambling and the violent content of many games, which led to aggressive behavior (e.g., see Brown, 1986). Attention soon turned from these negative preoccupations, however, to the more positive idea that game playing taught new skills and even supported old ones.

Some of the host of articles on the gaming phenomenon seem to be largely breathless attempts to prove that the writer is keeping pace with change. Black (1985, p. 82) for example starts by saying that because "in interactive literature you become . . . a participant . . . video gaming has Charles Dickens beaten hollow." Publishers have therefore "begun producing a series of real (sic) books . . . which . . . replicate the experience of video gaming off the printed page." This has had some initial success, but Black ends by realizing that "if you really want to become involved in a story, you can do it better in a book." Nevertheless Black surmises that what he calls "videracy" will spread so that his grandchildren will find it "easy to get by without a book, but impossible to cope in society without a computer;" this is considered possible because "the visual image is a natural language substitute for youngsters unwilling to do more than the minimum essential for survival . . . (but) . . . it is perhaps unfortunate that the visual image allows instant assimilation of certain types of information . . . while the printed word is slow and makes complex intellectual demands."

Black is saying here what has been explained previously, that picturacy is generally a less complex skill than is literacy, so that simple videogames can be used without literacy. Yet it is the print culture that has created the world of screen for picture and for computation. The screen and its pleasures are, therefore, a branch of the tree of the book, and if its user attempts to saw at the base of this branch it will fall. Our contribution here has been to identify the skills in what Black calls videracy more correctly than he has done and to make better deductions therefore than he has. In brief, one needs literacy and numeracy to program and to play with screen games and not just the moving picturacy and mobilacy that are involved in the early generation of pursuit games. Those who are sufficiently literate to operate computers (which themselves can train in literacy) will, to some extent, want books, thus sustaining the culture of the latter.

An opposite view has been offered in the warning by Haratonik (1984, p. 10) who played down the potential of "Pac Man as Pedagogue," noting that while computer-based screen games "would go a long way toward developing the logical, linear, sequential skills associated with literacy" this might be aborted by "a corporate thrust designed to provide a brave new world of entertainment disguised as knowledge to a mass society of semi-literates." This is to take a more Machiavellian view of the functioning of business enterprise in the American system than many others have taken, who would think perhaps that entrepreneurs would seek to sell to demand; if this was expressed in educational terms, this is what the products would cater to. Any marshaling of products into less demanding and away from more demanding materials would reflect rather than predetermine market requirements.

A more optimistic possibility has been presented by Greenfield (1984) and by Strover (1984) who explained that while preindustrial and industrial culture equipped its members to "handle simple two-variable problems . . . the information age concerns . . . the goal . . . to understand how large numbers of variables interact." The new challenge is to "think in terms of stochastic processes, game theory . . . or Markovian dynamics." Not only does this sound impressive, but it is also suggested that videogames are alluring and simulate the new world at large in "requiring the management of increasing numbers of variables during problem solving" (p. 12). Games are devised so that the player never does win but is made to feel just one step away from winning. In ascending a ladder of increasingly complex rules and phenomena the player comes to recognize the program of the game. Unless these programs build in stimulus randomness, however, (which some do), the player can eventually come to learn the exact pattern of challenges presented. In such cases screen games become boring and the likeness between video games and an advanced model of the information age collapses in favor of a better analogy, not fully expressed by the same writer, between more traditional games and pastimes, and the ability to cope with an environment presenting unpredictably altering values on each of several dimensions. Consider the case of a young child learning to be herdsman in an African society; he deals with variations in weather, motion of marauding animals and human enemies, and the waywardness of his own animals. Or, consider the soccer player or player of the game monopoly, preinformation age pursuits, which also involve multiple variables on which some unexpectedness of behavior occurs and must be handled. It may be that people who do not develop mastery over computer games suffer in some extent in self-esteem, whereas those who do become competent, though to a limited level, may have inflated ideas of their competence that would not equip them as well in the greater randomness of real life than that found on the nonwinning, but nonlosing, screen.

More usually, however, since computers are spreading quickly as devices essential to occupational functioning in commerce and industry, young people have to become competent in their use, and it is important to examine the ways in which adoption of computers has taken place. Watkins and Brim (1985) reported from their Michigan site that well over three fourths of teachers in elementary schools had used computers at some time with their classes. They estimated that pupils encountered an average of 1 computer-using hour per week, each, and teachers were eager to press for more. Notably, Watkins and Brim found that their teacher sample reported no sex differences in the development of computer operating skills. On a broader scale these authors cite a national U.S. survey in 1983 that reported 3% and 5% of the American population owned personal computers, but that the proportion among households with adolescents was 16%. Uses were more often said to be educational than was "mere" gaming, and if they did provide enhancement of skills then the purchasing patterns indicated an increase in knowledge gap between the advanced and the less advancing sectors of society.

A warning to this effect had already been sounded by Day, Barnett, Kim, and Miller (1984) on the basis of their survey of nearly 2,500 households in upper New York State; they found that adopters and intending adopters differed from nonadopters in being better off economically and in following friends who set the computer ownership fashion which they followed. Day concluded that a "computer knowledge gap may be developing which may systematically exclude members of the lower classes from the advantages of the information revolution."

One of the impediments in acquiring computer skills is described by Rauschenberg (1984) as computerphobia. Rauschenberg, who mentions the drive to implement "computer literacy" throughout the nation's high schools sees the difficulty for some individuals as a part of a more general syndrome of communication anxiety, and she has devised a questionnaire with which to measure this phenomenon. Curiously, individuals' measured computerphobic correlated significantly with an anxiety over public speaking rather than with anxiety involving getting on with other people one at a time. On the face of it, an interaction with a computer is a dyadic one, and it would therefore follow that a correlation between dyadic communication anxiety and computerphobia might be greater than that between public speaking and computerphobia. Rauschenberg does not discuss her findings at length, other than to suggest that highly computerphobic pupils would respond best in one-to-one tutoring. The result suggests, however, that marked differences exist among individuals in the ways in which they perceive the computerized screen socially. Some may regard it as an impersonal tool, inanimate even though it uses the ideas and information programmed into it by others; some may regard it as an individual and, if they do not fear speaking with individual strangers can readily strike up a fruitful acquaintance with this new electronic being (this has occurred, according to Hellerstein (1986) who reported not just uses of computerized bulletin boards for lonely hearts clubs and dating facilities, but that users also treated their terminals with some degree of anthropomorphism, sometimes giving them names, keeping them in bedrooms, and denying access to others). Others, however, who fear the scrutiny of strangers, are reluctant to "speak publicly" with a computer, which is encountered, as an actor over which one has little control. These individuals fear disapproval from the computer whose utterances they may not understand.

Rauschenberg acknowledges that "computerphobia is complex . . . the more we understand about the feelings and apprehensions of those who will use computers for communication, the better people can be prepared for technological effects on human lives" (p. 12). It is difficult to think of any research on "televisionphobia." Chen (1984), in seeking for common issues in TV and microcomputer research, seems mainly to discover differences between the two fields. To some extent both he and other American investigators, realizing the active role of the computer user have allowed this model to influence their view of how children encounter network television. Collins (1982, p. 10) wished to move "from a focus on program content and outcomes of viewing to an analysis of the cognitive tasks performed in viewing particular programs . . ." To an extent the model of an active viewer has been supported by British research discussed in Chapter 3, which has been based mostly on adult samples, though similar findings have been found with children (Greenberg et al., 1986). In short, people clearly select what they wish to see on a variety of dimensions of content. This selectivity implies an element of self-control in information processing, and individual differences in patterns of selectivity are also clearly demonstrable (Wober, 1980d), differences which are just as likely to be observed in American as in British samples.

The question of whether the amount of use of computers associates with more or with less use of television or whether the two are not linked may be an important one. If heavier television users are also greater users of computers, it could be argued that the skills and experience established with the older screen pave the way for the encounter with the new. In contrast, if a negative link is found it may be that television satisfies needs different from and complementary to those involved in computer use or that television simply occupies time that is unavailable for other purposes. It may be helpful to note, therefore, (Greenberg et al., 1986) that there was a significant positive relationship between amount of viewing of adult programs among a sample of children and their reported use of computers. There was a greater correlation between computer use and appreciation of adult programming seen, and while the link between amount of viewing and computer use collapsed to insignificance when partialling out appreciation, the latter did not reduce to insignificance when controlling for the amount of viewing. A plausible interpretation of this is that there is no evidence that habituation with screen use, measured by its amount of use across one week, either contributes to or impedes computer use; more likely is the interpretation that an element of critical maturity evidenced by appreciation of adult programming viewed is a correlate (though less likely to be a cause, than an effect) of the reported extent of use of computers.

Among other noteworthy results of this British survey were that reported computer use was markedly sex linked, with boys having a higher claimed use and experience than girls. There was no such distinct association between computer use and socioeconomic status, so at this early age in this one instance, it was not evident that a class-based competence gap was already growing. The result is practically similar to that in a much larger British survey (Cunnington and Associates, 1984) in which over 10,000 homes were involved, nationwide; computers were used in over 10% of households involving over 14% of the population, but this rose to 44% of children aged 12 to 15 (with a marked differential in favor of boys). Cunnington reported that the penetration of the different socioeconomic groups was even, but the tables show clearly that the lowest (DE) stratum, which also includes many single person and elderly households had a much lower incidence of computer access than did the other groups. The sex differential is confirmed by Gribbin (1984) reporting an Equal Opportunities Commission survey of 1,200 children in southern England. Gribbin explains that children consider that computers will be used at work equally by women and men, but schools delegate computer-instruction training to mathematics and science teachers, who happen to contain the largest proportion of men in an otherwise female dominated primary teaching profession. The EOC responded by sending its report and a computer comic called Load Runner (in which boys and girls share equal status) and other materials to every secondary school in the country.

In a more specialized paper on the uses of computers to aid mathematical learning in schools, a British Inspector of Schools, Fletcher, (1983) made a number of encouraging observations, though he pointed out worthwhile cautions as well. Generally noting the motivating features of the user-controlled screens, Fletcher observed that computers helped children perform some of the otherwise tedious "drill" tasks (such as learning multiplication tables) in pictorial form, with a confidential record of performance avoiding discouragements associated with traditional methods. Excitement has been generated widely and pupils work intensively and long so that "the outstanding implication . . . is that this energy should be developed" (p. 33). At the same time Fletcher enters some cautions; some schools are found, he says, where enthusiasm is waning—usually because the activity has become institutionalized in the wrong way—the fun has been banished. In a different way Fletcher doubts that computer languages are "really languages at all, or are they no more than methods of coding? . . . Codes are not designed as aids to thinking and they are usually of little help in concept formation. Computer languages assist certain styles of thinking and impede others . . . ; this therefore has implication for teachers of more than one subject" (p. 29). Whether Fletcher means that gains in mathematics may be offset by damage to English literacy is not explicit, but it does at least seem to be implicit. Nor has he, or have others, convincingly stated that rudimentary skills, such as multiplication tables, the ability to hold parts of calculations (in brackets) while broader operations are carried out mentally, or skill in dealing with orders of magnitude of units when adding zeros to multiply, are clearly assisted by computer operation in comparison with other methods of learning.

The essential role of good teachers in making sure that interactive screened resources work well is attested by Tidhar and Ostrowitz-Segal (1985) who report on experience with teletext instruction carried out in Israel. Not quite as flexible as personal computers with self-mounted and adjustable programs, the teletext in these cases nevertheless provided pages geared to a range of levels of competence. Perhaps more important, the pages could be used at each learner group's own pace (the screens were provided for four to five learners each). Though the broadcast trials were short, not exceeding 2 months, evaluation showed that the method was successful, particularly in primary schools. The authors report that the apparatus encouraged introverted children to speak out and children were happy to work independently in groups without constant teacher supervision.

Fletcher's warm approval of the potential of computers to assist thought reflects the endorsement of Paisley and Chen (1984, pp. 122–123) who referred to "the computer's power to mirror children's thought processes . . . (it) can lead children to engage in . . . thinking about one's own thinking." They see the concepts of a bug as a problem and debugging as problem solving as preparing users for acquisition of more advanced cognitive skills. This may be a generous thought. At least on some occasions debugging can otherwise be felt to be the defeat of a kind of design perversity by the application of arbitrary maneuvers. Nevertheless, since "instructive media can be designed to be nonpunitive and entertaining, they may provide an impetus to children's development of reading and language skills."

Paisley and Chen raise the McLuhanite contention that "exposure to interactive media may also affect cognitive style;" yet they had no evidence at that time to support such an idea. Instead of pointing to some aspect of sensory skill structure (that is to say, a development of skill in decoding visual, or auditory or olfactory or other codes to an extent that had not existed hitherto) Paisley and Chen consider that a way of applying one's existing cognitive structure might be affected by the use of interactive media; this is a reinforcement of "impulsive" to replace "reflective" thought. There is a need for some clarification here, as the authors say that "reflective children, who are often blocked by anxiety over being wrong can benefit by using well designed (computer) systems;" but this neglects that not all reflective children may be "blocked by anxiety" and it is not self-evident either that "impulsive thought" (if this is what used to be called [thoughtless] trial and error activity) is superior to reflective thought.

In all, Paisley and Chen insist, probably correctly, that as computers and other "interactive media become friendlier over time . . . the benefit differential between information haves and have nots who actually use the systems . . . increases." This is because, they say "interactive media offer extraordinary access to information, but only to those who understand the algorithms of information seeking" (p. 133). Having raised this spectre, Paisley and Chen promptly end their essay with faith in the future, in particular that "interactive media . . . may (sic) be able to provide children with the literacies and modes of thought that the future requires." This conditional optimism invites consideration of what the best conditions might be in which to maximize competence and skills across the whole population. Some of these questions lead to very awkward problems for particular societies. Thus, American society, unused to controls and restraints on equipment for self-expression and the spread of information may either "progress" in a direction of deepening social inequity, or devise ways of positive discrimination (as happened with "busing") to restrain the exploitation of information by some and to maximize its use by others. It is not uncommon to read in the press that 10 million American take narcotics. This group is unlikely to constitute a sector that is advancing in the deft manipulation of information through use of the best gadgets and networks becoming available; indeed, a retreat into a narcotized world may be for some a response to a fear of the galloping advance of others. In the very different Soviet society, while computer competence might be fostered and needed widely for macroeconomic and defense purposes, one can see that the society would be less keen to place terminals in every home to allow untrammeled interrogation of databanks, be they simple holiday guides; supermarket price lists; or more problematic legal and private records, histories, dictionaries, and other cultural resources.

SUMMARY:
THE SCREEN AND INDIVIDUAL SENSIBILITY

The question we have tackled here is a relatively unfamiliar one. People have been immersed from childhood in a world in which screens with moving pictures have been a part of their experience for a length of time second only to that of sleep. Does this presence of moving pictures with sound make people more skilled in moving picturacy, oracy, and musicacy to the detriment of their skill in literacy? At a level of measureable skills this may be a rather prosaic question; however, it goes further. More difficult to conceive of, this raises the possibility that the quality of one's experience of the world is radically different if one has this new profile of skills, compared with an older profile emphasizing literacy and allowing less place for moving picturacy. A further extension of this question is whether the changing screen will have new consequences for the sensory architecture of a person's ways of perceiving the world.

In exploring these issues we have made an analysis of the various skills involved in processing information acquired through each of the sense receptor systems. To emphasize the differences among these information routes, each skill has been given a provisional name reflecting the sense mode involved, and in some cases distinguishing between the skills necessary in constructing and in making sense of messages, encoding, and decoding. The purpose of this exercise has been to help to display the complexity of what does occur in processing information and to give a better chance of developing questions that address and clarify the various different possibilities, which may be blurred by the use of more conventional terms.

An example may help to illustrate what is meant. The British House of Commons declined to have their proceedings televised live; however, they had allowed live radio broadcasts for some years, so the television news had developed a method of portrayal whereby an artist's drawing of the Chamber was screened (still) while the sound track relayed recorded or sometimes live sound. The question then arose whether the public would be better served by having live pictures to accompany the live sound. An experiment was proposed, in which the proceedings in the House of Lords, which does permit live television newscasts would be taped and a parallel version made with artists illustrations only, as for the House of Commons. In conventional terms, pictures are information which should add to that in words heard on the sound track, so the Lords' live sight and sound material should engender better understanding and recall of material than the version with artist's drawing and sound. An analysis using the newly suggested terms would compare the two displays thus: The artist's picture, together with speech, would require little or no skill in still picturacy, but all the information accessed by ear would carry words, which would pass to the left side of the cortex to be processed. Little or no processing would occur in the right side of the cortex, which received only a still picture. In this condition attention might be fully applied to the auditory verbal material and would allow it to be stored, at least in part, in long term memory, for retrieval and meaningful integration with the perceiver's previous knowledge and attitudes.

In contrast, the moving pictures, together with the speech, would present an active task to the right side of the visual part of the cerebral cortex, whereas the spoken words occupied space in the left side. It then becomes an open question whether what is going on in the left side of the brain matches and enhances what is demanded of the right, or whether the presentation sequence, or the individual's ability to temporarily hold, match, and store leads to significant loss or confusion in information processing. It seems likely that, whatever the real outcome of the comparison, the more detailed system of identifying skills helps to recognize the complexity of the situation and what is entailed for the perceiver.

As with the illustration just discussed, the first question in this summary, whether the addition of television to a culture's sensory ecology changes the ways in which people are aware of the world, has to be answered conditionally. It probably depends on the extent to which the screen displaces the page. In turn, the kind of programming that prevails in a nation's television, and which partly determines the way in which this message system is used, eventually affects the balance between literacy and moving picturacy. In the future, the same kind of qualification must be applied in anticipating any developing effects of the changing screen.

Brown (1986) has compared what various message systems can do for children and, tellingly, has no chapter explicitly celebrating any easily identifiable or strong advantages for television. Nevertheless, in one case she cites certain merits of the moving picture. It helps children to remember actions and to recall the order in which events are portrayed better than does speech alone (this does not assert that television as commonly experienced, with flashbacks and other devices for disrupting temporal order is better than speech or print, or indeed than temporally logical television in conveying order). Because television contains much explicit information about facial and bodily expression, it enables viewers who have progressed in expressionacy to make inferences they might otherwise have to construe with more contribution of their own imagination, or not at all if they have portrayals of similar material in sound radio or print. Nevertheless, Brown is careful to point out that "the same verisimilitude that makes moving pictures so legible can also mislead young viewers" (p. 73); further, television narration tends to convey to children that events unfold more quickly than does print narrative. This may be an extremely important feature of screen culture and links with assertions made by some of the challengers reviewed in an earlier chapter, that television "makes children impatient," replacing any preferences that might be developing for deferred gratification with immediate gratification. The same possibility existed with cinema film, except that children experienced far fewer hours of it per week, when encoding styles were more leisurely overall; even the Keystone Kops' hectic chases were not as speedy or as numerous as the exploits of the hyperactive motorbikes, cars, or helicopters of latter day television.

Brown's chapter, which might have been on the merits of television, turns out to be more of a mitigation of its pitfalls. She closes by saying "television should not be incriminated as the enemy of children's education;" it is more a matter of "how it is used that determines its value to people" (p. 79). To this, bearing in mind what has been shown in Chapter 3, we should add that what is on offer influences how the screen is used, and that in turn can have certain directly formative effects on children (as with the perception of time) or indirect effects, if the screen detracts from the development of a more sophisticated literacy by more time spent with better quality material in print.

Not only does the potentially protelevision chapter turn out to be something of a rearguard defense, the next one is entitled "Does Television Stifle Imagination?" The answer, paraphrased, is possibly not; but an implied claim for a benefit of the screen may itself need some mitigation. Brown states (1986) "imagination can only use what memory has to offer" (p. 98), thus implying that the abundance of pictures viewers encounter probably provides a rich "pictabulary" from which the imagination can make enriched choices just as it can from a rich vocabulary. However, this seems to employ an unnecessarily limited model of the imagination, which operates not just at a concrete level, but also at an underlying structural one. In a way, the former can be thought of as "unimaginative imagination" (itself, an imaginative thought, at the structural level). Examples of unimaginative imagination include much of what happens in space fiction of the more ordinary kind. Masquerading as imaginative because it is set in space, the characters are given nonsense syllable names and have supposedly strange attributes (x limbs, y sense organs, arranged in unconventional fashion). They go through plot routines of threat, maneuvre, and resolution that are little different from the conventional drama of print fiction.

It is possible that unimaginative imagination may be served well by extensive experience of the screen; however, truly imaginative achievement operates at a deeper level. This dissolves ingredients, which are encountered and normally left as wholes, and recombines them in unexpected ways. Examples abound in *Alice in Wonderland* and in the works of numerous comedians; a contemporary political cartoon showed the island of Great Britain redrawn (slightly) as an aircraft carrier from which U.S. planes flew to attack Libya; no words were required to make its point. Similarly, existing elements may be recombined in new ways; thus, a teenager was asked for suggestions as to what society might be able to do with the multitude of plastic bags now available for trash; fitting them into wire frames under which to grow strawberries, or tying them as sails to small domestic windmills may be impracticable ideas thrown up, but they involve transformations and not just permutations of purpose. Again, Brown has perforce to lay a responsibility at the door not of television's potential, but of its actual performance: "children's TV programs don't always exploit their physical resources . . . we could feed children's imagination by upgrading the quality and diversity of the television they watch and by helping them use viewing experiences in the interest of their own personal expression" (p. 98).

In conclusion, Brown sets out three roles for adults, in guiding them how best to use message systems for children: historian, chef, and traffic cop. The historian develops and transmits a social perspective; the chef offers a wise choice of materials and suggestions as to what to consume and how to savor it, and the cop can lay down rules about what can be viewed and when. These three roles will be discussed further in the next chapter where we will have to take into account also that only a minority will even have read Brown's book, or others like it; perhaps a majority remain unequipped to be good chefs and are also unwilling to act as traffic cops, though they may need their good offices.

CONCEPTS EXPLORED IN THIS CHAPTER

Cassettary.   A term analogous to library—a store of cassettes.

Computerphobia.   The evident fear that some have in using computers; raises the question as to whether or why there is or is not an analogous televisionphobia, or a form of opposite which is gadget-hunger.

Descheduling.   One purpose of the use of VCR or audiocassette. Sometimes known as "time-shift" it should be used in preference, since time can not be and is not shifted; the schedule or position of a coded message can be, and is altered from what the original provider has generated.

Diffusion. A word used usually to refer to purchase or spread of some form of gadget or hardware, though it could refer to the ways in which skills spread within a society.

Empires of Message Systems. Scholars have asserted that a message system, such as print and now the screen, have had major formative effects on how societies are organized and even on how people think. These fields of effects are referred to in the metaphor of "empires."

Imagery Styles. Personal reports or claims of being able to experience mentally the equivalent of externally supplied messages, without their immediate presence. *Crossmodal* images "appear" in one sense field to accompany inputs arriving via a different medium; *intramodal* images are repeats of percepts, within the same medium; *automodal* imagery is the production of images in any medium, by choice.

Information Gaps. Related to unevenness of diffusion. Some people or sections of society become better informed or more skillful users of new message systems than are others.

Information Pathways. These connect message transmitters (which may be outside or even inside the receiver's body) with the receptor sense organs. It is these pathways that, in reference to the particular sense organs they reach, define an effective set of labels for different *media.*

Literacy. Literally, the skills involved in decoding and in encoding messages involving the code elements of letters; the term is used as a design example from which to construct other words referring to other coding skills, such as gesturacy, moving picturacy, and so on.

Message System. This is the whole apparatus of the industry which produces messages, the hardware through which they are dispatched, the medium, and the sense organs at which they are received, collectively understood as a system.

Sapir-Whorf-McLuhan Hypothesis. The notion that the nature of message systems in use affects an individual's ways of thinking, including imagery styles.

Unimaginative Imagination. Merely the random combination of a known array of ingredients, in contrast to simple imagination which may involve a dissolution of some ingredients to provide new elements for combination.

Videotext. Text displayed on a screen—unlikely to be psychologically different from text on a page. So-called videotex is an unsuccessful attempt to establish a jargon variant to refer to text delivered interactively, by cable. Teletext is a system of providing videotext in association with broadcast (and usually) picture signals and is not fully interactive.

CHAPTER 7

To Zion Or Gomorrah: The Highway of the Screen

INTRODUCTION: THE PROBLEM OF PLENTY AND THREE PHILOSOPHIES FOR ITS SOLUTION

Man's known history extends not much more than 5,000 years back, and for much of this time it has been possible to see that human creativity has posed problems for the management of surplus perhaps as often as nature has thrown calamity in society's path. The present ferment in the production of communications equipment is a good example of an acute problem of surplus, though it does not appear to be pitted against any opposing natural force or resistance. Indeed, it is this lack of external restraint that gives rise in some minds to questions about the wisdom of allowing or encouraging unfettered rein to science and engineering to produce and market whatever devices can be contrived.

The nuclear accident at Chernobyl may be a catalyst in affecting attitudes toward harnessing technology for the best. One British commentator referred to the political fallout from the event as likely to be more significant eventually than that from the radiation leak. The emigre Soviet scientist Zhores Medvedev wrote that "the best safety precautions of all have nothing to do with the proper design of machinery, but with the proper design of society." Writing opposite him in *The Times* on the same day (May 1, 1986) Sir Fraser Noble, one time progenitor of Britain's first Center for Mass Communication Research at Leicester University declared about broadcasting that "what we need is not more governmental or judicial intervention, but practical common sense operating with an informed social conscience and stern self-discipline. Broadcasters today have to meet a challenge, which is essentially the same as in 1969 (when Noble's committee on research presented its final report)—perhaps even harder to meet because of technological advances . . . as well as changing social attitudes." The voice was probably prophetically toned by the gravity of the other news of the day, but the stance was unusual and might be a sign of some shift from the breathless expansionism of the early 1980s toward some more searching questions about the role of mass distributional message systems, which is discernible in the climate of the late 1980s.

At the start of the decade as network broadcasters were followed by cable channels in the United States and the promise of more by satellite, it was easy to find observers such as the British *Sunday Times'* Industrial editor Roger Eglin (4 October, 1981) who wrote "space TV promises to be a bright 'sunshine' industry creating many thousands of jobs, particularly in the preparation of programme material . . . ;" his colleague John Petty (*Daily Telegraph*, 17 November 1981) reflected this with "cable television is spreading like a forest fire in the United States . . . already the Russians are said to be sub-titling programmes in English . . . the (British) Government is aware that it is in danger of being upstaged by more thrusting commercial enterprises abroad." A head of one British TV company (Lord Windlesham, *Times*, 3 December 1981) declared "one basic principle shines out . . . this is . . . the freedom of the individual to express himself, to speak and to be heard. In broadcasting the freedom to speak needs always to be matched by the freedom to receive, with artificial impediments—such as encoding or jamming—reduced to a minimum."

It has already been pointed out (Chapter 1) that broadcasting is mostly a process of *ad* rather than of *co* mmunication and that freedom of speech in encoding is actually an expensive function not freely available to all but secured only by a few. Nevertheless, aside from such reservations not often expressed then or even now, it was not difficult to pick up a rhetorical climate of opinion about communication developments, which held that progress meant plenty, and that more meant better.

It was certainly not the outcome of earlier models of audience research that the seers of the industrial and technical worlds took what later began to appear as a view of naively simple optimism. However, there is one way in which the activities of determining the future and of describing the present did interlock. There was a kind of moral simplicity about both enterprises. Stuart Hall (1980), in describing the development of his new Center for Contemporary Cultural Studies, stated that the aim was to move away from "research of a largely empirical kind, based on audience survey method, qualitative content analysis and a preoccupation with questions of the debasement of cultural standards through trivialisation, pinpointed in the issue of the media and violence" (p. 117); instead of behaviorist psychology, Hall and his colleagues wished to give weight to perspectives from traditions of sociology and literary criticism. Three terms of jargon or code are touchstones of this cultural studies approach: readings (the personal idiosyncrasies of decoding that make many diverse meanings from the same coded message), discourses (the readings that the critical researchers apply to the content before them), and hegemony (the power that the encoders are said to exert over the decoders but that seems at odds with the notion that the decoders interpret the messages they choose to hear in any way they want). This concern with hegemony reflects a Marxist perspective shared by many of the cultural analysts, but for the current discussion this stance is certainly not morally neutral. It implies what is socially good and bad, the television Zions and Gomorrahs of our title, and therefore what should be made to happen and what should be avoided. In short, the stance is prophetic rather than scientific in the old, mechanistic and morally neutral sense of the word.

This emerging group of studies is not merely spoken of among themselves by academics; they have carried their perspectives into the teaching of the subject in colleges and schools in Britain (e.g., Fiske and Hartley, 1978), Australia (e.g., Hodge, 1982), and the United States (e.g., Mosco, 1982; Rowland, 1983). They raise questions not only about *what* is going on and of *why* it has come about but also about *where* new technical developments might lead society and *whether* the unfolding possibilities are desirable. In raising these questions the critical theorists have contributed to an atmosphere in which the unfettered optimism of early technician journalists has evolved into a position in which disadvantages and drawbacks of new message systems are acknowledged and tackled, along with the potential advantages. In introducing a discussion of an optimistic technical determinism, Luyken (1986) places a question mark after his title and begins his text by pointing out that "the public debate . . . on how to design and implement . . . the so-called 'new media' or 'information age' . . . (is) extremely polarised in most of the countries preparing for it" (p. 181). Luyken shows how the feasibility of setting up satellite-linked channels has much to do with military and power political considerations, as well as with technical solutions for using natural and man-made resources. When all these are taken together, it becomes less obvious that what seem at first sight to be unfettered extensions of capacity, provision of messages, and freedom of expression are all aspects of the improvement of human experience.

THE GRAIL OF INNOVATION: INVENTION OVER INTERVENTION

At the outset of the 1980s a threefold model was offered as an analogy for what was happening in the thinking about communications enterprises (Wober, 1981b). Leading the field was the technical liberalism already described. In this philosophy, progress is a good thing; science and technology will extend their achievements, producing new devices, which either must be beneficial simply because they are the latest products of human intelligence, or which need simple rearrangements in the social order for their benefits to be realized without other parallel losses. Self-evident examples that reinforce this notion are the motor car and airplane outside the home and radio, television, refrigerators, and other labor-saving devices within it. A more thoughtful account of this philosophy is provided by McPhail (1981) who recounted the victories of the free press and of liberalism from Gutenberg onwards, relating the telecommunications revolution to this worthy pedigree. The Luddites who opposed the industrial revolution are derogated in this view as short-sighted ruffians; to the fore is Edison's invention of the phonograph and telephone, which public welcome validated as proofs of the beneficial momentum of technical discovery. The world of medicine over two centuries provided convincing evidence for this philosophy with a succession of successful medicines and life-saving treatments before biological engineering and concern about iatrogenic disease began to pose some problems in that field.

Underpinning this evidence of the successes of science over the last three centuries is a recurring theme in American literature, ideology, and entertainment, which lauds self-reliance in coping with the problems posed by the physical and social environments. Mankind is seen as constantly needing new territories to conquer; these might be the wild West, President Kennedy's New Frontiers of the Third World, President Johnson's new formations in the Great Society, the vantage points of proximate space, or the inner self of the "beat" generation (from which a rather hasty retreat was beaten). In this perspective, satellites are doubly convincing since they occupy new territory geographically, as well as in terms of human relations. Two possibly weak points of this philosophy were pointed out by Wober (1981b) in that the individual freedom for some humans to occupy new territory often conflicts with a "what about the Indians type of reservation" (p. 2), and that a corresponding individual responsibility to defeat hostile forces sometimes undercuts a broader societal authority often necessarily organized in federal agencies (Wober, 1984f). The dilemma is posed and played out in many Western movies and in some television shows, such as the *A-Team*, where the defeat of crime or of evil is in the hands of a self-appointed individual or small group, while "The Feds" or centralized authority embodied in the sheriff are portrayed as distant, sometimes corrupt, but generally ineffective.

A further paradox is revealed by a scrutiny of the lamentations of Postman (1986) who has eloquently described the empire of print in its most glorious form in America, alongside which he has set for comparison a derogatory account of that trivial world whose message systems are dominated by the pictorial screen. As Postman observes, the style of thought and indeed of action fostered by print is "linear;" in this, order prevails and progress is not only possible but becomes sought after. Thus, it is the dynamism derived from print that has fitted in with the approach (it is difficult to term it a doctrine) of technical determinism. It is ill-suited with the label of doctrine since it is tempting to hope that with an element of reflection, which accompanies anything as explicit as a doctrine, its failings or even fallacies would become more obvious and lead to its demise.

Where Postman (whom we have seen before, as a challenger in Chapter 4) has denied himself optimism may be in the very swamp of whose dangers he has so wittily written. For the message system of the pictorial screen is not "linear" in its thought-patterns but is reflective. It may be this very lack of linearity, of the impression that thought and science and technical development will and must march inexorably "onward" with time that will be the screen's saving grace. It replaces print with a more enfolding experience that is cut away from the previous progressiveness and which may eventually allow a more considered approach to where society will go next. Thus, the nature of the message system, which is currently dominant and which has been brought into existence by the previously dominant system, lacks the intellectual momentum to go much further. It remains a question whether the dynamic of an earlier message system will, through the actions of adventurous minorities, continue to reshape the nature of the message systems currently in place. Some of this direction is seen in the efforts of those who promote teletext and other uses of the screen as a moving print message system.

QUALITY BEFORE EQUALITY:
INTERVENTION HARNESSING INVENTION

This first approach to innovation, not only by welcoming it but also by pressing it forward without any bureaucratized impediment, is opposed by a more cautious stance. Proponents of this philosophy can be found within the British broadcasting systems, and have been copied or adapted for a number of other countries, for example with the NHK in Japan. It has frequently been said that the mechanisms of control in Great Britain are founded on a need to ration the use of the frequency spectrum equitably, but it is much more convincing to take the view that even if there was no frequency shortage, the British approach would still have been a regulatory one, based on perceptions of the need to conserve and promote quality. One journalist, Sean Day-Lewis (*Telegraph*, 8 June 1981), opposed his editor in a piece entitled "Satellite: More Means Worse?" Day-Lewis was concerned with a likely dearth of creative talent and ideas; he noted that the increase in narrow-casting (by VCRs) had meant that "the only clear addition to what is available on television is soft pornography." William Scobie (*Birmingham Post*, 16 November 1981) reported from Los Angeles that "America's appetite for the big stuff is big and getting bigger—and the films harder;" the *News of the World* (13 September, 1981) was more explicit "TV Menace of Porn Movies by Satellite," explaining that "sickening scenes of sexual perversion" were in prospect on unregulated satellite channels (which would be unavoidable if regulated ones were set up). Similar comments had been offered in the United States. Le Duc (1979) noted that an open skies policy would "debase European culture and destroy the European press, (so that) the wisest policy decision of all might be simply to suppress it (ie. DBS) now" (p. 242).

Some objective research, which reinforces these concerns, has been provided by Zillman and Bryant (1986). They showed volunteers (students as well as a broader adult sample) either commonly available pornographic films, including four kinds of explicit sexual encounter but not containing violence, or a "control" set of sexually innocuous comedies. In all, each group saw 6 hours of one or another kind of film in 1 hour sessions spaced over 6 weeks. On the seventh week, viewers were able to choose a videocassette from a range of six types of movies, which they were to watch while ostensibly waiting for another procedure. Those who had become accustomed to "mild" pornographic materials made more choices of viewing harder pornographic materials, including violence and bestiality, and viewed them for longer periods. The authors confront the argument that "people who have seen it all should get over it" and observe that sufficient evidence exists that, while moving toward the end of the range a number of viewers become harmed and may harm others in the process. Further, it is not known at what point along the continuum of hardness or depth of pornography appetites developing in this direction might eventually stabilize, though it is unlikely to be at the innocent extreme. To some extent, familiarity with what is viewed is followed by imitation, and the whole process is one in which a subculture of prurient or even deviant sexuality will have been helped into existence.

FEAR OF THE FRAY:
LEAVING PROGRESS TO SINK OR SWIM

A third philosophy is more like that of the ostrich, or of the Essenes in their time who, in face of the slings and arrows of misfortune withdrew from them and letting the world get on with its "developments" prepared for the millenium by a retreat into self-discipline and cleansing. In this view "progress" is a kind of disembodied natural force, which can neither be opposed nor deflected, controlled, or modeled. One is in the presence of this ideology when one encounters metaphors about the tide, which the Danish King Canute supposedly could not prevent from coming *in*, or about breaches in dykes, which can not be plugged by any heroic gestures with one finger, or even two. The first metaphor neglects that Canute took his courtiers to see that he had no power over the natural forces of the sea, but that just as surely as the tide came in, so too did it go out, and that if one was careful one need not get one's feet wet. The metaphor is better suited therefore to illustrating the second, conservative philosophy rather than the liberal one.

To return to what these philosophies may have been called 2,000 years ago, the first approach, of positive liberalism resembles that of the Sadducees, the party which adopted the modern Hellenism of the day. Their action in doing so raised the anxiety of others who at that time thought of the fearful example of dissolution in Gomorrah that invited destruction. The main party of the time who sought to conserve an ideal of Zion was that of the Pharisees who did not wholly avoid change but rather tried to harness and adapt the pressures for change within an existing view of an ideal society. Unforseen at the time was the Christian revolution, and some may like to think that an analog will arise in cultural terms at the present; however, it may be noted that this new society grew up outside the one in which the other three philosophies contended. Some argue that the New Way emerged from what seemed like Essene Escapism, and it will remain to be seen whether, in modern terms, a dynamic innovatory hybrid philosophy, and all the new forms of action and life that it may introduce, may spring from this least likely standpoint.

FORCES IN FAVOR
OF EACH PHILOSOPHY

As the 1980s progressed, developments in a variety of fields gave encouragement to those who favored each of these philosophies of technology. Scientific advances led to cheaper reception dishes; better ways of using cables; adding signals to existing broadcast channels, giving the user some measure of control over the material used; and so on. Such developments help convince some people that unfettered expansion is not only the most likely, but also the most desirable, course. On a much larger scale and in the opposite direction are the problems with the nuclear industry. Sweden held a plebiscite and decided that the country's nuclear power plants should be phased out entirely by the end of the century. In Austria a pressure group marched on a power station site and caused the cancellation of plans to build a large hydroelectric complex on the Danube. Several countries have witnessed the rise of Green parties with philosophies of conservation and a cautious use of new techniques; the reactor disaster at Chernobyl shows signs of being a milestone in the path of growth of these green parties.

A good research question for the communications industries is to examine what the public knows and understands about new devices and structures; this leads to further questions about what people want from, and, therefore, how it might be best to proceed with innovations. The Tunisian, Masmoudi stated at the International Institute for Communications conference in 1980 (quoted in McPhail, 1981) that the New World Information Order should above all, allow individuals, communities and nations to make known their aspirations, their concerns and their problems in struggling to shape a better future. Much that is known about the uses and gratifications (but also needs) associated with television has not shown, indeed has even failed to ask about, whether people want television for communication, that is for expressing, as well as for receiving ideas and information. The critical studies approach has underlined that people communicate laterally, that is with each other, on a basis of what they have viewed in common. This becomes more difficult, not easier, when there is a proliferation of channels, thus reducing the chance that two people have seen items in common and can discuss their experience together. Mostly, however, people want television for diversion, relaxation, and a release from the exercise of creative endeavor. From this background, might users want new screen devices so that they could really communicate with the originator of messages or via the sender back to the wider public? The QUBE project in Columbus, Ohio and small similar projects elsewhere have shown little sign of burgeoning; rather they have tended to be underused and uneconomic. Another research question is whether attitudes toward innovation in other fields might carry over to and eventually influence attitudes toward new screen devices.

The study quoted previously by Wober (1981b) began to deal with some of these questions. A London sample were asked to what extent they welcomed each of seven technical innovations. It was clear that some innovations were desired by substantial majorities, including birth control and video cassette recorders, both of which offer users greater control over their gratification planning. Other innovations received a mixed reception (pay TV meters and a channel tunnel), but some were clearly opposed. A satellite with five more TV channels was rejected by a similar majority as a proposal for more nuclear power stations. It was shown that items on an adapted scale of sensation seeking attributes were linked with others measuring the degree of welcome for certain technical novelties. Most of the correlations between measures of amounts of viewing of each of three program genres, and opinions about innovations were negative. Heavier viewers were likely to reject innovation. An exception was that heavier viewers of news and information programs were more likely to support nuclear power station expansion, though heavier soap opera viewers implied more anxiety in that they tended to oppose this innovation. In all, the study revealed a discriminating public, inclined to support some but not all changes, and revealing that where support exists, it is linked with a particular pattern of personality and behavior.

The picture of a public with differentiated attitudes toward innovation was also reported by Pion and Lipsey (1981). With an American sample they derived results on what people would like science and technology to accomplish for society. They wanted science to solve or at least to serve social problems, by improving health care and education and by reducing crime and pollution. Low on the list were science applications to defense and fundamental research (whose potential they may not perhaps have understood). Unfortunately, entertainment and communications were not dealt with explicitly in this research, but the goal of a less violent society may not be unconnected with the means of a measure of control over content and its scheduling on broadcast screen services. We have already seen in the previous chapter that investigators have identified what they call "computerphobia," and another has labeled "techno-stress" (Brod, 1984) as a painful sensitivity to being overwhelmed by hasty technical changes. Not everybody in Brod's view is hostile to new hardware; the "techno-anxious" are afraid of it, but another syndrome of dysfunction as Brod sees it is that of the "techno-centered" individual who becomes a lackey of the machine. At one extreme the "couch potatoes" made famous by Greenfield's book share a devotion they may not have realized with those at another extreme who are computer freaks, neither adaptation being, in the clinician's view, entirely sound.

Thus, the three main philosophies of innovation are not only proclaimed by their informed supporters, they are also manifest in the public at large in terms of patterns of behavior, often enacted without knowing that they exemplify some particular family of attitudes. As Slack (1984) has explained, these phenomena can be effectively understood in a combined program of theorization and research that encompasses several levels from those of traditions, goals, and competences in the society to personality and behavior patterns at an individual level, all linked by the traditional constructs of social psychology, which account for how the individual relates to the world about the constructs of attitudes and families of attitudes and ideals, which we can call philosophies.

Analysis of the three philosophies and their outcomes can effectively begin by elimination of the retreatist variant. Those who abstain from positive expression of goals and participation in action leave the field open to the innovators who exemplify what is sometimes called "technological determinism," though it would be as well to realize that it is not an inanimate entity that moves forward on its own but rather one which is served and propelled by those whose interests it serves. This power of interest is most clearly seen when two techniques collide; for example, the dish manufacturers were seriously incommoded when the satellite channels effectively scrambled their signals to protect against unfettered use of what are expensively produced goods (Miller, 1986). Neither the dish hardware nor the scrambling technique are autonomous products of a march of technical progress; they are developments produced and offered as an equation between service (to purchasers) and profit (to providers).

In the climate of a world of unrestrained innovators, the unfolding pattern of pressures and events can either be awaited with detachment or predicted to some extent with the aid of generalizations based on observation of actual behavior, both at an individual and a system level.

There are two scenarios that can be pictured in this world of unrestraint, which will now be described.

DARWIN IN DANTELAND: THE ITALIAN SYNDROME

When legislation broke the 25-year hold of the state broadcasting organization, RAI, which provided two channels, and in 1977–1978 allowed whomsoever was able to run a television station in any city to do so, a large number of entrepreneurs set up shop. Hundreds of local stations were established, but it soon became clear that in order to attract viewers and thus advertising revenue, the broadcasting content had to seek sensationally populist levels. The principles of behavior that determined this are the known facts about needs and gratifications, and the almost thermodynamically determined laws of viewing behavior, which indicate that less demanding and more arousing material will be more readily viewed by more people than will more demanding and less arousing material (Chapter 3). No great market of the mind or emporium of art was opened. Although some referred to the "richness and variety of TV offerings," pointing out that the average set could receive 15 stations and was actually pretuned to an average of 9 (Capocasa, Denon, and Lucchi, 1985), a choice, which might be related to the comparatively very slow spread of videocassette recorder ownership (Italy had 3% of households owning one, when Germany stood at 20% and estimates of over 40% were available for the United Kingdom), Italian programming did not become famous for any regular haul of Emmys, Golden Roses, or other marks of professional esteem on the international festival prize circuit.

In effect, the most agile operators survived and grew larger by amalgamations and economies of scale. It would be inaccurate to give the impression that Italian television was totally deregulated, as a constraint remained that operators could not broadccast centrally and network by relay; they had to transport tapes from city to city to simulate the condition of local broadcasting independence. Mastery of motor transport and organization became one condition of survival of the fittest in this modern scene of swift evolutionary struggle. Less than a handful of large networks eventually emerged. Ironically, once the broadcasting majors had become large enough to become highly visible, they also became more sensitive about their images and, with their consolidated economic position, can even afford to buy or make some better quality programming.

In terms of the metaphor heading this chapter, the vehicles of Italian broadcasting culture tottered for some time toward the direction of Gomorrah, bearing a product which, if not always sordid was also not celebrated for its quality. The many vehicles were replaced by a few, more powerful ones, which gave a better performance. In the medium term, the state broadcaster RAI survived and remained the peak time market leader, providing a yardstick to varied program schedules similar to those of reputable networks in other developed nations; this has provided a model of which the newcomers take note. Indeed, when socialist France chose a consortium to run its new Canale 5, the contractor was Berlusconi, the largest of the Italian newcomers, who provided a rhetoric based on quality, but an initial schedule which made its greatest appeal with tested American movies and miniseries. When political decisions removed Berlusconi from the French scene, he was able to start operations in Spain.

THE HIGH HOTHOUSE JUNGLE

This metaphor presents an option different from the Italian model, still reflecting a low level of intrusive regulation, but which has probably not been truly set up in any society. Even the United States has some mechanisms of restraint in the FCC and the NAB, with various consumerist and quality seeking pressure groups also exerting an influence. Nevertheless, the ideal of this model would require something like the conditions found in a high hothouse: an abundance of energy or wealth in the society, from which giant growths would certainly spring. This jungle of broadcasting bodies would present a different aspect to observers with different levels of acuity. At one level, the profusion would nevertheless seem to be sameness and monotony. The hundreds of programs and series, like trees of the Amazon forest, would mostly be of similar structure and genre in order to compete and survive in the same conditions. At another somewhat naive level, it could be felt that the plenty was a sign of variety and choice. Ten quiz shows, varieties of instant coffee, or compact motor cars are in this view an index of twice as good a life style as offered by five each of these commodities. At an extremely sophisticated level, like that of the tropical botanist or in screen terms the semeiologist, the spectacle would be of a real abundance; yet the richness would lie in the differences of detail rather than of major structure.

Something of the flavour of this prospect was reported in the British weekly *Campaign* (28 November 1986) whose reporter Charles Dawson attended an annual program market at France's Cannes. Most of the 700 buyers present were from Europe, accounting for what may soon be the largest and most complex market in the world. In 1985 there were 57 national, seminational, or transnational TV stations; in 1986 this grew to 61, and by 1990 well over 100 were anticipated. Whereas in 1985, the 17 European countries were estimated at having required nearly 190,000 program hours, the 1990 figure was forecast as 470,000 hours. While quantity was therefore going to burgeon, there was no commensurate suggestion that variety, expressed in terms of new program types and variants, would multiply in like measure. In fact the prospect was simply for "more of the same;" if anything, the pointer to the future led past a figure of 43% of Europe's public broadcasters time consisting of entertainment toward the nearly 80% of private-sector broadcasters' time consisting of entertainment.

TELEVISION TARZANS AND INDIANA JANES

Among the branches of the maze of networks in the High Hothouse Jungle, the viewers who would be most successful at making the best of their surroundings would be those who could effectively take care of themselves in both a hostile and tranquil environment. Such viewers would know the ropes, move from branch to branch of the networks without falling, avoid traps and pitfalls, and always survive any dangers in a healthy fashion. Such adepts would be termed by less literate observers as television literates, but as we have argued in the previous chapter, these adaptive abilities are strictly speaking not literacy but a variety of other skills, which might best be given the general name of "TDC" or "Television Decoding Competences." TDC would join with Television Encoding Competence to form the overall skills we may term Television Coding Competences.

In the days of more informed concern about television's effects, in the United States there have been several projects to promote TDC and, albeit at a more professional level, TEC. For example, the CBS network has distributed scripts of programs for schoolchildren, which form an effective introduction to understanding how programs are put together and to some extent how they function in viewers' experience. An understanding of this kind does not necessarily equip one with TEC or the ability to design and achieve expressions according to one's intentions using screen materials. Less ambitious, had it been the product of a major network but very ambitious as the enterprise of a small group of academics, have been the courses devised for classwork by Singer, Zuckerman, and Singer (1980) which were based originally in New England but which have taken root in many American and Canadian schools, and the work of Dorr, Graves and Phelps (1980) at the Annenberg School in Los Angeles, which is similar in methods and scope. Both groups successfully showed that young children could become much more critically aware as viewers to know what television was doing, in effect enhancing their television decoding competence.

In a particularly important area of applied education Huesmann (1986) tackled the situation that youngsters with a high diet of screen violence would tend to distinguish less effectively between reality and fantasy and would tend to identify with aggressive characters, which would explain the observed fact that they had somewhat higher levels of personal aggression than were found among low level violence viewers. Taken through a course that addressed these possible ways of decoding screen violence and suggesting new ways of being more sensitive to its consequences, youngsters developed less aggressively than did others who had no such course. In effect, a television decoding competence had been inculcated, with beneficial effects.

These North American initiatives, like European ones (e.g., Gunter, 1984) seek to equip ordinary viewers to become benefit maximizers. This implies that they would also be harm minimizers. Their defenses would thus lie in their own hands and judgment. The menaces outlined by some of the challengers described in Chapter 4 would not so deeply threaten viewers equipped with the degree of insight that such courses in TDC would bring because the viewers would see the threats for what they are and avoid them. This is the theory, and it runs parallel to the doctrines of the consumerists who believe that when armed with check-lists of measured qualities and attributes purchasers will more likely buy better quality refrigerators or any other product. This is undoubtedly true in many cases; yet, it only calls forth more subtle arts of marketing such as are practiced by beer and soap and other mass consumption producers, which manage to sell their commodities in many cases not according to subjectively discernible attributes but by product image and personality. In a similar manner, this phenomenon exists in the world of intangibles, perhaps even more so. Indeed, the control option or innovation philosophy that looks to an educated self-reliance may have to admit to two important weaknesses; one is that some Tarzans will trip and sustain injuries more often than if they inhabited a less hazardous environment. The other is that not all people can or even want to succeed in becoming such Indiana Janes.

These doubts do not and should not deter those who offer courses in TDC, at whatever level, but neither should they obscure what is likely to be another truth: that they can only reach a tip of the iceberg in terms of enabling the population to cope for itself in making the best of its screen facilities. It would be a pity in some opinions, if inevitable in others, if the screen cornucopia to come was fed by a small population sector of skilled technocrats who provide a spate of products of a humdrum similarity. Whether these products were reached and used via broadcast ground-stations, via satellites or dish or cable, or bought or borrowed on cassette, if the contents continue to consist of a fictional mixture much as before, the means of delivery may make little difference to the harms and benefits that might be produced among individuals, or to the overall screened package, which increasingly constitutes public culture.

PACMAN'S LUNCH:
THE DEVOURING SCREEN

In one widespread image of the future screen, a survivor, clearly identified with the representative user-viewer, resurrects itself after each welter of dangers has done its worst, healthy and well enough to play its next game of life. Much has been written about what Pacman can teach players in terms of motor and possibly some more advanced cognitive skills. Less has been developed about the social psychology of being Pacman, and this question now invites our attention. Pacman may die, but his death is temporary and involves no pain; Pacman is not wounded so that he communicates suffering of a physical or mental kind. Importantly, Pacman is not so often Pacwoman. There is a Ms Pacman but whether the prefix or suffix gives the dominant meaning remains debatable, and the creature is less well known than her predecessor. Those who ask why women or girls are sometimes found to be less willing venturers into future screen space might start with the matter of the gender of Pacman. While in an earlier generation it was Alice who ventured through the looking glass, whatever her success, today's adventuress into the world of the screen generally has to do so in masculine guise.

However, the image of Pacman is not used here to study patterns of success but to throw up in contrast the question of failure. Many of the early screen games provided little or no invitation to identify with destructibility. Other creatures, sub-human, were sent packing, or were eaten until the adventurer had some humorous and easily deniable accident. But what of those who are less than adept in this dangerous "territory" who are neither Tarzans or Janes in a jungle, if that is the nature of the unfettered world of the screen to come?

It is hoped that there will be schools for survival; but will these be schools with any hidden or actual drop-out rate that is substantial? Such a hazard seems likely. The purely information processing part of decoding screen entertainment, the moving picturacy, the musicacy, the oracy, and the gesturacy are taken to be almost universally possessed, at least to a sufficient extent to give a convincing impression to outsiders that viewing is for everyone a useful and rewarding experience. Yet this goes little further than a merely perceptual level of competence. At a level of social perceptions and responses, it would take intensive courses in citizenizing the viewer whom society at the same time provides with a screen environment that is wild in many ways. Most people can and do qualify as vehicle drivers; they have to do this because they operate lethal weapons (although licences are not required, in some societies, for firearms). Yet what is termed the "accident rate" (in order to obscure the demotic desire for equal access to all for this great facility of independent mobility) is not wholly composed of accidents. Accidents are one part of a larger category of events that should be called mishaps, a major part of which are caused by operator weaknesses that are identifiable and which, in an industrial setting, would be minimized by more rigorous procedures of selection to supplement any training that operators receive.

Using the screen is obviously not as immediately hazardous as driving a vehicle, which can kill at 20 miles per hour; however, enough has been researched (and discussed in Chapter 4) to raise sufficient possibilities that long-term misuse of the screen, for example by viewing too many programs or playing too many games based on violence (particularly if the suffering is experienced mostly by the weaker in society) or by over loud listening, could demean the viewer and through his or her further actions harm or in other ways diminish the overall social good.

In all, the world of the high hothouse jungle is another where the survival of the fittest is the order of the day. The survivors we meet here are not the providers of the fare but are to be found among those consumers who are not consumed themselves. Others who appear to survive or who are indeed eager users are perhaps a little like Pacman's lunch; they keep coming up to form the next meal for this persistent little monster. The fit person is the Tarzan or the Jane whose survival is serial and goes beyond the symbolic screen death. In surveys when people were asked if some aspect of television such as misleading or overpressing advertising, or violent material was harmful, substantial proportions would say such things did harm someone else, but they denied it harmed themselves. The identification with the notion of indestructibility was therefore already in place well before Pacman's birth, even while the forces of danger were acknowledged to exist.

SCREENS OF EDEN: THE GREEN IDEAL

Quite different from the philosophies of freedom or of minimal control over innovation are those which seek to add wisdom to technology, to give it a human concern. To treat technology as a person or a superperson may be a kind of idolatry, allowing applied science considerable powers of autonomy and assuming they will be exercised benevolently. Activists and thinkers who gather under the Green banner (not the Islamic one) are concerned with individual freedom but consider it to be served in some cases by taming technology to which they do not ascribe a supernaturally irresistible character. Two thousand years ago this philosophy was that of the Pharisee party, which sought to identify the enduring ideals that were universally true but which made considerable accommodation between new and old ways of pursuing such ideals. Although compromise was recently seen as moral weakness in the wake of appeasement of midcentury fascist excesses, if the new task is to adapt to changes otherwise dictated by circumstances created by the inventions of technology, then the passive acceptance of such changes becomes the course of appeasement. To attempt to defy technical change by prohibiting its scope of application may turn out to be unworkable, while to compromise presents difficult problems of choice and assessment and probably constitutes what is truly the tough rather than the weak option. Currently, such thinking relates to the ways in which nuclear power and other energy production, chemical fertilizers, medical drugs, and now new, as well as existing, screen devices are used and should or perhaps should not be used.

In effect, Green philosophies or methods are already in place in most broadcasting systems across the world. The question now is not how or whether to get such philosophies into action but whether or how or to what extent to keep them there. It has been pointed out repeatedly that new screen techniques bypass and challenge systems of broadcasting control or regulation of content. What has not been realized so often is this broader contradiction, that while developments in other fields are gradually persuading more people that controls are desirable they may simultaneously become persuaded that this direction of development should be reversed in the world of entertainment and information.

The problems of control revolve about how and why it should be accomplished, if at all. And the latter question can be divided into two sections, one dealing with the contents themselves and the second with their arrangement, or scheduling. Why certain contents should be provided, answers in part to the population's expressed needs and desires, and its demonstrable preferences in behavior, usually for entertainment of various kinds followed by news and discussion provided in an entertaining fashion. A second source of pressure for provision comes from creative people; some are driven to seek new forms of drama using electronically aided ways of making and altering visual images; others try new forms of comedy; a third group of pioneering journalists wish to take cameras where they have not been before and, either as a by-product or even intentionally, blur the boundaries of privacy. This whole matter of private and public space will be examined in further detail, but will be preceded by a discussion that shows that some researchers maintain that certain kinds of material produce harm and imply a need for their restraint.

One of the possible kinds of harm is to the privacy of nonprofessional participants in the making of programs, of which several examples have been given (Wober, 1985d). Before building a case for the protection of privacy it will be useful to underpin its importance with existing compelling arguments. A good starting point is the speech to Congress made on 6 January 1941 by President F. D. Roosevelt enunciating Four Freedoms, which define a set of rights that individuals universally should expect to enjoy (Mazrui, 1972). These rights comprise the "freedom of speech and expression, freedom for every person to worship God in his own way, freedom from want and freedom from fear" (p. 53). The third of these deals with the physical absence of hunger and maintenance of health, but the three others are psychological and cultural. The first two in particular imply the need for each individual to develop in the ways determined by personal inheritance and local culture to become oneself fully. In all the western societies, as well as most others, this entails the conservation of a private sphere for each person which can be articulated or revealed at that person's own desire. That privacy right is echoed by privacy need as a construct of personality structure has been shown in several surveys (Wober, 1978d, Durkin, 1981). Some people express a greater privacy need than do others, but all need it to some extent, depending on other attitudes, such as those toward swearing and bad language or toward certain other screen materials.

A good starting point for an exploration of the realms of private and public space, and how the former is symbolized and protected is to be found in the biblical books of Genesis and Leviticus. In the former, God reviewed his work and set aside a day for rest. This rest was not just a physical recuperation, not needed by the Divine Being, but a psychological respite from the days and the world of work, which involve others and very often do so in conflict. The Sabbath also offers social behavior, but this is intended to be of a special kind, where all are at rest and not bringing pressures to bear on each other as happens during the days of work. In the book of Leviticus a number of rules are laid down concerning what are now called prohibited categories of marriage; but they more directly refer to sexual relations and, in making boundaries to access between certain categories of people help to define a territory of privacy. Of greatest importance, these injunctions appear as operationalizations or definitions of the concept holy. God set aside a holy day of rest and renewal or maintenance of the self; the Sabbath is holy; holiness consists in not dealing wrongly with others in a variety of ways that safeguard wholeness (the two words holy and whole have the same root), and holiness is loving one's neighbor as oneself.

The bases of respect for others and a right to develop and renew oneself are thus laid at the roots of the experience of western cultures and through them, of many others. Integral to the notion of privacy as an opportunity for wholeness is the corollary of boundaries of one's individual existence. These boundaries are of the present, between oneself and others, and in more distant time between one's existence in this life and whatever lies outside it. It is probably these boundaries and their symbols that provide the fuel for much literature and comedy and that suggest sensitivities that certain kinds of restraint (from within) or control (from without) would be welcome in the culture of public utterance that modern societies manage to project on screens in every home. These privacy needs, the boundaries that protect them, and the symbols that signify them are of course ideal territory for the attention of social psychologists and social anthropologists.

Where these considerations become important in understanding the role that television plays in people's lives is in examining the ways in which the material that people see on their screens either serves or impedes the functions that religions are trying to deal with. These functions include the management of concerns that everybody has about the mysteries and the familiarities of life, about the sacred and the profane, about the private and the public, and about the boundaries that separate and help to define these pairs of opposites. Many have made the claim that, in the words of Gerbner and Gross (1976) "our chief instrument of enculturation and social control, television may function as the established religion of the industrial order." Before that, another American, Michael Novak (1975), exclaimed that "television shapes the soul" (p.

194); his argument was that television as a common experience across the nation contains a "mythic structure" of prime time news and fiction which pits symbols of the forces of good and evil in conflict in "classic forms of moral heroism" (p. 19). Yet Novak also claims that "television . . . has vested interests in new moralities . . . (and) the present system is effectively a form of social control." Novak's colleague in the same symposium wrote "TV shows . . . seethe with myths and heroes. They guide decisions, inform perception, provide examples of conduct. Does that make our mass-media culture 'Religious'? I do not think we can explain its grip on people in any other way . . . ." Looking at the program makers rather than at their audience Bakewell and Garnham (1970) had earlier referred to "the new priesthood;" the parish of this priesthood and its ministry were by no means fully explored, but the implication that television constituted a religion was clear.

A number of reservations have to be set alongside these resonant utterances. One is that television is a vehicle for the explicit messages of various recognized religions, which in the United States run their own channels or programs: in Great Britain, the particular religion which is constitutionally linked with the very central symbols of the state does not seek to use television evangelically, but its presence is felt at moments of particular importance in the metaphysical life of the nation. In Holland the television system has been split up into parts each of which is organized by a political or religious faction, so the distinction between television as a carrier and an author is more in evidence. Perhaps a more important negation of the idea that television is itself a religion, in the United States, is that a religion has an external source of validation for the ways it enjoins upon its followers. Real religions have a God, and even Marxism has a notion of historical development whose inevitable laws can be discerned by scientific inquiry and map out the general course of events that will take place on earth. Television lacks either kind of particular supernatural fount of authority for the myths and norms which it propagates, how ever pervasive and forceful these may be. Nevertheless, there is the function that has been previously outlined of setting boundaries to help organize individuals' experience of existentially important matters, in which what television does closely resembles one important part of what religions do.

What is this function of boundary maintenance? To explain this we need a theory, which starts by supposing that humanity is able to see itself and to realize that life is short, though mysteriously important, and it is set in a larger and even more mysterious context. We want to know where we come from, why, and where we go if anywhere. We want to make life safe, and its safeness is distinguished from what is dangerous, that threatens to damage or end life. What is safe is light, is life, is clean; what is dread is dark, is death, is dirty. Organized religions provide some answers to these questions of existential anxiety, and particular attention is paid to easing the anxiety that attends presence at the portals of life, that is, its beginning and its end. Fiction shows death happening to other people, obviously not to oneself or to ones with whom one closely identifies. Thus, "goodies" die less often than do "baddies;" where it happens, the death of goodies has to be handled with greater dramatic delicacy than the demise of baddies. This may be another way in which television falls short of being like a true religion; religions make strenuous efforts to teach adherents to respect and value the lives of others, whereas much of the material of screen fiction, which includes cinema as well as television, shows others as getting short shrift.

What used to be thought of as the first portal of life, childbirth, is an event that might be thought of as equally fraught with anxiety as is death, given that an individual in both cases is at the threshold of existence, thus demonstrating the threat of nonexistence. Accordingly it was supposed that portrayal of real childbirth in full frontal detail, on television, would be something that viewers would not wish to see (Wober and Reardon, 1978). However, two surveys found that explicit childbirth was something which twice as many people were willing to watch, as said they would be unwilling to see it. This suggested that the initial conjecture should be reformulated. The child does not spring from oblivion but has been within the mother for nine months; childbirth is nowadays relatively a safe procedure, one with a virtually guaranteed happy outcome, and any childbirth shown on television has almost certainly been screened so that "real death" is not going to be shown "live." It may be that instead, it is the moment of conception that is more fraught with existential anxiety. In keeping with this, half the sample in both of the surveys were unwilling to see real heterosexual intercourse portrayed on television, and less than a third were willing to watch it.

It is not quite sufficient to try to explain this reluctance by the hypothesis that people would shun viewing intercourse because it exposes their own privacy (by identification) or that of the actors, for it is no less revealing of bodily privacy than is explicit childbirth. This returns to the possibility that viewing intercourse may be declined because it carries some buried reminder of the converse of life. It may be, however, that a further distinction has now to be made between intercourse of a promiscuous kind, which viewers will assume has been staged with contraception so that no possibility of new life really exists, and intercourse of a dedicated kind intended to produce life. It is in the latter case only that aversion might be expected, and the reasons might be at least two, including the problem of existential threat, and second concern for the privacy of the child to come. Viewers may sense the difficulty that would attend a meeting, however unlikely, between oneself and a child that sprang from an intercourse that had been witnessed, as a piece of information that would rob such a child of a most important facet of the privacy of its origins.

The idea that the portals of life are threatening places is not very surprising, and, given also that people are very unready to watch real killing on television, and the peaceful death of a person known to one even less than that of a stranger, the available evidence supports this theory.

These explicit possible or actual portrayals are, however, less difficult to incorporate into a theory than is a whole range of events and behavior that may be said to symbolize indirectly the great transitions. Among the phenomena we may consider here are eating (ingestion of life-giving substance), excretion (discarding of what is not life-giving, and thus symbolic of the threshold between life and death), and bad language.

The social psychological significance of eating, as shown on television, has not extensively been studied. It is likely, however, that it is seldom shown. Actors approach their food but are seldom seen to eat it; even people in advertisements are seen to lift food toward their mouths, but chewing and swallowing are less "tasteful" to portray. This reluctance to show eating invites explanation (if the fact of the matter is true), and one explanation could be that eating is partly symbolic of the act of procreation. Indeed, some advertisements do appear to make deliberate use of this possible undercurrent of meaning. It goes without saying that defecation is unmentionable and unshowable, being the symbolic opposite of eating, namely, standing for death; but micturition is occasionally shown, being related to drinking, which may be less existentially potent a symbol than is eating. Also, drinking of alcohol may not be assimilated as a message linked in meaning with procreation but is accepted at its explicit level as a case of social rather than sexual intercourse. On British television it is clear that people who symbolize the integrity of the culture are most unlikely to be shown eating or drinking, let alone excreting. The theory outlined suggests that people in counterpart roles elsewhere would not be portrayed in such a way either. The elected American President may not be in quite such a durably symbolic centrality as is the British monarch, but it is also unlikely that the President would be seen eating or drinking or excreting. It is not sufficient to answer such a possibility with the reply that it would be undignified to provide such a portrayal, as that would invite the next question—why is the privacy of the President more precious than that of an ordinary citizen. Indeed, in some respects this is not so; very intimate details of Presidential physiology and functioning have been provided by word of mouth on American television, when it was a matter of informing the nation about the President's viability and health. But these things were reported, not shown, and then only when it was explicitly to sustain the belief in the viability of the President.

It could be envisaged that in some societies for a chief to be seen eating might be taken to symbolize worldly success, with harvests, military operations, or diplomacy. In such circumstances, screen portrayals of such activity would be welcome. On the other hand, it could also be envisaged that to show a Queen giving birth might serve as a great public affirmation of her royal existential (not political) authority and her function of enhancing and prolonging the social order. That such a thing is utterly remote in Great Britain is partly because the public functions of the monarch have come to be firmly delineated from the private life of the royal family, which is given considerable protection. Further, television has no status as an acknowledged religion in itself in Great Britain. In fact, when radical comedy presents puppet images of the Queen and her family in positions of ridicule, while his may affect the attitudes of those who choose not to reject the message of such comedy, while perhaps enjoying its methods, it also demonstrates that the institution of television is far from being some sort of quasi state religion.

Nevertheless, television has been used skillfully in Great Britain to being home to the mass of people the ways in which the monarch has a role in unifying society, and who does so, moreover, through a mechanism involving what is a state religion, namely the Anglican Church (Episcopalian in the United States). Interestingly, it has been American sociologists who have had a prominent place in describing the ways in which Royalty has interconnected via television with the political life of Great Britain. Shils and Young (1975) have pointed out that the coronation is a supreme ritual in which the Sovereign takes an oath to maintain divine laws and is anointed in demonstrating a link with the prophetic validation of biblical kings. All this is now telecast making it a national (as well as international) experience, and Shils and Young argue that this is renewed every Christmas when the Queen telecasts a personal message. Later on, Blumler, Brown, Ewbank and Nossiter (1971) reported on attitudes towards the Queen and the Prince of Wales at the time of the latter's Investiture, televised from Caernarvon Castle. Blumler et al. refer to a "political religiosity," which engenders a "kind of commitment (that) reinforces the disposition of subjects to obey the secular authorities" (p. 170).

In the United States, the foundational structure of the state and its chief symbols are quite different, but they include events such as the Presidential inauguration, the annual messages to the nation, and tangible symbols such as the flag, the federal Capitol and state capitol buildings representing the Constitution (by which religion is explicitly disestablished). It could be argued that in transmitting such images, American television fulfills some of the functions of a religion; but this argument would have to be sustained by a convincing demonstration that such a portrayal of the Constitution as a kind of quasisupernatural entity (perhaps, as a doctrine brought into public focus from a realm of Universal truth, by a quasiprophetic group of Founding Fathers) both pervaded the rest of broadcast and now cable television and was not effectively undercut by other symbol systems, including the messages of recognized religions on their own channels and programs. One might doubt that television would pass such a test of the case that it itself constitutes a religion.

A more realistic interpretation of matters is that viewers have psychological and philosophical needs that religions have evolved to meet. Television caters for some of people's needs at these levels, but probably not either in the United States or in Great Britain as an exclusive, explicit and established system which can be called a religion by fulfilling the two criteria necessary for this designation (namely, that it shows people the rules of a good life and that it explicitly ascribes authority for these rules to a supernatural entity which is not available for appeal to change or modify the rules). Instead, television mediates the operation of existing established religions, of which there can be only one in any developed society, for example, a denomination of Christendom, or Islam, but not two concomitantly. Television also furthers the functioning of non-established religions and of others which are of long standing and perhaps established in neighboring countries. Thus, TV coverage of the Pope's journeys, not least to Poland and the Philippines, may have done much to strengthen awareness and the influence of the Roman Catholic Church in these nations, in the first of which Marxism is the established philosophical system and in the second of which there is a strong minority Muslim movement.

Television may also mediate the appeal of "religions" which the Bible would have unhesitatingly referred to as false ones. In modern terms, the demigods are the Lennons and the Presleys, both of whom have had their moments of demigodliness; for example a BBC program called *Elvis Lives* (17 December 1980) showed an orator in the United States declaring "He is the Messiah of Memphis" and hinting at a "second coming;" and Relics of Elvis Presley were treated as if they were sacred, and a baby named Elvis Presley Patterson was believed to be by some a reincarnation of the singer. The clatter of these cases passes by, however, and television is not seen as having more true service to one minor cult than to another.

In all, it is not easy to see television as a religion in itself, though some of the symbols to which it adds currency and strength serve some of the functions that religions also promote. These functions include a shoring up of the awareness of the presence and wholeness (if not quite holiness) of life by certain kinds of treatment of death and of symbols that could stand for death and certain kinds of treatment of birth and of symbols that stand in turn for that. These functions in indirect ways can help conserve the experience of privacy and in so doing may serve the first two of President Roosevelt's four freedoms. There are many simple and explicit ways in which these freedoms can be served: the freedom to listen (to news) which, though not quite the same as freedom of expression does provide people with the opportunity to encounter views with which they approve; there are the opportunities to identify with worthy characters whom one admires, and this range of opportunity has continued to be extended especially for people of ethnic minority groups. However, there are indirect ways in which television can and does convey the idea that privacy is a necessary facet of every person's life and, what is more, is available and valued in the culture. Considerable thought has to be applied in detecting these indirect routes of functioning, one of the strong contributions of the school of critical studies.

The whole of this section is provided to illustrate the contention presented earlier concerning the need to control television's content. To a considerable extent, a number of restraints are exercised by program makers even in countries where there is relatively little official control.

We have noticed the restraints on the portrayal of excretion, even of eating, on abuse of the treasured symbol systems of national identity and esteem, and even of the portrayal of the act of procreation (except in circumstances where it is probably understood to have circumvented that outcome). To the list of such restraints which appear not to require explicit injunction it is possible to add a number of others. Thus, in British television the advertising channels do not permit commercials for alcoholic drinks to use any form of appeal that suggests that alcohol drinking is an effective route to sexual conquest; and programs are required to refrain from any portrayals of hangings or suicides, certainly in material shown before 9 p.m. when it is considered that screen fare should consist of material suitable for family viewing.

It was also mentioned that positive reasons may exist for control of scheduling of programs for positive public service reasons quite apart from any interests that the entrepreneurs have for seeking programs that will sustain large and continuous audience sizes. There is considerable room for more research in the area now to be discussed, but persuasive pointers exist to suggest that a good case is there to be made. The theorizing here is in the tradition of social psychology developed by Schachter, Berlyne, and others, which holds that emotion is a psychological counterpart of the physical construct of energy; both are scalar entities; that is, they have quantity but not direction. Giving direction to psychological energy, or emotion, is cognition, in effect putting a name or a signposting direction to release the flow of energy and this then becomes motion or action.

In program viewing terms, Zillman (1971) has argued that arousal engendered by seeing aggressive movies, if not given some particular direction for outlet may decay in a matter of a few minutes. A second program that is also aggression provoking will serve to sustain levels of arousal, but a happy ending (Zillman, Johnson and Hanrahan, 1973) can reduce the potential for aggressive behavior. This raises the possibility, shortly to be investigated in Great Britain, that an arousal-reducing program screened and viewed after an aggression-provoking one could dissipate the affect that had initially been aroused, or at any rate turn it around so that it might be released as good-humored boisterousness. To reinforce the notion that longer-term transformations of affect can be achieved, that is, outside the structure of a given program, researchers who have investigated the effects of violent erotica, which have been shown to increase beliefs in rape myths and other manifestations of readiness to victimize women, have needed to employ debriefing techniques that remove the unpleasant effects brought into being to demonstrate a positive effects hypothesis. Specifically, Malamuth and Check (1981) state that "a debriefing concerning the falseness of (such) stimuli has beneficial long term effects in reducing subjects acceptance of rape myths" (p. 445).

The reasoning following these pieces of evidence and their applicability to the consequences of certain patterns of television scheduling is simple. If violent action adventure programming is shown, such aggressive potentials as are engendered in some viewers may well be dispelled or transmuted into other forms if viewers have an opportunity to see an arousal dissipating program after the provocative one. For a television channel to mix its schedule in such a way would enable it to argue that it had served a positive social function, while still satisfying the desires among certain entrepreneurs to show violence-containing materials, and a willingness among large audiences (see Chapter 3) to view such material. It is almost certainly true that if there are many available channels, and that on one or another there will be more violent material to be seen, some viewers will move from channel to channel seeking such material. In this case it can reasonably be argued, however, that such viewers are to be held responsible for their own generation of aggressive potential.

This selective search for antisocial resonance could only be thwarted by a supergreen system of control, of which some might say Swedish practice is an example, in which violent material is quite scanty indeed. This may be one reason why, as Roe (1983) explained, when videocassette recorders became widely owned, particularly young viewers used them to devise and indulge in diets of violent content that were much greater than what had gone before. This led to a "moral panic," a term that seems to be used in a context that carries a coded implication that such a panic is irrational or immature or at any rate out of place. Nevertheless, not only did the moral panic apparently subside, so did the initial surge of viewing of such material. This does not deny, however, that a new equilibrium developed after the availability of materials has changed in a particular way is probably one which involves more violence viewing than was possible hitherto, and this may promote a dispersed, but detectably increased, proclivity to aggressive behavior among a small but significant proportion of the population.

FROM GREEN FIELDS
TO THE PAINTED DESERT

With the increase in numbers of channels available on air or by cable, and the parallel increase in the numbers of households with more than one set and the quickfire spread of videocassette recorders, a philosophy of control inspired by green ideals becomes virtually impossible to implement. Much as they have been anticipated by those who welcome the situation, the new colors of the developing screen environment are those of the painted desert, strident and varied. What those modern Sadducees who welcome this latter-day Hellenism might feel is a pleasure that the pampered population living in Wendy Box country and fed with a filtered diet of viewing experience are now to live in a new atmosphere.

The changing screen has brought considerable benefits for many. In television's first 30 years, vision reception has improved tremendously, adding color and size to the picture. New improvements are anticipated to resolution, screen size, and to sound quaity. The public want all these things. The changing screen has brought information channels based on text, which allow an increasing measure of interaction, or the ability or necessity for the viewer to determine what comes next, and even to go back on what has been seen before. This has been regularly used by owners, though the ownership of such facilities has proceeded at a much slower rate than that of recorders. Since these machines give access to films of one's own determination, there has been much support in spending for the shelf in the shop just as much as for the shelf of the air, in terms of choice of movies; but the air has so far won the favors of the audience in Great Britain, where public service broadcast channels continue to provide a service of high quality. The opposite is the case in certain Middle Eastern countries where personal recorders are used to avoid what the nation's services provide.

Self-determination is the ideal proposed by the advocates of unfettered change, something with which publics will certainly agree. If this determination is used by sufficient numbers to generate an atmosphere that begins to cause the culture to resemble that of the Cities of the Plain, Sodom and Gomorrah, most publics would resist such a movement. The power of choice is not likely to be used by the majority to produce an ideal culture of a New Jerusalem; nor would publics be likely to be happy with externally applied controls that sought to reach such an ideal. In the end, majorities of most publics would prefer to find the culture of their screen worlds to be positioned somewhere between the extremes of Zion and Gomorrah. In such a future, internal and external controls would find a point of balance that is acceptable to each society. The service of this study has been to map out backwards the lines of roads and where they have come from, to the present, and by so doing to point to directions that are available for movement ahead, with something of the consequences of travel along each way.

CONCEPTS EXPLORED IN THIS CHAPTER

Biblical Metaphors.   Or examples of philosophy that correspond to present day approaches to innovation are available. The Sadducees were the party of accepting modernism from the Greeks, come what may; the Pharisees were the "green" party of intention to react to innovation with due care for what it might do to society. The Essenes were the group who turned away from worldly events and let them develop as they may.

Boundary Maintenance.   This is a function which individuals need, to help maintain and regulate their privacy. Program contents invite examination to judge the extent to which they symbolize maintenance or jeopardize it. Certain activities, such as eating, drinking, excreting, procreating, and dying, at different levels either may symbolize or actually show the boundaries of existence, which are precious in ways that may promote anxiety or security.

Privacy.   As a fundamental universal human need and hence a right, as a psychological counterpart to the rights to health and bodily security is discussed as a good, which is not infrequently put in jeopardy by the functioning of television. In particular, nonprofessional participants in program making need to be careful about the welfare of their privacy.

Religion.   A system of regulation of the social and moral order that is essentially based upon a suprahuman (and thus unchallengeable) source of authority. In this view, television may serve but is not itself a religion.

TCC.   Or Television Coding Competences includes both a decoding and an encoding variant. These competences are what have been referred to in earlier chapters in others' terms as "literacies," or in suggested new terms for example as "moving picturacy," "oracy," and the rest. Courses have been devised that aim to teach people these skills, and they are reported to help youngsters to achieve a better experience from their use of the screen.

Technical Determinism.   Usually called technological determinism, it is the approach which considers that new inventions and technical developments will and must be allowed to influence and sometimes produce major changes in society. An opposite doctrine has not yet been named but would assume that social science has advanced sufficiently so that the results of technical innovations can, to some extent, be forecast. Armed with the forecast a society can and should make an informed decision about how to adopt technical innovations.

References

Adoni, H., Cohen, A. A., & Mane, S. (1984). Social reality and television news; perceptual dimensions of social conflicts in selected life areas. *Journal of Broadcasting*, 23, 33–49.

AGB Cable & Viewdata. (1983). *Report on first cable marketing monitor*. London: Author.

Airey, L. (1984). Social and moral values. In R. Jowell & C. Airey (Eds.), *British social attitudes. The 1984 report* (pp. 121–144). Farnborough: Gower.

Alexander, A. (1985). Adolescents' soap opera viewing and relational perceptions. *Journal of Broadcasting & Electronic Media*, 29(3), 295–308.

Allen-Mills, A. (26 January 1984). TV Turned Off For a Month. Daily *Telegraph*.

Altheide, D. L. (1985). *Media power*. Beverly Hills, CA: Sage.

Alvarado, M., & Buscombe, E. (1978). *Hazell: The making of a TV series*. London: British Film Institute/Latimer.

Anderson, D. R., & Lorch, E. P. (1979). A theory of the active nature of young children's television viewing. Paper presented at the Society for Research in Child Development, Biennial Meeting, San Francisco.

Anderson, D. R., & Lorch, E. P. (1983). Looking at television: Action or reaction? In J. Bryant and D. R. Anderson (Eds.), *Childrens Understanding of Television*. New York: Academic Press.

Antonius, G. (1938). *The Arab awakening*. London: Hamilton.

Appel, V., Weinstein, S., & Weinstein, C. (1979). Brain activity and recall of TV advertising. *Journal of Advertising Research*, 19(4), 7–15.

Aske Research Ltd. (February 1977). *Programmes viewers like to watch. Report to the Independent Broadcasting Authority.* London: London Graduate Business School.

Aske Research Ltd. (November 1980). *Attitudes to episodes and programmes. report to the independent broadcasting authority.* London: London Graduate Business School.

Aske Research Ltd. (November 1981) *Some insights from Canada. report to the independent broadcasting authority.* London: London Graduate Business School.

Atkin, D. J. (1986, October). The regulation of politically offensive speech on cable. Paper presented at the Sixth International Conference on Culture and Communication, Temple University, Philadelphia.

Bakewell, J., & Garnham, N. (1970). *The new priesthood: British television today.* London: Allen Lane.

Baptista-Fernandez, P., & Greenberg, B. S. (1982). The context, characteristics and communication behaviours of blacks on television. In Greenberg, B. S. (Ed.), *Life on television. Content analysis of U.S. TV drama.* Norwood, NJ: Ablex.

Barlow, G., & Hill, A. (1985). *Video violence and children.* London: Hodder and Stoughten.

Barwise, T. P. & Ehrenberg, A. S. C. (1982a). Glued to the Box? Patterns of TV Repeat Viewing. *Journal of Communication, 32,* 22–29.

Barwise, T. P. & Ehrenberg, A. S. C. (1982b). *The liking and viewing of regular TV programs: Cincinatti pilot study. Report to the Markle Foundation.* New York: Authors.

Barwise, T. P., Ehrenberg, A. S. C. & Goodhardt, G. J. (1979). Audience appreciation and audience size. *Journal of the Market Research Society, 24* (4), 269–289.

BBC (1973). *Till Death Us Do Part as Anti-Prejudice Propaganda.* London: British Broadcasting Company.

BBC (1984). *Annual Report.* London: BBC.

Bechtel, R. B., Achelpohl, C., & Akers, R. (1972). Correlates between observed behaviour and questionnaire responses on television viewing. In E. A. Rubinstein, G. A. Comstock, & J. P. Murray (Eds.), *Television and social behaviour: V. 4. television in day to day life: Patterns of use.* Washington, D.C.: Government Printing Office.

Becker, S. L. (1984). Marxist approaches to media studies: The British experience. *Critical Studies In Mass Communication, 1,* 66–80.

Belhassen, C. (1986). Le journal de Cathie Behhassen *Telerama No. 1891, 9,* 51–53.

Belson, W. (1978). *Television violence and the adolescent boy.* Farnborough: Saxon House.

Beniger, J. R. (1983). Does television enhance the shared symbolic environment? Trends in labelling of editorial cartoons, 1948–1980. *American Sociological Review, 48,* 103–111.

Beville, H. M. (1985). *Audience ratings: Radio, television, cable.* Hillsdale, NJ: Lawrence Erlbaum Associates.

Black, J. (1985). Interactive Games. *Intermedia, 13,* 82–84.

Blumler, J. G. (1979). The role of theory in uses and gratifications studies. *Communication Research, 6,* 9–36.

Blumler, J. G., Brown, J. R., Ewbank, A. J., & Nossiter, T. J. (1971). Attitudes to the Monarchy: Their structure and development during a ceremonial occasion. *Political Studies, 19*(2), 149–171.

Blumler, J. G., Nossiter, T. J., & Brynin, M. (1986). Broadcasting finance and programme quality: An international review. In Home Office (Ed.), *Research on the range and quality of broadcast services*. London: Her Majesty's Stationery Office.

Bourdieu, P. (1980). The production of belief: Contribution to an economy of symbolic goods. *Media, Culture and Society, 2*, 261–293.

Bouwman, H. (1984). Cultivation analysis: The Dutch case. In G. Melischek, K. E. Rosengren, & J. Stappers (Eds.), *Cultural indicators, an international symposium*. Vienna: Verlag Der Osterreichisches Akademie Der Wissenschaften.

Bowman, G. W., & Farley, J. W. (1972). TV viewing: Application of a formal choice model. *Applied Economics, 4*, 245–259.

Boyd, D. (1984). The Janus effect? Imported television entertainment in developing countries. *Critical Studies in Mass Communication, 1*, 379–391.

Briggs, Lord. (1976). Visual Literacy: A current problem of needs and resources. In *Vision and hindsight. The future of communication*. London: International Institute for Communication.

British Broadcasting Corporation. (1976). *A–Z of the BBC*. London: BBC.

Broadcasting Yearbook (1984). *Broadcasting yearbook, 1984*. New York: Author.

Brod, C. (1984). *Technostress: The human cost of the computer revolution*. Reading, MA: Addison-Wesley.

Bronowski, J. (1973). *The ascent of man*. London: British Broadcasting Company.

Brown, L. K. (1986). *Taking advantage of media. A manual for parents and teachers*. Boston: Routledge and Kegan Paul.

Caine, Sir. S. (1968). *Statement on TV policy. Paying for TV? A supplement to Hobart Paper No 43*. London: Institute of Economic Affairs.

Cantor, M. G. (1980). *Prime time television. Content and control*. London: Sage.

Cantor, M. G., & Cantor, J. (October, 1986). The Internationalization of TV Entertainment. Paper presented at the Sixth International Conference on Culture and Communication at Temple University, Philadelphia.

Cantor, M. G., & Pingree, S. (1983). *The soap opera*. Beverly Hills: Sage.

Capocasa, A., Denon, L., & Lucchi, R. (1985). Understanding Audiences of TV Commercial Breaks: What People Do, How They React, How Much They Recall? European Society For Marketing Research Conference. Amsterdam: ESOMAR.

Cerulo, K. A. (1984). Television, magazine covers and the shared symbolic environment, 1948–1970. *American Sociological Review, 49*, 566–570.

Chen, M. (1984). Computers in the Lives of our Children: Looking back on a Generation of Television Research. In R. E. Rice (Ed.), *The new media: Communication research and technology* (pp. 269–286). Beverly Hills: Sage.

Colbert, M. (1976). The Appreciation of Comedy and Light Entertainment Programmes Special Report. London: Independent Broadcasting Authority, Research Department.

Collett, P., & Lamb, R. (1985). *Watching people watch television. Final report to the IBA*. Oxford: Department of Experimental Psychology, Oxford University.

Collins, W. (1982). Cognitive Processing in Television Viewing. In D. Pearl, L. Bouthilet, & J. Lazar. *Television and behaviour: Ten years of scientific progress and implications for the 1980s* (pp. 9–23). Washington DC: National Institute for Mental Health.

Compaine, B. (1984). *Information technology and cultural change: Towards a new literacy?* Cambridge, MA: Harvard University Center for Information Policy Research.

Cullingford, C. (1984). *Children and television.* Farnborough: Gower Press.

Cumberbatch, G. (1985). Sorting Out Little White Lies from Nasty Pieces of Work. Guardian.

Cunnington & Associates. (1984). *Home computer usage and attitude survey.* London: Author.

Csikszentmihalyi, M., & Kubey, R. (1981). Television and the rest of life: A systematic comparison of subjective experience. *Public Opinion Quarterly, 45,* 317–328.

Daily Star. (1985, May 16). Smelly Telly on the way. *Daily Star,* p. 5.

Darmon, R. Y. (1976). Determinants of TV viewing. *Journal of Advertising Research, 16,* 17–20.

Dasen, P. R. (1972). Cross-Cultural Piagetian Research: A Summary. *Journal of Cross Cultural Psychology, 3*(1), 23–39.

Davidson, R. J. (1984). Hemispheric Asymmetry And Emotion. In K. R. Scherer & P. Ekman (Eds.), *Approaches to emotion.* Hillsdale, NJ: Lawrence Erlbaum Associates.

Dawson, C. (1986). Is programming the key to the television revolution? *Campaign,* 28 November, pp. 57–85.

Day, K. D., Barnett, G. A., Kim, K. L., & Miller, D. M. (1984, May). The Diffusion of Home Computers: Differences Between Adopters, Planners and NonAdopters—1983. Paper presented at the International Communication Association Annual Convention, San Francisco.

De Fleur, M. C., & Ball-Rokeach, S. (1973). *Theories of mass communication.* London: Longman.

De Kerckhove, D. (1985, July). Four arguments for the defence of television. Paper presented at the Seminar: Media, Culture, Lifestyles. MEDIACULT, Vienna.

Dominick, J. R., & Pearce, M. C. (1976). Trends in network prime time programming 1953–1974. *Journal of Communication, 26,* 70–80.

Dominick, J. R., & Rauch (1972). The image of women in network TV commercials. *Journal of Broadcasting, 16,* 259–265.

Doob, A. N., & MacDonald, C. E. (1979). Television viewing and fear of victimization: Is the relationship causal? *Journal of Personality & Social Psychology, 37,* 170–179.

Dorr, A. (1986). *Television and children: A special medium for a special audience.* Beverly Hills: Sage.

Dorr, A., Doubleday, C., Kovaric, P., & Kunkel, D. (1983, October). Televised Television Literacy. Los Angeles, CA: School of Education, UCLA.

Dorr, A., Graves, S. B., & Phelps, E. (1980). Television literacy for young children. *Journal of Communication, 30*(3), 71–83.

Douglas, M., & Wollaeger, M. (1982). A Typology Of The Viewing Public. In R. Hoggart & J. Morgan (Eds.), *The future of broadcasting.* London: Macmillan.

Durkin, K. (1981). *Viewers' reactions to the house communion programme.* Canterbury: University of Kent, Social Psychology Research Unit.

Durkin, K. (1984). The transmission and reception of mass media messages about male and female roles. In J. S. Caputo, (Ed.), *Dimensions of communication.* Lexington, MA: Ginn & Co.

Durkin, K. (1985a). Sex roles and television roles: can a woman be seen to tell the weather as well as a man? *International Review of Applied Psychology, 34,* 180–201.

Durkin, K. (1985b). Television and sex role acquisition. 1: Content. *British Journal of Social Psychology, 24,* 101–113.

Durkin, K., & Hutchins, G. (1984). Challenging traditional sex role stereotypes in careers educational broadcasts: The reactions of young secondary school pupils. *Journal of Educational Television, 10*(1), 25–33.

Ehrenberg, A. S. C. (1968). The factor analytic search for program types. *Journal of Advertising Research, 8,* 55–63.

Ehrenberg, A. S. C. (1985, February 14). What is the BBC worth? *New Society,* pp. 248–250.

Ehrenberg, A. S. C., & Barwise, T. P. (1982). *What does UK television cost?* London: London Graduate Business School.

Eisenstein, E. L. (1979). *The printing press as an agent of change. Communication and cultural transformations in early modern Europe.* New York: Cambridge University Press.

Elias, N. (1962). *The civilising process.* Oxford: Blackwell.

Ellul, J. (1980). *The technological system.* New York: Continuum Publishing.

Emery, M., & Emery, F. (1975). *A choice of futures: To enlighten & inform.* Canberra: Center for Continuing Education, Australian National University.

Emery, F., & Emery, M. (1980). The vacuous vision: The TV medium. *Journal of the University Film Association, 32,* 27–32.

Eron, L. D., Huesmann, L. R., Lefkowitz, M. M., & Walder, L. O. (1972). Does television violence cause aggression? *American Psychologist, 27,* 253–263.

Espe, H., & Seiwert, M. (1986). European television-viewer types: A six nation classification by programme interests. *European Journal of Communication, 1,* 301–325.

Factor, J. (1985). *Childhood and children's culture.* Melbourne: Australian Children's Television Foundation.

Featherman, G., Frieser, D., Greenspun, D., Harris, B., Schulman, D., & Crown, P. (1979). Electroencephalographic and electrooculographic correlates of television watching. Final Technical Report. Hampshire College, Amherst, MA.

Feshbach, S., & Singer, R. D. (1971). *Television and aggression.* San Francisco: Jossey-Bass.

Fiddick, P. (1985, 10 January). Research. *The Listener.* page 25.

Fife, M. (1981). Television and the Black Community. In H. A. Myrick & C. Keegan (Eds.), *In search of diversity.* Washington, DC: Corporation for Public Broadcasting.

Fiske, J., & Hartley, J. (1978). *Reading television.* London: Methuen.

Fletcher, T. J. (1983). *Microcomputers and mathematics in schools.* London: Department of Education and Science.

Foster, E. D. (1982). *Understanding broadcasting.* Reading, MA: Addison Wesley.

Frank, R., Becknell, J., & Clokey, J. (1971). Television program types. *Journal of Marketing Research, 8,* 204–211.

Frost, W. A. K. (1969). The development of a technique for TV programme assessment. *Journal of the Market Research Society, 11,* 25–44.

Fujio, T. (1982). *High definition television. Technical monograph No. 32.* Tokyo: Nippon Hoso Kyogai.

Gaddy, G. (1986). Television's impact on high school achievement. *Public Opinion Quarterly, 50,* 340–359.

Gagnon, D. (1985). Videogames and spatial skills: An exploratory study. *Educational Communication and Technology Journal, 33*(4), 263–275.

Gandy, O. H. (1981). Toward the production of minority audience characteristics. In H. A. Myrick & C. Keegan (Eds.), *In search of diversity*. Washington, DC: Corporation for Public Broadcasting.

Gandy, O. H. (1982). *Beyond agenda setting. Information subsidies and public policy*. Norwood, NJ: Ablex.

Gandy, O. H. (1985, April). Inequality: You don't even notice it after a while. Paper presented at the Thirteenth Annual Telecommunications Policy Research Conference, Airlie, VA.

Gaziano, C. (1983). The knowledge gap. An analytical review of media effects. *Communication Research, 10*(4), 447–486.

Geerts, C. (1980). Trois semaines de television en Belgique francophone. Brussels: Radio Television Belgique, Francaise.

Gensch, D., & Ranganathan, B. (1974). Evaluation of television program content for the purpose of promotional segmentation. *Journal of Marketing Research, 11*, 390–398.

Gerbner, G., & Gross, L. (1976). Living with television: The violence profile. *Journal of Communication, 26*(2), 173–199.

Gerbner, G., Gross, L., Eleey, M. F., Jackson-Beeck, M., Jeffries-Fox, S., & Signorielli, N. (1977). Television violence profile No. 8: The highlights. *Journal of Communication, 27*(2), 171–180.

Gerbner, G., Gross, L., Eleey, M. F., Jackson-Beeck, M., Jeffries-Fox, S., & Signorielli, N. (1978). Cultural indicators, violence profile No. 9. *Journal of Communication, 28*(2), 176–207.

Gerbner, G., Gross, L., Signorielli, N., Morgan, M., & Jackson-Beeck, M. (1979). The demonstration of power: Violence profile No. 10. *Journal of Communication, 29*(3), 177–196.

Gerbner, G., & Signorielli, N. (1979). Women and minorities in television drama, 1969–1978. Unpublished report, Annenberg School of Communications, University of Pennsylvania, Philadelphia.

Gerbner, G., Gross, L., Morgan, M., & Signorielli, N. (1982). Television's contribution to political orientations. *Journal of Communication, 32*(1), 100–127.

Gitlin, T. (1981). *The whole world is watching*. Berkely: University of California Press.

Gitlin, T. (1982). Prime Time Ideology: The hegemonic process in television entertainment. In H. Newcomb, (Ed.), *Television: The critical view*. New York: Oxford University Press.

Goodhardt, G. J., Ehrenberg, A. S. C., & Collins, M. (1975). *The television audience*. Farnborough: Saxon House.

Gould, P., Johnson, J., & Chapman, G. (1984). *The structure of television, Television: The world of structure/Structure: The world of television*. London: Pion.

Gould, M. S., & Shaffer, D. (1986). The impact of suicide in television movies; evidence of imitation. *New England Journal of Medicine, 315*(11), 690–693.

Glasgow University Media Group. (1976). *Bad news*. London: Routledge & Kegan Paul.

Glasgow University Media Group. (1980). *More bad news*. London: Routledge & Kegan Paul.

Greenberg, B. S. (1964). Person to person communication in the diffusion of news events. *Journalism Quarterly, 41*, 489–494.

Greenberg, B. S. (1986a, March). Some uncommon television images (The Drench-Drench Hypothesis). Paper given at the Society for the Psychological Study of Social Issues Conference on Television as a Social Issue, New York City.

Greenberg, B. S. (1986b). Teletext in the United Kingdom: Patterns, attitudes and behaviours of users. In J. Salvaggio & J. Bryant (Eds.), *Media use in the information age: Emerging patterns of adoption and consumer use.* Hillsdale, NJ: Lawrence Erlbaum Associates.

Greenberg, B. S., Richards, M., & Henderson, L. (1980). Trends in sex role portrayals on television. In B. Greenberg (Ed.), *Life on television.* Norwood, NJ: Ablex.

Greenberg, B. S., Gunter, B., Wober, M., & Fazal, S. (1986). *Children and their media.* London: Independent Broadcasting Authority Research Department.

Greenfield, P. M. (1984). *Mind and Media.* London: Fontana.

Gribbin, M. (1984, August). Boys muscle in on the keyboard. *New Scientist, 30,* 16–17.

Gross, L. (1984). The cultivation of intolerance: Television, blacks and gays. In G. Melischek, K. E. Rosengren, & J. Stappers (Eds.), *Cultural indicators: An international symposium.* Vienna: Verlag Der Osterrcichisches Akademie Der Wissenschaften.

Guizzardi, G. (1986). *La narrazione del carisma. I viaggi di Giovanni Paolo II in televisione.* Rome: Radio Televisione Italiano.

Gunter, B. (1984). Television and the young viewer. II. Teaching television literacy. *Head Teachers' Review,* Summer, 19–24.

Haldane, I. R. H. (1970). Measuring television audience reactions. *Proceedings of Thirteenth Annual Conference of the Market Resaerch Society.* London: Market Research Society, pp. 59–85.

Hall, S. (1980). *Culture, media, language: Working papers in cultural studies 1972–1979.* London: Hutchinson.

Hannah, M. St. C. (1982, May). The video revolution—sociological change, marketing opportunities, research nightmare. *Admap,* 296–301.

Haratonik, P. (1984, May). Pac-man as pedagogue. Paper presented at the International Communication Association Conference, San Francisco.

Harris, G. and Booth, D. A. (1986, September). Sodium preference in food and previous dietary experience in six and twelve month old infants. Paper presented at the Developmental Section of the British Psychological Society, Annual Conference, Exeter.

Hartley, J. (1984). Encouraging signs: Television and the power of dirt, speech and scandalous categories. In W. D. Rowland Jr. & B. Watkins (Eds.), *Interpreting television: Current research perspectives.* Beverly Hills: Sage.

Hartshorn, D. J. (1983). Children And Video Films At Home. *Educational Studies, 9,* 145–149.

Hawkins, R., & Pingree, S. (1980). Some processes in the cultivation effect. *Communication Research, 7,* 193–226.

Head, S. W. (1976). *Broadcasting in America* (3rd ed.). Boston: Houghton Mifflin.

Hedinsson, E. (1981). *Television, family and society: The social origins and effects of adolescents' TV use.* Stockholm: Almqvist & Wiksell International.

Hellerstein, L. (1986, May). Electronic messaging and conferencing with an emphasis on social use: An exploratory study. Paper presented at the International Communication Association, Chicago.

Henry, H. (1978). TV audience research: Now what? *Admap,* June, 280–282.

Himmelweit, H., Swift, B., & Jaeger, M. J. (1980). The audience as critic: An approach to the study of entertainment. In P. Tannenbaum (Ed.), *The entertainment functions of television.* Hillsdale, NJ: Lawrence Erlbaum Associates.

Hirsch, P. (1980a). An organisational perspective on television (aided by models from economics, marketing and the humanities) In S. Withey and R. Abeles (Eds.), *Television and social behaviour: Beyond violence and children.* Hillsdale, NJ: Lawrence Erlbaum Associates.

Hirsch, P. (1980b). The scary world of the non-viewer and other anomalies: A reanalysis of Gerbner et al's findings on cultivation analysis. Paper presented at American Association for Public Opinion Research.

Hobson, D. (1982). *Crossroads—The drama of a soap opera.* London: Methuen.

Hodge, R. (1982). Culture as communication: Towards a theoretical basis for communication studies. *Australian Journal of Communication, 1 & 2,* 76–83.

Howard, J., Rothbart, G., & Sloan, L. (1978). The response to "Roots:" A national survey. *Journal of Broadcasting, 22*(3), 279–288.

Huesmann, L. R. (1986). Cross-national communalities in the learning of aggression from media violence. In L. R. Huesmann & L. D. Eron (Eds.), *Television and aggression: A cross national perspective.* Hillsdale, NJ: Lawrence Erlbaum Associates.

Hughes, M. (1980). The fruits of cultivation analysis: A re-examination of some effects of television watching. *Public Opinion Quarterly, 44,* 287–302.

Hulten, O. (1979). *Mass media and state support in Sweden.* Stockholm: The Swedish Institute.

Hur, K. K. (1981). Impact of "Roots" on black and white teenagers. *Journal of Broadcasting, 22*(3), 289–298.

Hurwitz, D. (1984). Broadcast ratings: The missing dimension. *Critical Studies In Mass Communication, 1,* 205–214.

IBA (1974a). *Attitudes to broadcasting.* London: Author.

IBA (1974b). *Television and children.* London: Author.

IBA (1975). *Love thy neighbour.* London: Author.

IBA (1984). *Annual report.* London: Author.

Irvine, S. H., Irvine, M., Auburn, M., & Auburn, T. (1984, March). *Peter Tavy turns off. Report to the independent broadcasting authority.* Plymouth: Plymouth Polytechnic, Department of Psychology.

Jakubowicz, K. (1985). Mass and communication revisited. *Intermedia, 13,* 37–41.

Jankowski, G. J. (1985, September). The Global Context: The Broadcasters' Responsibility. Paper presented at the International Institute of Communications Conference, Tokyo.

Johnson, J., & Ettema, S. J. (1982). *Positive images: Breaking stereotypes with children's television.* Beverly Hills: Sage.

Jones, M., & Dungey, J. (1983). *Ethnic minorities and television. The attitudes of immigrant communities to television programmes with special reference to light entertainment and drama.* Leicester: Centre For Mass Communication Research.

Kaneko, T., Yoshida, T., Shinod, N., & Hitoshi, M. (1986, July). Psychophysiological effects of 1-hour watching of TV programs on EEG, heart rate, eye blinking and eye movement. Paper presented at the 21st International Conference of The International Association for Applied Psychology, Jerusalem.

Katz, E. J., Blumler, J. G., & Gurevitch, M. (1973). Uses and gratifications research. *Public Opinion Quarterly, 37,* 509–523.

Kieras, D. (1978). Beyond pictures and words: alternative information processing models for imagery effects in verbal memory. *Psychological Bulletin, 85*, 532–554.

Kirsch, A. D., & Banks, S. (1962). Program types defined by factor analysis. *Journal of Advertising Research, 2*, 29–31.

Klapper, J. T. (1960). *The effects of mass communication.* New York: Free Press.

Knill, B. J., Pesch, M., Pursey, G., Gilpin, P., & Perloff, R. M. (1981). Still typecast after all these years? Sex role portrayals in television advertising. *International Journal of Women's Studies, 4*, 497–506.

Krugman, H. (1970). *Electroencephalographic aspects of low involvement: Implications for the McLuhan hypothesis.* Cambridge, MA: Marketing and Science Institute.

Krugman, H. (1971). Brain wave measures of media involvement. *Journal of Advertising Research, 11*, 3–9.

Krugman, H. (1979, January 29). The Two Brains: New evidence on TV impact. *Broadcasting*, p. 14.

Large, M. (1980). *Who's bringing them up?* Gloucester: TV Action Group.

Larson, R. & Kubey, R. (1983). Television and Music. Contrasting media in adolescent life. *Youth and Society, 15*, 13–31.

Last, R. (1985). Rough Sketches. *The Daily Telegraph*, 14 January, p. 9.

Le Duc, D. R. (1979). West European broadcasting policy: Implications of new technology. *Journal of Broadcasting, 23*(2), 237–244.

Lehmann, D. R. (1971). Television show preference: Application of a choice model. *Journal of Marketing Research, 8*, 141–173.

Levy, M. R. & Fink, E. L. (1984). Home video recorders and the transience of television broadcasts. *Journal of Communication, 34*, 56–71.

Levy, M. R. & Windahl, S. (1984, May 24–28). Audience activity: A conceptual survey and research agenda. Paper presented at the International Communication Association, San Francisco.

Leyens, J. P., Parke, R. D., Camino, L., & Berkowitz, L. (1975). Effects of movie violence on aggression in a field setting as a function of group dominance and cohesion. *Journal of Personality and Social Psychology, 32*, 346–360.

Liebert, R. M. & Baron, R. A. (1972). Some immediate effects of televised violence on children's behaviour. *Developmental Psychology, 6*, 469–475.

Liebes, T. (1984). Ethnocentrism: Israelis of Moroccan ethnicity negotiate the meaning of "Dallas." *Studies in Visual Communication, 10*, 46–72.

Little, A. D. Inc. (1980). *Pay television services via direct broadcast satellite: Demand and impact in the 1980s. Report for the Comsat General Corporation.* Denver: Author.

Livingstone, S. M. (in press). The implicit representation of characters in Dallas: A multidimensional scaling approach. *Human Communication Research.*

Livingstone, S. M. & Greene, G. (1986). Television advertisements and the portrayal of gender. *British Journal of Social Psychology, 25*, 149–154.

Lull, J. (1982). How families select television programs. A mass observational study. *Journal of Broadcasting, 26*, 801–811.

Luyken, G. M. (1986). Direct broadcasting satellites: A concept for the future? *Media, Culture And Society, 8*, 183–197.

MacDonald, J. F. (1985). *Television and the red menace: The video road to Vietnam* New York: Praeger.

Malamuth, N. M. & Check, J. V. P. (1981). The effects of mass media exposure on acceptance of violence against women: A field experiment. *Journal of Research in Personality, 15,* 436–446.

Mander, J. (1978). *Four arguments for the elimination of television.* New York: Morrow.

Manes, A. L. & Melnyk, P. (1974). Televised models of female achievement. *Journal of Applied Social Psychology, 4,* 365–374.

Manstead, A. S. R. & McCulloch, C. (1981). Sex-role stereotyping in British television advertisements. *British Journal of Social Psychology, 97,* 209–220.

Mazrui, A. A. (1972). *Cultural engineering and nation building in East Africa.* Evanston: Northwestern University Press.

McCain, T. (1985). The invisible influence: European audience research. *Intermedia, 13,* 74–78.

McCombs, M. E. & Shaw, D. L. (1972). The agenda-setting function of mass media. *Public Opinion Quarterly, 36,* 176–187.

McGuire, W. J. (1974). Psychological motives and communications gratifications. In J. G. Blumler, & E. Katz (Eds.), *The uses of mass communications.* Beverly Hills: Sage.

McLuhan, M. (1962). *The Gutenberg galaxy.* London: Routledge & Kegan Paul.

McPhail, T. L. (1981). *Electronic colonialism: The future of international broadcasting and communication.* Beverly Hills: Sage.

McQuail, D., Blumler, J. G., & Brown, J. R. (1972). The television audience: A revised perspective. In D. McQuail (Ed.), *Sociology of mass communications* (pp. 135–165). Harmondsworth: Penguin.

Menneer, P. (1981). *Towards qualitative research: The BBC viewpoint.* London: BBC.

Meneer, P. (1984). AIs and audiences: How the BBC uses AIs. In *Annual review of BBC broadcasting research findings. London: BBC Data.*

Merton, R. K. (1957). *Social theory and social structure.* Glencoe: Free Press.

Metz, R. (1975). *CBS: Reflections in a bloodshot eye.* New York: New American Library.

Miller, J. (1986). Scrambling the dish man's business. *Intermedia, 14,* 8.

Monten, K. (1985). *Hemelektronik I Sverige, 1985.* Stockholm: SR/pub No 3.

Morgan, M. (1980). Television Viewing and Reading: Does more equal better? *Journal of Communication, 30,* 159–165.

Morley, D. (1980). *The 'Nationwide' Audience.* London: British Film Institute.

Morley, D. (1986). *Family television: Cultural power and domestic leisure.* London: Comedia Publishing Group.

Mosco, V. (1979). *Broadcasting in the United States. Innovative challenge and organisational control.* Norwood, NJ: Ablex.

Mosco, V. (1982). *Pushbutton fantasies: Cultural perspectives on videotex and information technology.* Norwood, NJ: Ablex.

National Institute For Mental Health, (1982). *Television and behaviour: Ten years of scientific progress and implications for the eighties. Volume 1: Summary report.* Rockville, MD: Author.

Nemo, J. (1980). A better way of funding TV in the UK. *Admap,* August, 400–402.

Neuman, W. R. (1981). The ebb and flow of social research on television. In W. R. Neuman (Ed.), *The social impact of television.* New York: Aspen Institute.

Newcomb, H. M., & Hirsch, P. M. (1984). Television as a cultural forum: Implications for research. In W. D. Rowland, & B. Watkins (Eds.), *Interpreting television: Current research perspectives.* Beverly Hills: Sage.

New Society (1985, 21 February). Education: Getting to grips with graphicacy. New Society, p. 12.

Nielsen (1984). *Nielsen report on television.* Northbrook, Ill: Author.

Nolan, T. (1981). Untitled article, in *TV Guide,* 8 August 9–12.

Novak, M. (1975). In D. Cater & R. Adler (Eds.), *Television as a social force: New Approaches to TV criticism.* New York: Praeger. pages 9–23.

O'Bryant, S. L., & Corder-Bolz, C. R. (1978). The effects of television on children's stereotyping of women's work roles. *Journal of Vocational Behaviour, 12,* 233–244.

Osgood, C. E., Suci, G. J., & Tannenbaum, P. H. (1957). *The measurement of meaning.* Urbana, Ill: University of Illinois Press.

Ott, J. (1976). *Health and light.* New York: Pocket Books.

Owen, B. M., Beebe, J. H., & Manning, W. G. (1974). *Television economics.* Lexington: D.C. Heath.

Paisley, W., & Chen, M. (1984). The second electronic revolution: The computer and children. In R. Bostrom (Ed.), *Communication Yearbook VIII.* Beverly Hills: Sage.

Palmer, E. L. (1983). *US children's television in crisis: An international perspective on our tradition, vision and values.* Melbourne: Australian Children's Television Foundation.

Palmer, P. (1986). *Children's uses of television.* London: Routledge & Kegan Paul.

Palmgreen, P. (1984). The uses and gratifications approach: A theoretical perspective. In R. Bostrom (Ed.), *Communication yearbook VIII* Beverly Hills: Sage.

Peacock, A. (1986). *Report of the Committee on Financing the BBC.* London: HMSO Cmnd 9824.

Pearl, D., Bouthilet, L., & Lazar, J. B. (1982). *Television and behaviour: Ten years of scientific progress and implications for the eighties.* Washington, DC: U.S. Government Printing Office.

Phillips, W. (1986, November). Pandora's Box—Will British television go the Italian way? *Admap,* 496–501.

Pilkington Committee (1960). *Report of the Committee on Broadcasting.* London: Her Majesty's Stationery Office.

Pingree, S., & Hawkins, R. (1980). U.S. programs on Australian television: The cultivation effect. *Journal of Communication 31*(1), 97–105.

Pion, G. M., & Lipsey, M. W. (1981). Public attitudes toward science and technology: What have the surveys told us? *Public Opinion Quarterly, 45*(3), 303–316.

Poindexter, P. M. (1980). Non-News viewers. *Journal of Communication, 30,* 58–65.

Poindexter, P. M., & Stroman (1981). Blacks and television: A review of the research Literature. *Journal of Broadcasting, 25*(2) 103–122.

Postman, N. (1982). *The disappearance of childhood.* New York: Delacorte Press.

Postman, N. (1986). *Amusing ourselves to death.* London: Heinemann.

Pottle, J. T., & Bortz, P. I. (1982). *The impact of competitive distribution technologies on Cable television.* Denver: Brown, Bortz and Coddington, for the National Cable Television Association.

Prue, T. (1979). The rate for the job. *Options,* Spring, 11–19.

Rao, V. R. (1975). Taxonomy of television programs based on viewing behaviour. *Journal of Marketing Research, 12,* 355–358.

Rauschenberg, G. S. (1984, May). Electronically assisted communication and communication apprehension. Development and preliminary evaluation of an instrument to measure computer phobia. Paper presented at the International Communication Association, San Francisco.

Real, M. (1984). The debate on critical theory and the study of communications. *Journal of Communication, 34*(4), 72–80.

Reeves, B. & Lang, A. (1986, May). Emotional television scenes and hemispheric specialisation. Paper presented at the International Communication Association, Chicago.

Reeves, B., & Thorson, E. (1986). Watching television. Experiments on the viewing process. *Communication Research, 13*(3), 343–361.

Richardson, A. (1977). The meaning and measurement of mental imagery. *British Journal of Psychology, 68,* 29–43.

Roberts, E. J., & Lemieux, P. H. (1981). *Audience attitudes and alternative program ratings: A preliminary study.* Cambridge, MA: Television Audience Assessment Inc.

Roe, K. (1983). The influence of Video Technology in Adolescence. *Media Panel Report No 27.* Lund: University of Lund, Department of Sociology.

Roe, K. (1985). *The advent of cable systems in Sweden. The programme output of seven cable-TV channels.* Report No 5. Lund: University of Lund, Department of Sociology.

Rosengren, K. E., & Windahl, S. (1972). Mass media use as a functional alternative. In D. McQuail (Ed.), *Sociology of mass communications.* Harmondsworth: Penguin.

Roth, L. (1983). *Inuit media projects and northern communications policy. Communication and the Canadian north.* Montreal: Department of Communications, Concordia University.

Rothschild, M., Thorson, E., Reeves, B., Hirsch, J. E., & Goldstein, R. (1986). EEG activity and the processing of television commercials. *Communication Research, 1986, 13,* 182–219.

Rowland, W. D. (1983). *The politics of TV violence.* Beverly Hills: Sage.

Rowland, W. D., & Watkins, B. (1984). *Interpreting television: Current research perspectives.* Beverly Hills: Sage.

Rubin, A. M. (1977). Television usage, attitudes, and viewing behaviors of children and adolescents. *Journal of Broadcasting, 21,* 355–369.

Salomon, G. (1979). *Interaction of media, cognition and learning.* San Francisco: Jossey Bass.

Schiller, H. I. (1981). *Who knows: Information in the age of the fortune 500.* Norwood, NJ: Ablex.

Schlesinger, P. (1978). *Putting reality together.* London: Constable.

Schneider, K. C. (1979). Sex roles in television commercials: new dimensions for comparison. *Akron Business and Economic Review,* Fall, 20–24.

Scott, R. (1980). *A report from the working party on new technologies.* London: Broadcasting Research Unit.

Segnit, S., & Broadcast, S. (1973). Life style research. *European Research, 1,* 6–13.

Setlow, C. E. (1978, December 31). TV Ratings—There just might be a better way. *New York Times.*

Sheehan, P. W. (1971). Individual differences in vividness of imagery and the function of imagery in incidental learning. *Australian Journal of Psychology*, 23, 278–288.

Sherman, M. (1985). Visual decoding of radio commercials. Earsight vs eyesight. In *Proceedings of the ESOMAR conference at Englefield green*. Amsterdam: E.S.O.M.A.R.

Sherman, B. L., & Dominick, J. R. (1986). Violence and sex in music videos: TV and rock 'n' roll. *Journal of Communication*, 36, 79–93.

Shils, E., & Young, M. (1975). The meaning of the Coronation. In E. Shils (Ed.), *Centre and periphery: Essays in macrosociology*. Chicago: University of Chicago Press.

Siceloff, J. (1983). *First go for firewood*. Pomona, CA: Author.

Signorielli, N. (1984). The demography of the television world. In G. Melischek, K. E. Rosengren, & J. Stappers (Eds.), *Cultural indicators: An international symposium*. Vienna: Austrian Academy of Sciences.

Silberstein, R., Agardy, S., Ong, B., & Heath, D. (1983). *Electroencephalographic responses of children to television*. Melbourne: Australian Broadcasting Tribunal.

Silvey, R. (1974). *Who's listening. The story of BBC audience research*. London: Allen and Unwin.

Singer, J. L. (1977). Imagination and make-believe play in early childhood: Some educational implications. *Journal of Mental Imagery*, 1, 127–144.

Singer, D., Zuckerman, D. M., & Singer, J. L. (1980). Helping elementary school children learn about TV. *Journal of Communication*, 30(3), 84–93.

Slack, J. D. (1984). *Communication technology and society: Conceptions of causality and the politics of technological intervention*. Norwood, NJ: Ablex.

Steiner, G. (1965). *The creative organisation*. Chicago: University of Chicago Press.

Strover, S. (1984, May). Games in the information age. Paper presented at the International Communication Association, San Francisco.

Swanson, G. E. (1967). The frequency structure of television and magazines. *Journal of Marketing Research*, 7, 8–14.

Tan, A. S., & Tan, G. K. (1985). Television use and mental health. Department of Mass Communications, Texas Tech University, Lubbock, Texas. Unpublished manuscript.

Taylor, L., & Mullan, B. (1986). *Uninvited guests*. London: Chatto and Windus.

Television Audience Assessment (1983). *The audience rates television*. Cambridge, MA: Author.

Television Audience Assessment (1984). *Commercial effectiveness and viewers' involvement with television programs: A literature review*. Cambridge, MA: Author.

Television Digest, Inc (1984). *Television Cable Factbook*. Washington: Author.

Thomas, H. (1962). *The truth about television*. London: Weidenfed and Nicholson.

Thorson, E., & Reeves, B. (1986). Prediction of memory for commercials from over-time patterns in occipital and frontal alpha. School of Journalism And Mass Communication, University of Wisconsin (Ms).

Tidhar, C. & Ostrowitz-Segal, L. (1985). Teletext In Israel: A New Instructional Tool. *Journal of Educational Television*, 11(3), 161–169.

Tuchman, G. (1978). The symbolic annihilation of women by the mass media In G. Tuchman, A. Daniels, & J. Benet (Eds.), *Hearth and home: Images of women in the mass media*. New York: Oxford University Press.

Turkle, S. (1984). *The second self: Computers and the human spirit.* New York: Simon and Schuster.

TV World (1980, August). UK Cable Bill. *TV World, 3*(10), 6.

UNESCO (1981). *Three weeks of television. An international comparative study.* Paris: Author.

Valaskakis, G. (1983). *Communication and the Canadian north.* Montreal: Department of Communication Studies, Concordia University.

Valaskakis, G. (1985, May). Northern native communications: The influence of Canadian theoretical and research interests on current programs and policy. Paper presented at International Communications Association, Honolulu.

Valenzuela, N. A. (1981). Blacks in public broadcasting: Developing a research agenda. In H. A. Myrick & C. Keegan (Eds.), *In search of diversity.* Washington, DC: Corporation for Public Broadcasting.

Volgy, T. J., & Schwarz, E. (1984). Misreporting and vicarious political participation at the local level. *Public Opinion Quarterly 48,* 757–765.

Wakshlag, J. J., & Wober, J. M. (1985). Qualitative and scheduling factors affecting viewing behaviour. In *Seminar on broadcasting research.* Englefield Green. Amsterdam: E.S.O.M.A.R.

Walker, J. L. (1980). Changes in EEG Rhythms during television viewing; preliminary comparisons with reading and other tasks. *Perceptual And Motor Skills, 51,* 255–261.

Waln, V. G. (1984, May). The tactile communication system: Directions for communication research. Paper presented at the International Communications Association, San Francisco.

Watkins, B., & Brim, D. (1985, May). The adoption and use of microcomputers in home and elementary school. Paper at the International Communication Association, Honolulu.

Webster, J. G., & Wakshlag, J. J. (1982). The impact of group viewing on patterns of television program choice. *Journal of Broadcasting, 26*(1), 445–455.

Webster, J. G., & Wakshlag, J. J. (1983). A theory of television program choice. *Communication Research, 10,* 430–446.

Weinstein, S., Appel, V., & Weinstein, C. (1980). Brain activity responses to magazine and television advertising. *Journal of Advertising Research, 20*(3), 57–63.

Wells, W. D. (1969). The rise and fall of television program types. *Journal of Advertising Research, 9,* 21–27.

Wilkus, E., Woelfel, J., Barnett, G., & Fontes, N. McLuhan hot and cool: An empirical test. Buffalo, NY: State University of New York, Department of Psychology.

Williams, R. (1973). *Television, technology and cultural form.* London: Fontana.

Williams, T. M. (1985). *The impact of television. A natural experiment in three communities.* London: Academic Press.

Wilson, K. (1986). The Videotex industry: social control and the cybernetic commodity of home networking. *Media, Culture and Society, 8,* 7–39.

Winn, M. (1978). *The plug in drug.* New York: Bantam Books.

Witkin, H. A. (1967). A cognitive style approach to cross-cultural research. *International Journal of Psychology, 2*(4), 233–250.

Wober, J. M. (1971). *English girls' boarding schools.* London: Allen Lane.

Wober, J. M. (1974). Unwilling viewing of TV programmes. London: Independent Broadcasting Authority, Research Summary, 14 June.

Wober, J. M. (1976). *Psychology in Africa.* London: International African Institute.

Wober, J. M. (1976, May). Week 37–75. Some Aspects of a Week's Televiewing Among The Audience In The Midlands. London: Independent Broadcasting Authority, Research Department, Special Report.

Wober, J. M. (1978a). Close encounters of a broadcast kind: A new field for psychological research. *Bulletin of the British Psychological Society, 31*, 381–385.

Wober, J. M. (1978b). Televised violence and paranoid perception: The view from Great Britain. *Public Opinion Quarterly, 42*, 315–321.

Wober, J. M. (1978d). Psychologists and the intrusion of broadcast 'programmes' on personal privacy. *Bulletin of the British Psychological Society, 31*, 1–2.

Wober, J. M. (1979a, October). Interests Apart. An exploration of the ideal of complementary programming. London: Independent Broadcasting Authority, Research Department, Special Report.

Wober, J. M. (1979b, November). Attitudes towards an absent service. public opinions during the ITV strike, on aspects of ITV and BBC 2. London: Independent Broadcasting Authority, Research Department, Special Report.

Wober, J. M. (1980a, January). Chance and Choice. Changes in the distribution of viewing across programme types when their availability is altered. London: Independent Broadcasting Authority, Research Department, Special Report.

Wober, J. M. (1980b, April). Fiction and Depiction. Attitudes of fifteen television series and the novels from which they were made. London: Independent Broadcasting Authority, Special Report.

Wober, J. M. (1980c, April). A Box For All Seasons: The ebb and flow of television viewing, and appreciation, over a whole year. London: Independent Broadcasting Authority, Research Department, Special Report.

Wober, J. M. (1980d, June). Patterns of personality and of televiewing. London: Independent Broadcasting Authority, Research Department, Special Report.

Wober, J. M. (1981a, September). Television and Women: Viewing patterns and perceptions of ideal, actual and portrayed women's roles. London: Independent Broadcasting Authority, Research Department, Special Report.

Wober, J. M. (1981b, December). Pyramids Or Chariots—The satellite question. The degree of welcome for telecommunications and other innovations. London: Independent Broadcasting Authority, Research Department, Special Report.

Wober, J. M. (1981c, December). Broadcasting and the Conflict in Ireland: Viewers' opinions of two series, and their context. London: Independent Broadcasting Authority, Research Department, Special Report.

Wober, J. M. (1981d). Assessing the patterns and experience of viewing television. In S. H. Irvine & J. W. Berry (Eds.), *Human assessment and cultural factors*. New York: Plenum Press.

Wober, J. M. (1982a, February). New Scales for Old? A preliminary experiment on the possibility of developing multiple means of programme assessment. London: Independent Broadcasting Authority, Research Department, Special Report.

Wober, J. M. (1982b, July). The Falklands: Some systematic data on viewing behaviour and attitudes concerning television coverage of the Conflict. London: Independent Broadcasting Authority, Research Department, Special Report.

Wober, J. M. (1982c, August). Programme Type and Audience Size: Resisting the pull of peaktime and pointing towards ways in which greater choice may be used. London: Independent Broadcasting Authority, Research Department, Special Report.

Wober, J. M. (1983a, February). Enjoyment and Strength of Impression. New scales for programme assessment weighed in the balance and found wanted. London: Independent Broadcasting Authority, Research Department, Working Paper.

Wober, J. M. (1983b, October). Broadcast Media and Sensotypes. London: Independent Broadcasting Authority, Research Department, Reference Paper.

Wober, J. M. (1984a, April). The Psychological and Economic Value of TV. A Pointer from Peter Tavy. London: Independent Broadcasting Authority, Research Department, Working Paper.

Wober, J. M. (1984b, May). Appreciation, Enjoyment and Impact: A National Survey. London: Independent Broadcasting Authority, Research Department, Research Paper.

Wober, J. M. (1984c, May). TV's Menu, The Viewers' Order. London: Independent Broadcasting Authority, Research Department, Working Paper.

Wober, J. M. (1984d, July). Television And The Ages of Man. London: Independent Broadcasting Authority, Research Department, Research Paper.

Wober, J. M. (1984e, November). Voting In Europe. Television and viewers' involvement in the 1984 European Parliamentary Election. London: Independent Broadcasting Authority, Research Department, Working Paper.

Wober, J. M. (1984f). Viewers Or Vigilantes: Options on Violent Pornography. *Intermedia, 12*(2), 20–23.

Wober, J. M. (1984g). Cinderella Comes Out, showing TV's Hits and its Myths. *Media, Culture and Society, 6,* 65–71.

Wober, J. M. (1985a, February). Screens And Speakers. Ownership, use and ideas on payment for electronic devices for entertainment and information. London: Independent Broadcasting Authority, Research Department, Working Paper.

Wober, J. M. (1985b, April). The Primacy of Print Over Screen? Some indications from a young teenagers' survey. London: Independent Broadcasting Authority, Research Department, Working Paper.

Wober, J. M. (1985c). Sensotypes: Their Signs And A Search For Sources. Paper given at the Seminar on Media, Culture, Lifestyles, MEDIACULT, Vienna.

Wober, J. M. (1985d). Does television hurt people? In E. Denig & A. van der Meiden (Eds.), *A geography of public relations trends.* Dordrecht: Martinus Nijhoff Publishers.

Wober, J. M. & Dobie, I. (1978). The role of wrestling as a public spectacle: audience attitudes to wrestling as portrayed on television. London: Independent Broadcasting Authority, Research Department, Special Report.

Wober, J. M. & Fazal, S. (1984). Citizens of Ethnic Minorities: Their prominence in real life and on television. London: Independent Broadcasting Authority, Research Department, Special Report.

Wober, J. M. & Reardon, G. (1978, May). Tolerance and Taboo. Exploring the content and structure of attitudes concerning television documentaries. London: Independent Broadcasting Authority.

Wober, J. M. & Reardon, G. (1983, May). Enjoyment and Strength of Impression: A confirmatory study. London: Independent Broadcasting Authority, Research Department, Special Report.

Wright, C. (1975). *Mass communication.* New York: Random House.

Young, B. M. W. (1975). How should broadcasting be financed? *Independent Broadcasting, 5,* 2–5.

Zillman, D. C. (1971). Excitation transfer in communication-mediated aggressive behaviour. *Journal of Experimental Social psychology: 1,* 419–413.

Zillman, D. C., & Bryant, J. (1986). Shifting preferences in pornography consumption. *Communication Research, 13*(4), 560–578.

Zillman, D. C., Johnson, R. C., & Hanrahan, J. (1973). Pacifying effect of happy ending of communication involving aggression. *Psychological Reports, 32,* 967–970.

Index